THE ULYSSES VOYAGE

Tim Severin was born in 1940 and educated at Tonbridge School and Oxford University. He has sailed a leather boat across the North Atlantic in the wake of St Brendan, captained an Arab sailing ship from Muscat to China and been awarded the Founder's Medal of the Royal Geographical Society. He has written nine books, translated into more than 25 languages, on the history of exploration, and lives in County Cork, Ireland.

Also by Tim Severin
The Brendan Voyage
The Jason Voyage
The Sindbad Voyage

THE
ULYSSES
VOYAGE
Sea Search for the Odyssey

TIM SEVERIN

Drawings by Will Stoney
Photographs by Kevin Fleming

ARROW BOOKS

Arrow Books Limited
62–65 Chandos Place, London WC2N 4NW

An imprint of Century Hutchinson Limited

London Melbourne Sydney Auckland
Johannesburg and agencies throughout
the world

This edition first published in Great Britain
by Hutchinson 1987

Arrow edition 1988

© Tim Severin 1987
© Illustrations Will Stoney 1987
© Photographs Kevin Fleming 1987

This book is sold subject to the condition that it shall
not, by way of trade or otherwise, be lent, resold, hired
out, or otherwise circulated without the publisher's
prior consent in any form of binding or cover other
than that in which it is published and without a similar
condition including this condition being imposed on the
subsequent purchaser

Phototypeset by Input Typesetting Limited, London SW19 8DR

Printed and bound in Great Britain by
Anchor Brendon Limited, Tiptree, Essex

ISBN 0 09 954420 2

Contents

Maps

Photographs

All photographs copyright by Kevin Fleming

The Illustrators

Drawings

Will Stoney drew the sketches which illustrate this story of the Ulysses Voyage and they are very important to an understanding of the tale. A full crew member of *Argo*, Will was asked not only to sketch scenes along *Argo*'s route which he found worth recording, but was also given the difficult task of depicting the landscape at key landfalls as it would have appeared to Ulysses and his companions in the Late Bronze Age. To do this, Will had to sketch the topography precisely but omit modern features such as roads, telephone poles, hotels, concrete jetties and so forth which are superimposed on the original landscape and distract the historical view. A technical artist by profession, Will worked under less than ideal conditions – guarding his sketch pad in a plastic bag against the spray – but the quality of his drawings does more than any words to portray the scenes which would have greeted the men returning from the Siege of Troy, and given birth to some of the legends within the *Odyssey*.

Photographs

Kevin Fleming took all the photographs in this edition of the book, and the excellence of his work needs no proclamation. It is self-evident. Assigned to the project by the *National Geographic Magazine*, Kevin's diligence in being in the right place at the right time in order to get the right shot was an object lesson in professionalism. As a result, he has provided – for the first time in all the dozens of commentaries about the *Odyssey* – actual *photographs* of some of the key sites in Homer's tale. Kevin was a good companion and has been most generous in allowing his photographs to add to the excitement of the story.

Crew List

Argo's complement varied from as few as seven to as many as a dozen crew members at any one time. Several of the team will be met in the following pages but the full list of volunteers who came aboard to share in the adventure and research is:

Jonathan Blows
Nazem Choufeh
Andrew Dillon
Tony Fairhead
Costas Ficardos
David Gahan
John Kelly
John Littlewood
Cormac O'Connor
Ali Pasinar
Clive Raymond
Mark Richards
Bora Sahinoglu

Ida Severin
Andrew Steele
Will Stoney
Theodor Troev
Peter Warren
Brian Watkins
Peter Wheeler
Dick Whelehan
Rick Williams
Derry Woodhouse
Gerry Wrixon
Erzin Yirmibesoglu

Author's Note

Another expedition to explore the borderline between fact and fiction in an ancient tale has once again brought together excellent colleagues from previous ventures, introduced new crew members, and enlarged my circle of friends and advisers. In writing this account of the Ulysses Voyage one of my happiest responsibilities is to thank them for all that they have done.

The role of Sarah Waters was, as before, central to the project. Assisted by Constance Messenger, she ran the home office and looked after the multitude of details that make such an endeavour run smoothly from its first planning to the final gathering-in of the results.

In England Colin and Rosemary Mudie – from whose drawing board had come the original design of *Argo* in preparation for rowing the 1,500 miles of the Jason Voyage – advised on how we might overcome our lack of oarsmen when following Ulysses. Mariner and Zodiac both helped with equipment, as did Telesonic Marine, allies for the third time in preparing a 'Severin expedition'. It was a pleasure, too, to contact once again Gerald Dennis and his team of painstaking sailmakers at Maldon in Essex. Ten years earlier they had made the sails for the Brendan Voyage, and now they made with equal skill the new square sail for *Argo*. While mulling over the possible landfalls, I received helpful advice from Rod Heikell, author of *The Greek Waters Pilot*.

In Turkey I don't know how we would have managed without the help of my remarkable 'Turkish family' –

the Akcas. Irgun had looked after the equipment for *Argo* during the winter, and when the crew arrived in Istanbul to begin preparing the galley for launch, Mukaddes could arrange anything, and did – instantly. Every day we were in Turkey, we met with kindness and co-operation, and in particular I remember the help from Dr Hasan Souda in Canakkale, smoothing our path. He was introduced by Ali Pasinar, *Argo*'s fishing expert. None of us will forget Ali's guided tour of the Bosphorus as we sailed away to the Aegean. I only regret that such episodes must fall outside the scope of my present tale.

In Greece 'Uncle John' Vasmadjides was waiting to help us. He was as indispensable and generous with his time and counsel as when we were preparing the Argonaut project. Another ally from those days, Stas Rodopoulos, was again on hand to help, and so too was Vasilis Delimitros, builder of *Argo* and loyal to his creation. The Ulysses Voyage gave me the chance to meet a man whose work I had long admired – Paddy Leigh Fermor – and thanks to his introduction I went on to meet some of his former associates in the Cretan Resistance who then acted as my guides to their island. In particular I would like to thank Manoussas Manoussakis whose energy and passion for scholarship ensured that I got to see the remote places that are likely to have been associated with the legend of Polyphemus the Cyclops.

Other scholars unstintingly gave advice which was beyond my competence: Jim Mavor, archaeo-astronomer at Woods Hole, explained the star direction as Ulysses sailed away from Calypso's island. Dr John Harvey advised on the fabled lotus plant and the mysterious 'moly', antidote to the witch Circe's spells. Martin Sands from the Royal Botanic Gardens at Kew not only produced further details on both plants but by an extraordinary stroke of luck proved to be an authority on the flora of Paxos, which I was to suggest as Circe's island. Monique Kervran was once again a mentor for the field archaeology, with her fresh outlook on age-old problems and a truly international experience in field work. In France, too, I owe a debt to Professor Paul Faure who put me on the track of the *triamates* ogres. Following his directions I was fortunate to find the Doctors Shaw, a husband and wife team, at Kommos who took time away from their excavations to explain the site. And when I came to the crucial phase of writing up the story of the voyage and needed to turn to a Homeric expert, Professor John Luce of Trinity College, Dublin, was courtesy itself. He was extraordinarily kind – and patient – in setting me straight on matters of Homeric scholarship and sifting out my worst errors. The mistakes which remain, as well as my interpretation of all the expert advice I have been given, continue to be my responsibility.

The launching, running and writing up of an unsponsored expedition means that somewhere in the background are the professionals – editors, publishers, literary agents – without whose help the project could never be paid for. Again the same people who assisted previous ventures have brought the Ulysses Voyage to print: so my thanks to the Sheil and Wallace agencies in London and New York, Harold Harris my editor since the Brendan Voyage, now joined by Richard Cohen, and to Bill Graves, Elie Rogers and Merle Severy at the National Geographic Society in Washington. One of the great luxuries in producing another volume is the feeling of confidence I have in working with them.

TIM SEVERIN
Co. Cork, Ireland
1986

A Note on the Translation of Homer

The translation of the *Odyssey* selected for use in this book was made by E. V. Rieu and first published by Penguin Books in January 1946. It was chosen for its readability and popularity: it has been reprinted forty-one times since it first appeared, which must be a record. Other translations do differ on certain points of language – there is enough ambiguity in Homer's vocabulary to keep scholars occupied for the foreseeable future – and some offer their translations in verse. But Rieu's rendering of the *Odyssey* into English was the version we carried on *Argo*, and a reader who may be encouraged to reread Homer's immortal tale in full will find the Penguin Classics edition readily available.

PROLOGUE

The Riddle

No single poet – Dante, Goethe or even Shakespeare – has had a more pervasive influence on the cultural foundation of the West than the shadowy figure we call Homer. His name is so familiar that it is easy to overlook just how long his work has been our heritage. Homer described events that took place, as far as we can tell, at roughly the same time as the Exodus. Before the Old Testament was complete, his works were already the basic scrolls in a cultured man's library. By the time Jesus was born, so much had been written about Homer and his work that it would be a very long time before any of the Apostles could challenge his leading position as the most intensively studied author in Western civilization. All this Homer accomplished with just two poems – the *Iliad* and the *Odyssey* – written in a language that the Greeks of the classical era already found so old-fashioned that they had difficulty in understanding some words, while in our own century a lexicon to elucidate his vocabulary runs to 445 densely written pages without solving dozens of doubtful meanings. Yet this ambiguity never cloaked Homer's essential genius. His characters are so timeless, the phrases so elegant, and the mosaics of the word pictures so vivid that his tale of one man's extraordinary journey 3,000 years ago has never been eclipsed. With the *Odyssey*, the subject of this book, Homer composed such an evocative saga that its very title has been retained as the word to describe lengthy travels.

Homer's genius has always been irresistible to the

inquiring mind. In the early days of the Roman empire there was a time when educators considered that Homer provided the foundation for all useful knowledge – whether history or geography or rhetoric. Today an echo of that variety survives. Archaeologists, historians, folklorists, all continue to dissect Homer's work and find – or think they find – fresh insight. After more than 2,000 years of research it seems almost inconceivable that anything can be added to the awe-inspiring mass of scholarship that has been piled on those two poems.

No one, then, can tackle Homer lightly. But for me, intrigued by the mix of truth and fiction in stories of early voyages and travels, the bait was laid early and the trap was very tempting. The *Odyssey*'s adventures – with the Cyclops and Sirens, Scylla and Charybdis, and Aeolus, the Ruler of the Winds – had been introduced as childhood tales. Then, studying the history of exploration at Oxford, I encountered a few of the dozens of theories about the *Odyssey*. Some claimed the tale was pure fantasy, others traced real routes to plausible sounding places which they said the hero Ulysses (to use the Latin version of his Greek name, Odysseus) had actually visited. Still other commentators proposed explanations which seemed more fantastic than if the *Odyssey* had been a fairy tale in the first place.

Finally, in 1981, I fell firmly into the jaws of the trap. That year I began to prepare an expedition to investigate the route of Jason and the Argonauts to fetch the Golden Fleece. I wanted to build a replica of an early Greek galley, assemble a crew of volunteers and row and sail the vessel from Greece to Soviet Georgia along the route that Jason took. But everywhere I turned to study Jason, I kept on stumbling across Homer and the *Odyssey*. The stories of Jason and Ulysses are closely intertwined. Homer, I discovered, seemed to have borrowed ideas from the story of the Argonauts. He even mentioned Jason's ship by name. To try to sort out the overlap, I found myself compiling two separate catalogues of file cards, one labelled 'Jason', the other 'Ulysses'. There were cross-references, contradictions, similarities, and the two catalogues continued to grow side by side. In 1984 we made the Jason Voyage. We successfully rowed and sailed our galley, the 54-foot *Argo*, from Greece to Soviet Georgia at the eastern end of the Black Sea. There we found our Golden Fleece among the Svan people of the Caucasus mountains who showed us the ancient technique of submerging sheep-skins in the stream-beds so that grains of alluvial gold were trapped in the wool. By August that year we had brought *Argo* back to Istanbul for her winter lay-up, pulled ashore, courtesy of the Mayor, among the luxury yachts of the very rich in the city's most exclusive boat park. But I already knew that the galley's role was far from over. My boxes of file cards held the research into the *Odyssey*'s text; and I would not be satisfied until I had tried my hand at solving the longest running geographical riddle in the world: quite simply, that riddle asked, was the *Odyssey* the story of a real voyage? And if so, where did Ulysses go?

Clearly there had to be some truth in Homer's tales. Troy, the city whose siege by a Greek expeditionary force is the subject of the *Iliad*, was real. Its ruins have been found on the coast of Anatolia and studied with minute care. Mycenae, the capital of King Agamemnon who, Homer tells us, led the besieging army, has been excavated. So too – and *Argo* was to take us there – has the palace home of King Nestor, leader of the second most important Greek contingent. Several of the world's most gifted archaeologists and historians have been drawn into the search for the remarkable world that Homer described. In their hunt for the historic facts within the Homeric poems these experts pioneered techniques which changed the entire science of archaeology. They made international reputations as well as furious controversy. As we shall see, the same giants of scholarship appear again and again in the Homeric context, for each of them found it difficult to dig at Troy without wondering about Mycenae, or to investigate Mycenae without searching for the ruins of Ulysses' home or Nestor's palace. The links in the chain of their discoveries led on and on, crossed and recrossed in confusion, and still no end is in sight.

The scholars tended to concentrate on the *Iliad*, for this story is based on land and in a specific spot – before the walls of Troy. Here the archaeologists could dig, lay bare the walls and streets, compare sherds of pottery from one site to the next, and establish the lifestyle of the time. The *Odyssey* has been far more difficult to pin down. The spade is not the right tool to investigate a tale of far voyaging which might contain clues to the wandering of a man who lived 3,000 years ago. Nothing is more tantalizing or more puzzling than Homer's geography in the *Odyssey*. It is like a detective story about a series of murders where even the corpses are so bizarre that perhaps they may only be hallucinations as they lie littered along the trail. Homer sends Ulysses to a country whose inhabitants eat a wonderful plant that makes them forget their homes, then to visit cannibal giants who live in caves and tend flocks of sheep and goats but somehow gather crops that grow without any attention. There is an island encircled by steep bronze walls where lives a man who can control the winds by bottling them up in a leather sack. Soon afterwards Ulysses' squadron is wiped out by cannibals who massacre the crews in a death trap of a harbour with an entrance so narrow that they cannot escape.

As the trail continues, the curious episodes become even more curious. Ulysses and his surviving companions recuperate on an idyllic island ruled by a witch who can turn men into animals. A day's sail away they visit the lobby of Hades where Ulysses consults with the spirits of the dead and then, continuing on the homeward route, he and his crew row past the beach of the entrancing Sirens, daemons whose sweet singing lures sailors to their deaths. They narrowly evade a dangerous whirlpool in a narrow strait, but a six-headed monster living in a cave in a cliff-face snatches up six men from the deck and devours them. When the rest of the crew commit the sacrilege of killing and eating the cattle of the Sun God on his sacred island, their ship is sunk as punishment, and all are drowned except for Ulysses who clings to the wreckage. He is cast up in the pleasant realm of the demi-goddess Calypso and becomes her lover. From there the hero escapes in a makeshift boat, only to be sunk again and washed ashore in the kingdom of a seafaring people, the Phaeacians, who entertain him in the palace of their king Alcinous, before finally transporting him home in one of their swift ships. He had been nineteen years away from home.

Many-headed monsters are fantastic, and so too is the one-eyed Cyclops whom Ulysses blinded in his cave during the homeward journey. But were they pure inventions, or was there some real foundation to each legend? Did Homer have such extraordinary originality of mind that he could dream up such a remarkable string of bogeys without a shred of reality on which to hang his tales? And even if Ulysses' adventures were imaginary, did Homer *think* that they took place somewhere real? Or was his geography, like his fantastic creatures, without any footing in this world? 'You will find the scenes of the wanderings of Odysseus,' scoffed

Eratosthenes, the world's first scientific geographer in the third century BC, 'when you find the cobbler who sewed up the bag of winds . . .'

But Eratosthenes was a rare sceptic. His doubts about the reality of the *Odyssey* did not stop his contemporaries from trying to make geographical sense of it by trying to work out which were the lands where Ulysses met his adventures. The Greeks of the classical period treated the *Iliad* as real history, and modern archaeology has proved them at least partially right. Many of their finest scholars were equally sure that the scenes of the *Odyssey* were stages on a real voyage by a real man and they could identify the islands and harbours he had visited.

'As when some skilful man overlays gold upon silver . . .', observed Strabo, the most influential classical geographer of all, 'so he [Homer] took the Trojan War, an historical fact, and decked it out with his myths; and he did the same in the case of the wanderings of Odysseus.' Strabo, writing in the time of Augustus Caesar, listed half a dozen leading geographers who had already tried to unravel the mysteries of the *Odyssey*. Their efforts to locate Ulysses' wanderings have been repeated over the centuries by pedagogues of every hue – historians, armchair travellers, classicists, archaeologists, eminent novelists, even a British prime minister, Gladstone. Conflicting theories have placed Ulysses' wanderings in Italy, in the Black Sea, in Spain, out in the Atlantic, in the Indian Ocean, off Ireland or Norway. Scarcely a year goes by without a new interpretation of the text. In the last decade theories have despatched Ulysses as far as the high Andes in South America or as near as the Adriatic which, it was recently claimed by a Yugoslav sea captain, contains every scene of every adventure.

I checked the various theories against the charts.

The Riddle

Every scene that Homer mentions has been differently located by a score of experts. His physical descriptions (and they can be frustratingly vague) are matched against a variety of real places, and each one is claimed to be precise, but they are rarely in the same location. Ulysses' vessel jumps up and down the length of the Mediterranean like the knight on a chessboard. It skips over inconvenient land masses, skids around capes, travels at speeds that would do credit to a modern cruise liner in its attempts to link up sites that appear to be suitable. Only a tiny handful of the modern commentators were themselves sailors, even fewer had sailed the possible routes. No one had any firsthand idea of how a Late Bronze Age galley might travel.

Astonishingly, no one seemed to have asked themselves the basic question – if there was a real Ulysses and he made a real voyage, surely after the Siege of Troy, which reputedly lasted ten years, he would have been anxious to return home as quickly as possible. If so, what was the normal route he would have taken? Could this route have provided the scenes of the *Odyssey* without any of the dramatic leaps of navigation? Maybe this question was never asked because there was a risk that it could turn out to be an anticlimax, a question that might destroy one charm of the tale, the idea of Ulysses as the great explorer venturing beyond the horizon. On the other hand if such a straightforward route fitted the details of the *Odyssey* then something much more important would result: the riddle of the *Odyssey* would be solved on a rational basis that would bring Ulysses back from the unreal fairyland where the too fantastic and impractical interpretations had effectively consigned him.

So I knew what I would do: I would take *Argo* from Troy to Ithaca, Ulysses' home in the Ionian Islands off the west coast of Greece, following the track that a Late

Map 1 Central and Eastern Mediterranean with the sites traditionally identified with Ulysses Wanderings

YUGOSLAVIA

CORSICA

Bonifacio
Port Pozzo

• Rome

ITALY

Monte Circeo
(Circe's Home)

▲ Mt. Vesuvius

SARDINIA

Sirens

GULF OF KOTOR

ALBANIA

Saseno Is.

Meliboea

Thessa

TYRRHENIAN SEA

Aeolian Is.
(Ruler of Winds)   Strongyle

Lipari   Ganzirra

SICILY
(Thrinacia)

Mt Etna ▲

Cyclopes

STRAITS OF MESSINA
(Scylla & Charybdis)

IONIAN SEA

Ionian Is.

Ithaca

GREECE

Mycenae

Olympia
Peloponnese
Sparta

Gozo
(Calypso's Home)

Malta

TUNISIA

Jerba Is.
(Lotus-eaters)

MEDITERRANEAN

GULF OF SIRTE

N

Thrinacia   Sites traditionally identified with
            Ulysses wanderings

0   400 km
0   200 miles

LIBYA

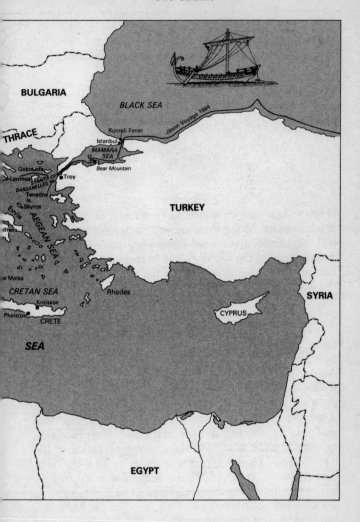

BULGARIA

THRACE

BLACK SEA

Jason Voyage 1984

Rumeli Fener

Istanbul

MAMARA SEA

Bear Mountain

Gokceada

Lemnos STRAITS OF
DARDANELLES ■Troy
Tenedos Is.

Skyros

Evvia

AEGEAN SEA

thens

TURKEY

e Malea

CRETAN SEA

Rhodes

Knossos

Phaistos■

CRETE

SEA

CYPRUS

SYRIA

EGYPT

Bronze Age sailor would have chosen if he was a prudent man. Along that 'logical' route, as I thought of it, I wondered if we would find sites that matched the descriptions in the *Odyssey* and perhaps uncover explanations for some, if not all, of the extravagant tales. I did not aspire to answer thorny questions of history or linguistics or land archaeology. Those were matters best left to the experts. Their work gave me the basic tools – encyclopaedias, concordances, translations, commentaries, all the scholarly apparatus that had accumulated over two millennia of studying Homer. My approach would be practical – geographical and maritime. It would be from a commonsense viewpoint – the stern deck of a replica Bronze Age galley. For this purpose *Argo* was ideal. Built for twenty oarsmen, she was precisely the size and style of craft that Homer mentions in the *Odyssey* as the standard voyaging galley of her day. Already I knew something about Bronze Age navigation, for on the 1,500 miles of the Jason Voyage we had gone from northern Greece, passed through the Dardanelles within sight of Troy, crossed the Marmara Sea and penetrated the Straits of the Bosphorus, and coasted all the way to the furthest reaches of the Black

Sea. Thus I had some concept of the distances we could expect Ulysses to have travelled each day, the limitations under oar and sail, the weather that his ship could withstand or not, the method of navigating by line-of-sight from headland to headland. This experience I now proposed to apply to the *Odyssey*. But first, before embarking on the voyage, I had to know our quarry. Who was Ulysses? Indeed, who was Homer?

1
Bard and Hero

Homer was a woman, so runs one theory. Another claims that he was a blind man. A third, that he was not a single individual but a panel of poets. A fourth, that he composed the *Iliad* but not the *Odyssey*. The academic views are no more consistent about the identity of Homer than the conflicting theories about the route of the *Odyssey*. The truth is that no one has yet discovered who Homer was, or precisely when he lived, although some shrewd calculations have been made. At best estimate he lived some time in the eighth or seventh centuries BC, that is some 500 years after the Siege of Troy and the unfolding of the events he described. It is also agreed that he (or they) was a bard, that is, a professional teller of sagas.

Just possibly – and this is where the theory of the blind man comes in – Homer drew a word picture of himself in the *Odyssey* rather as some film directors give themselves a walk-on part in their script. At the court of hospitable King Alcinous, there is a teller of tales whom, according to the *Odyssey*, 'the Muse loved above all others, though she had mingled good and evil in her gifts, robbing him of his eyes but lending sweetness to his song'. A favourite of the court, he was led to his special banqueting place by an equerry and seated on a silver-studded chair in the centre of the company. At his back was one of the great pillars of the hall and on it the equerry hung his 'tuneful lyre' and 'showed him how to lay his hand upon it. At his side he put a basket and a handsome table, together with a cup of

26

wine to drink when he was thirsty'. Thus equipped, the minstrel entertained the assembled company with 'a lay well-known by then throughout the world, the Quarrel of Odysseus and Achilles'.

Whether or not this was meant to be Homer himself, at least it tells us how the *Odyssey* and the *Iliad* were used and so warns us to beware. In Albania, in the west of Ireland and among Australian aborigines the techniques of living bards have been studied to see how accurately they hand on their verses and change them. They learn the verses not by rote and memory but in general terms of plot. Stock lines and phrases are repeated, but the bard is free to improvise and polish within the ground rules of his craft. Thus the oral poetry of the saga was a living, changing tale and what we have from Homer is not precisely what the first saga-tellers composed. Nevertheless, as we now know, their sources may be very ancient. Recently a Harvard scholar spotted a Homeric-sounding phrase in a fragment of a Bronze Age chronicle on a clay tablet that dates from close to the time of the siege. So it is possible that the first account of the siege was composed in the lifetimes of men like Agamemnon and Ulysses.

It is at the siege that the *Iliad* gives us our only glimpse of what Ulysses actually may have looked like. Homer provides a typically oblique, not a direct, description of the man. He was, says the poet, short in stature but broad in the shoulder and chest. At first encounter he gave the impression of being stiff and clumsy, what might be described today as something of a yokel. But the moment he began to speak, that impression was dispelled. He had a great voice uttered deep from the chest and his words were like 'the snow-flakes of winter' so that 'no man could contend with him'. Several incidents in both the *Iliad* and the *Odyssey* flesh out the shadow. Ulysses was clearly very strong.

He was a noted warrior when it came to the rough and tumble of hand-to-hand combat and he could throw the discus further than his rivals. He alone was able to bend and string the great bow which had formerly belonged to a legendary archer by the name of Eurytus, and once it was strung he was deadly accurate with it. Unusually for someone who was so stocky, there is also the claim that Ulysses was a good runner, fast enough to be a leading contender in foot races. The overriding impression, however, is of a burly man with tremendous stamina. During two shipwrecks on his voyage home he displayed phenomenal powers of endurance. On the first occasion his entire crew was drowned when a sudden tempest smashed their galley, but Ulysses was strong enough to haul himself onto a piece of wreckage, the main keel timber, and ride it like a liferaft until he came to shelter. The second time he had to abandon a small skiff in a storm and swim a prodigious distance to reach land where he survived a battering on the rocks as he tried to come ashore. In sum the image of Ulysses is of a powerfully built, rather rough-seeming man with the tenacity and physique of a born survivor.

But it was Ulysses' character, more than his appearance, which really interested Homer. The prime quality which Homer repeatedly mentions is his 'resourcefulness', meaning both his wiliness and his ingenuity. Again and again the adventures in the *Odyssey* and the events of the siege portray Ulysses as a man of great cunning who could twist words and situations to his advantage. By modern moral standards he was not an exemplary character. Ulysses would rarely tell the truth if he could think of a better lie. He was arrogant, grasping, bore grudges and, while extremely suspicious of strangers, was almost as mistrustful of men he had known a long time. Above all, he never lost sight of his own self-interest.

In Homer's eyes these qualities were admirable rather than odious, and Ulysses' behaviour was understandable if not always commendable. It is also true that by some curious process of character assassination Ulysses' qualities were to be blackened by mythographers as more and more legendary material built up around him. Whether this additional material was pure invention or whether it came from genuine early traditions we cannot say, but the effect was almost to turn Ulysses the hero into Ulysses the villain.

He was the only son of Laertes, ruler of the small and barren island of Ithaca. His mother was Anticleia, daughter of a famous rogue and thief named Autolycus from whom Ulysses was said to have inherited his cunning and duplicity. One tale says that Autolycus gave his baby grandson his name on a visit to see the boy in Ithaca. He was to be called Odysseus, Autolycus suggested, to commemorate the odium under which his grandfather had lived as a consequence of his constant thieving.

Ulysses' childhood was spent in the turbulent atmosphere of a petty chiefdom struggling to hold its own among rival neighbours. Conditions must have been similar to those of Scots clans in the Highlands squabbling for limited quantities of territory and cattle and for prestige. In fact the first journey which Ulysses is supposed to have made away from home was to cross from Ithaca to the mainland to try to recover some stolen sheep. It was on this errand that he acquired the great bow of Eurytus, given to him by the archer's son who was in the same area trying to recover some stolen mares. About this time, too, we get an initial hint that Ulysses was not one for fair play. Not content with the great war bow, he searched for poison to smear on the tips of the arrows. His request for special poison was turned down by one mainland chief, but Ulysses persevered and eventually obtained what he wanted from the ruler of the Taphians, a coastal people notorious as pirates.

Ulysses next appears in folk history among the many suitors who assembled at the court of King Tyndareus of Sparta to seek the hand in marriage of princess Helen, alleged to be the most beautiful woman in the world. Here tradition begins to credit Ulysses with his characteristic shrewdness. The impecunious young man from the insignificant chiefdom of Ithaca realized that he had no chance of winning Helen in competition with suitors from much larger and more important kingdoms. So he quietly struck a bargain with King Tyndareus, who was growing alarmed by the sheer number of rivals for his daughter's hand. The king feared that when the choice was announced, fighting would break out among the disappointed suitors. Ulysses told Tyndareus that he would solve the problem in return for a promise by the king to speak to his brother King Icarius recommending Ulysses as a suitable husband for his daughter Penelope. When Tyndareus agreed, Ulysses explained his scheme. Before announcing the winning suitor, Tyndareus was to extract a binding promise from all the claimants that they would protect the winner from any harm which might befall him as a result of marrying Helen. Without this prior undertaking, no suitor would be eligible to be considered as Helen's husband. Naturally all the hopeful young men agreed and took the oath – including the dissembling Ulysses who already knew that he was not under consideration as a real candidate. Rich and powerful Menelaus, brother of the King of Mycenae, was selected as Helen's husband. As events turned out, Ulysses' scheme rebounded. It was this binding oath of mutual support among the suitors which Menelaus evoked after Helen ran away with a

Trojan prince, and Menelaus and King Agamemnon were raising troops to attack Troy and win her back.

Characteristically – and here the later tradition begins to underline Ulysses' self-interested nature – Ulysses tried to evade the call-up. Why should he leave Ithaca and go off hundreds of miles to Asia Minor to campaign against the Trojans? So when the recruiting delegation from Agamemnon and Menelaus arrived in Ithaca, he pretended to have gone mad. The visitors found him in a field, wearing a madman's hat and tilling the soil with a plough yoked to a horse and an ox. Instead of corn seed, he was scattering the furrows with salt. Unfortunately for his ruse Palomedes, son of Nauplius, was as cunning as he was, and penetrated the trick. Snatching up Telemachus, Ulysses' infant son, he laid the baby in front of the ploughshare so that Ulysses was forced to swerve aside to avoid injuring his baby, and thereby reveal his sanity.

This story of Ulysses' feigned madness, and Palomedes' counter-trick, is not found in Homer but surfaces in later tradition. It makes a colourful introduction to Ulysses' involvement in the Trojan War, and has a sequel which is one of the most damning episodes in his life although once again this is part of later tradition and not an original Homeric story. According to one version Ulysses took his revenge on Palomedes by a truly foul trick. He forged a letter from the Trojans to Palomedes and hid it in his tent with some gold. He then denounced Palomedes as a Trojan spy and manoeuvred the Greeks into stoning the innocent man to death. Another, more blunt, version merely claims that Ulysses and his friend Diomedes lured Palomedes on a fishing trip and drowned him.

Diomedes frequently shows up in Ulysses' company in Homer's account of the siege. On one occasion they both penetrated the Trojan lines on a night-time scouting mission, captured a Trojan spy and, having successfully interrogated him, killed him. The information they gained allowed the Greeks to win an important skirmish against the Trojans. Twice more Ulysses disguised himself in order to penetrate the Trojan defences, actually climbing into the city itself. Once he entered the city to identify the real Palladion, a wooden statue which was possibly some sort of city totem. As long as the Palladion was held safe in Troy, legend said, the city could not be captured. Ulysses identified the real Palladion which had been hidden among several copies, and on his second mission, again with Diomedes, stole it out of the city.

Besides establishing Ulysses as bold and ruthless, Homer stresses that he was very valuable to the Greek cause as a persuasive negotiator, the man with the voice 'like winter snowflakes'. It is in this capacity that he is credited with two short voyages which may have some bearing on the travels of the *Odyssey*, though again the information is traditional and not Homeric. At the beginning of the campaign, when the Greek fleet was assembling, Ulysses is reported to have gone to the island of Skyros in the Aegean to recruit the Greek champion Achilles. Later, during the campaign itself, Ulysses returned to the same island of Skyros to recruit Achilles' son, Neoptolemus. Whether he made two visits to Skyros or just one (there may be repetitions in the saga-telling) it is interesting that Skyros lies on the route which Ulysses was to take later in the *Odyssey* and was a natural stop-over on his homeward route. The inference is that Ulysses was thoroughly familiar with the islands and sea lanes of this part of the Aegean.

As for the wooden horse, a trick said to have been devised by Ulysses and certainly his most spectacular contribution to the campaign, no scholar has yet come up with a satisfactory explanation for what the wooden horse really was. The most skilled Greek carpenter built it, six men including Ulysses and Menelaus hid inside it, and the horse was left outside the gates of Troy while the Greek fleet pretended to sail for home. The Trojans emerged from their defences and debated what to do with the wooden horse. Some wanted to burn it; others, to bring it into the city as a trophy. Finally the Trojans decided to haul the horse into Troy, and were obliged to break down a section of the wall to get it in. Helen was suspicious and walked round the outside of the horse, calling out the names of the hidden men in the voices of their wives. The ambush would have been discovered if Ulysses and Menelaus had not prevented their companions from calling back. That night the Trojans celebrated their apparent victory and while the garrison was off guard the armed men slipped out of their hiding place, lit a signal fire to recall the Greek fleet, and opened the gate of the city to the invaders. Troy was put to the sack and, according to later accounts, Ulysses once again acted in character. A Trojan named Antenor had helped him during one of his secret scouting missions inside Troy, so Ulysses made sure that Antenor was not harmed in the final attack. But after the city had fallen and the victors were deciding what should be done to the vanquished, he showed his ruthless streak. He insisted that Priam's last surviving grandchild should be murdered so that no male descendant of the Trojan king would survive to claim the throne.

This, then was the 'hero' Ulysses. Homer's original figure had been resourceful, self-interested, and a braggart, but admirable rather than odious. As time went on, and stories about him multiplied, Ulysses' qualities were downgraded and he was vilified almost beyond recognition. Here, I thought, was a lesson which should put us on our guard. Perhaps a similar distortion had

been applied by the classical treatment of Ulysses'
wanderings. Homer's original scheme of Ulysses'
journey may have been changed beyond recognition by
later writers and later traditions. I hoped that the way
to find out what was true and what was false was to
return directly to Homer's own story in the *Odyssey*,
disregard later interpretations, but call on the modern
archaeological record. So the logical place to start was
Troy itself, to see what we could learn from the
discovery of the actual site of Homer's 'beetling Ilium'.

2
Troy

Hakki, a Turkish shipwright in the old wooden-boat tradition, had looked after the galley lovingly in her winter quarters. He had repaired the ribs cracked during the previous summer's voyage to Soviet Georgia and kept the Aleppo pine of her hull drenched with linseed oil against the cold of winter. He had also carved two new steering oars from solid pieces of Turkish oak and reinforced them with bronze splints, because *Argo*'s original steering oars had both snapped in the Black Sea, been repaired, and snapped again. Her sail too was new. The previous one had rotted in the damp of the Black Sea and was too thin and flimsy. The replacement was hand-stitched in linen and painted with the head of a Bronze Age nobleman. His portrait was enlarged from a tiny enamel and gold medallion which had once decorated a chalice in old King Nestor's palace. Found among the debris by the archaeologists who excavated the site, the medallion is now displayed in the National Museum of Athens. I thought it only fitting that *Argo*'s crew should sail under the gaze of a man of Ulysses' own epoch.

Argo's crew was thoroughly international. When we set out from Istanbul we numbered five Irishmen, four Britons, two Turks, an American and a Syrian. Several members of my previous team from the Jason Voyage – Mark Richards the rowing master, Peter Wheeler my former second-in-command, burly Cormac O'Connor an Irish fisherman, and Peter Warren – had promised to find time to join later during the trip. As the weeks went by, and people joined or left the vessel according to the amount of free time they could spend aboard, we would also be accompanied at various stages by an Australian merchant-navy officer, an English accountant, a Turkish student, a retired Greek airline pilot, and a Bulgarian journalist. One English volunteer was on short leave from his job in a Gulf state and asked to spend 'a couple of days' with us. He got so beguiled by the lifestyle aboard *Argo* that he left us three weeks later realizing he had only just enough time to dash back to London, change planes and return immediately to the Gulf. We never did learn whether he found time to visit the family in England who had been expecting him.

Shipwright Hakki had taken such pride in looking after *Argo* that he was looking decidedly melancholy as he waved us goodbye from the yacht club and we crossed over to the European shore to pick up last-minute supplies. There two of the Irish contingent went ashore to see the sights. 'We leave at ten', I warned them as they sauntered off. At 10 a.m. when they had not returned, I ordered *Argo* to sea and left our two luckless sightseers ashore. They returned to the dock and were taken aback to find us gone, with all their clothes, passports and money aboard *Argo*. Frantic negotiations persuaded a Turkish fishing-boat skipper to take them aboard and set out in pursuit of the galley, now running fast away from the Golden Horn with wind and current in her favour. Eventually our strays did catch up with us. But it cost them a wild panic and a hefty tip to the fishing boat, and never again did anyone miss the sailing time.

Newcomers to galley sailing soon picked up the daily shipboard rhythm. Each night we anchored in a small port or quiet bay, and the crew like their Bronze Age predecessors went ashore to sleep on the beach. Dawn saw us rolling up sleeping bags and paddling out in the rubber dinghy so that we could hoist anchor and be underway as we ate a simple breakfast of bread and fruit purchased the previous evening. When we had a following breeze there was very little work to be done except to learn how to handle the twin steering oars which had to be twisted in opposite directions to control the ship, a curious sensation for those who were used to steering modern yachts. With thirteen men aboard we were below the galley's proper complement of twenty oarsmen and far too short-handed for rowing any distance, so we devised a makeshift system of fixing the dinghy's spare outboard engine on a wooden bar projecting over the galley's side. In a flat calm this motor-on-a-stick worked remarkably efficiently, though I worried whether this unorthodox arrangement would be sufficient in a gale or perhaps be swamped when the sea got rough. Events would prove these worries were well-founded, but for the moment we sped along gaily, and in just five days of exhilarating downwind sailing came from Istanbul to Troy. The only strenuous activity was to prepare the leather straps which held the oars. The leather was too stiff and had to be made supple by smearing the straps with mutton fat and then pulling them rapidly back and forth around the vessel's rail. The sight of eight half-naked men sitting in the sunshine, facing the rail and sawing away rapidly with the leather straps looked like a class of manic body-builders.

When *Argo*'s anchor dug into the sandy floor of the little bay of Entepe close to Troy on the south shore of the Dardanelles Straits, I began to grasp the complexity of the investigation I had chosen: today Ulysses would not recognize the Trojan coastline. The pleasant little Turkish hamlet of Entepe is now the closest sensible anchorage for a galley whose crew might wish to visit the site of Troy. But Entepe is at least three hours' march from the ruins, whereas in Ulysses' time the entire Greek fleet, said to have numbered a thousand ships, had been drawn up on a beach within easy striking distance of the city. In 1977 a team of American and Turkish geomorphologists sank boreholes in the 2½-mile-wide plain which now separates the ruins of Troy from the Dardanelles Straits. Their drilling revealed that when Troy was first founded some 6,000 years ago, the city stood on the shores of a large shallow bay which extended inland from the strait. A ramp leading down from the north gate of the city would have come directly to the beach and a convenient landing place for ships. But the two rivers which flow past Troy, the Menander and the Simoes, bring down so much gravel and silt that they have gradually choked up this bay. When King Agamemnon's armada arrived, the bay had noticeably shrunk and Troy was almost half a mile from the water's edge. Today, after another 3,000 years, the same silting has been accelerated by drainage and land reclamation so that Turkish farmers now tend fields of cotton, beans and wheat above the spot where Ulysses and his squadron may once have put fresh tar on the hulls of their ships ready to relaunch them from the beach for the long journey home.

You do not have to drill boreholes to detect these dramatic changes. You need only compare the most recent charts for navigating the Dardanelles against the first accurate coastal surveys prepared 100 years ago. The differences are striking. The Trojan embayment is now a stagnant saltwater lagoon where even a punt would find it difficult to thread a path between the ridges of sand and shingle, and the coastline has pushed further out to sea. Inland the irrigation work has straightened out the bends and meanders of the Simoes and Menander. Oddly enough, I found this reassuring. It showed that it is possible to use current changes, still

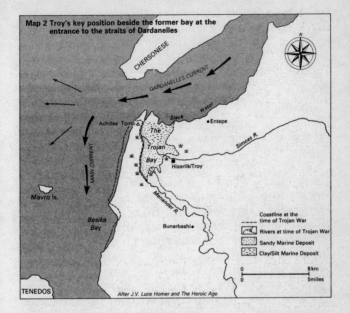

Map 2 Troy's key position beside the former bay at the entrance to the straits of Dardanelles

in progress, to interpret ancient alterations to coastlines. What is happening in front of Troy on the south shore of the Dardanelles is the same process of silting and infill that has been going on since the Trojan War. Of course the boreholes and soil tests are the controlled, scientific way to quantify the precise extent of the ancient bay at particular times. But a general overview on the spot, supported by a comparison between the most recent and the original charts, can establish the way the coast has been remodelled since the days of the great siege. The need to appreciate these changes, we were to find, would be crucial to our research when we came ashore in the territories of the one-eyed Cyclops and Charybdis, the legendary whirlpool.

The nineteenth-century map I was using for the

comparison at Troy was one prepared by the Royal Navy in 1872. During the next four months these nine-teenth-century Admiralty charts were to be irreplaceable. Together with *Argo*, they were the primary tools in the maritime search for any geographical facts within Homer's *Odyssey*. Without them it would have been impossible to begin to place Ulysses' wanderings in context. Unexpectedly, therefore, my first debt in the practical experiment was not to the renowned archaeologists who had uncovered Troy, but to an anonymous host of naval technicians, draughtsmen, and humble boat pullers, who had placed in my hands an effective means to come to grips with the mystery of Homer's geography. They were men from the time when the Royal Navy was the premier map-making organization in the world, and their achievement is still so remarkable that few modern maps have yet surpassed their finesse and accuracy in many out-of-the-way corners of the Mediterranean. For half a century survey parties of the Victorian Navy measured and sketched, climbed mountains to establish their triangulation points, criss-crossed bays in small rowing boats to take countless soundings with lead and line, scrambled onto isolated rocks to obtain their precise co-ordinates, interviewed the local fishermen to learn the names they called the various coastal features, measured tides and currents, dredged up samples from the bottom. All this data they carefully wrote up in the sailors' handbooks known as the Sailing Directions and collated into meticulous hand-drawn charts which the Naval Hydrographer's office engraved beautifully on steel plates on which the descendant maps still depend. Among these stalwart and dedicated surveyors one man was to play a key role for us – the slightly comic-sounding Captain Spratt.

Thomas Abel Brimage Spratt was the epitome of a Victorian scientist-sailor. His father was a hero of

Trafalgar, the renowned limping Commander James Spratt, who had dived into the sea from HMS *Defiance* and swum, cutlass in teeth, to the French 74-gun *Aigle*, boarding her single-handed. Climbing in through a stern window, he found his way to the French poop deck and threw himself on the French crew, one man against several hundred. In the mêlée he killed two French seamen, and was grappling with a third when he fell from the poop deck to the main deck, killing his opponent but injuring himself badly. He was saved by the timely arrival of a full boarding party from *Defiance* but his gallantry had cost him his career. His wounds left him with one leg shorter than the other and he retired to Teignmouth where he became renowned as a long-distance swimmer.

It was here that Thomas was born in 1811, and naturally at the age of 16 he was entered into the Royal Navy by his redoubtable father. But naval battles were in short supply by then, and in 1832 Thomas Spratt was posted to the Mediterranean aboard the survey ship *Mastiff*. For the next thirty-eight years he was to spend his professional career surveying the coasts of the Mediterranean, finishing up as a vice-admiral and a leading authority on the coastal maps of the Mediterranean. Significantly he also became a keen antiquarian. When the successful archaeologists came to search for the site of Troy, they carried with them what was known as 'Spratt's Map'. This was a wonderfully detailed drawing of the countryside around Troy which Thomas Spratt, then only a midshipman, had executed in company with a German professor of classical antiquities in the summer of 1839 while the British fleet happened to be lying at anchor nearby. All three great archaeologists of Troy – Heinrich Schliemann, Wilhelm Dorpfeld and Carl Blegen, whom we shall shortly meet – used 'Spratt's Map', and it struck me as remarkable that as we set out aboard *Argo* to research the *Odyssey* we would be relying on the work of exactly the same map-maker whose skill had contributed to the discovery of Troy. Nothing, it seemed to me, better illustrated the continuing fascination and unsolved mystery of Homer's poems. But where the archaeologists had employed the work of Spratt and his Royal Navy colleagues on land, we intended to use them in the manner for which they had been designed – from the sea.

For 250 days a year, the pilots and fishermen of the Dardanelles will tell you, the wind blows from the north down the straits. Under the wind runs the current, spewing southward at speeds of up to three knots as it pours from the Sea of Marmara into the Aegean. To row against that wind and stream was impossible for a Bronze Age ship. I realized how extraordinarily lucky we had been the previous year going out of the Aegean Sea towards the Marmara in the wake of Jason and his Argonauts. Then we had been blessed with a rare southerly wind which had sent *Argo* skimming forward over the surface of the water at six to seven knots, but the land had moved past at only half that speed as the mass of water on which we floated slid in the opposite direction. The rarity of the south wind and the adverse current add up to one good reason why ancient Troy was sited where it is. Early ships had been obliged to wait for day after day at the south end of the Dardanelles, hoping for the change in wind direction to let them proceed. Where they waited, they set up their impromptu markets, swapped trade goods, and Troy was built. Some historians have suggested that their harbour was not in the great now-vanished bay, but further round the point in a place called Besika Bay. But this notion ignores the powerful Dardanelles current which spreads fan-shaped once it leaves the straits, hindering the vessels coming up from the Aegean. The strongest arm of this current flows towards Besika Bay and makes it an awkward place to reach by oar and sail. Canny shipmasters in early vessels would have known to approach by the northerly route around the island now called Gokceada just as Jason and the Argonauts did. They would have much preferred to moor in the great bay, well sheltered from the hostile wind and current and perfectly poised to catch the first breath of the heaven-sent south wind that would let them break out and claw their way up the Dardanelles.

The second lesson I learned at Troy was drawn from the celebrated story of the long search for the site of the semi-legendary city and its eventual discovery. The man who must be credited with the 'discovery' of Troy is Heinrich Schliemann, a flamboyant businessman turned archaeologist who was so utterly convinced that the *Iliad* and the *Odyssey* were based on truth that he ignored the majority of professional scholars when they argued that the poems were works of fiction. Driven by his naïve and romantic conviction Schliemann, who was endowed with the most phenomenal physical energy, spent his fortune and his health in seeking tangible evidence that Agamemnon, Menelaus, Nestor, Ulysses and all the rest had really lived. First Schliemann looked for the scenes of Ulysses' homecoming in the Ionian Islands (where we shall encounter him later) and then in 1870 came to excavate for Troy and soon dumbfounded the experts when he successfully located the site of Homer's fabled city at a location called Hisarlik, 'the place of the castle'. Schliemann 'found' Troy by an energetic combination of logic, intuition, self-confidence, and the wholesale borrowing of ideas from previous researchers who had been scouring the area looking for the elusive city. He succeeded where much more learned men before him had failed, not just because he *believed* in Troy but because he boldly judged the clues in Homer taken all together rather than relying on one single factor.

The clue that had been misleading most of his predecessors was the most arresting topographical feature about the Troy that Homer had described – the presence of hot and cold springs. In 1795 a French savant by the name of Choiseul-Gouffier claimed he had found just such hot springs by a place called Bunarbashi, five kilometres south of the real Troy. Near the springs was an imposing hill, crowned by an ancient citadel. Traveller after traveller visited the spot, and were all convinced that this was the site of Troy, finding detail after detail that apparently coincided with Homer's text. But they were wrong. The basic flaw in their identification was that their site was much too far away from the two rivers Menander and Simoes which Homer had also implied flowed near the city. What was needed to identify Troy was a combination of several clues, whether the position of rivers, springs, harbour and coast-line, which added up to the same location. Schliemann, with his unshakable conviction that Troy would conform to the whole scenario of Homer's *Iliad*, disregarded the single false clue of the hot and cold springs and looked elsewhere. Thus he succeeded in finding what the others had missed. The message for us was clear: at each site in Homer's *Odyssey* we should try to match a variety of clues, and not be swayed by a single piece of evidence.

Schliemann's romantic faith in the underlying truth of Homer had its brilliant and happy result when the novice archaeologist found Troy. But what is astonishing is that Schliemann only had to dig in the spot where, on 'Spratt's Map', Troy was virtually marked with an x. Five years after the discovery of the misleading hot springs, another travelling scholar had

identified the site of Novum Ilium, the classical Greek
city of New Troy named in honour of its Homeric
predecessor. Midshipman Spratt had conscientiously
marked its location on his excellent map, doubtless
advised by his learned German colleague, and written
across it 'Ilium Novum?'. Here were to be seen the ruins
of classical Greek buildings. The place bore the same
name as Homer's city, and fragments of more ancient-
looking pottery were lying on the surface of the soil.
Yet it was another thirty years before anyone thought
to dig under New Troy to see if perhaps Old Troy lay
beneath. If ever there was an example of overlooking
the obvious, it was the events leading up to the discovery
of Troy itself. Aboard *Argo* it was worth remembering
that the simplest of explanations needed to be
considered, even the most self-evident.

With Troy found at last, the chance had come for
everyone to judge how the real place measured up to
Homer's picture of it. Schliemann's enthusiasm now
carried him adrift. In a series of sensational archaeological campaigns he tore into the hill of Hisarlik with the
help of hundreds of workmen wielding pick-axes and a
miniature railway to carry away the spoil. He dug down
to the ruins of a city which he announced was the very
same Troy that Agamemnon's troops had sacked. He
found armour which he claimed was worn by the
Trojans from the *Iliad*, and gold jewels which had
adorned Queen Helen herself. Now it was Schliemann
who had gone wrong. He had dug too deep, and he
was excavating a city that was far older than Homer's
Troy. It was left to the second of the three great archaeologists who worked at Troy – Wilhelm Dorpfeld – to
point out the error. Schliemann had poached Dorpfeld,
a young trained archaeologist, from another archaeological site at Olympia in mainland Greece and brought
him to Hisarlik. The new assistant was scholarly, pains-

taking and thorough. He soon explained to the whirlwind amateur Schliemann where he had erred, and
when Schliemann died in 1894 his mantle fell on
Dorpfeld who proceeded to excavate a citadel which
conformed splendidly to Homer's story. The ruins
appeared to coincide with the date of the siege, and had
wide streets and fine houses encircled by a beautifully
built defensive wall with fortified gates and watchtowers. Anyone with the least imagination could picture
it manned by the Trojan sentries gazing down at the
watch fires of the besieging Greek army. This, Dorpfeld
announced in his magisterial way, was the real Troy,
Homer's Troy.

This time it was Dorpfeld who had been led astray.
A few Homeric experts still claim that Dorpfeld's Troy,
known as Troy VI as it was the sixth city on the site,
was the Troy that Homer had in mind. But the majority
opinion now accepts the findings of the third and last
great excavator of Troy, the American archaeologist
Carl Blegen, who identified the next city above it, Troy
VIIa, as the Troy that was besieged and sacked at the
time of Homer's Trojan War. Blegen's argument is
highly technical, based on careful analysis of the
pottery, comparison with sites in contemporary Greece,
and by cross-reference with dates in Egypt and Anatolia,
plus the fact that the splendid walls of Dorpfeld's Troy
seem to have been thrown down not by sack, but by
an earthquake. Troy VIIa, so Blegen claimed, was
destroyed by a genuine sack.

But what emerges is that although an actual Troy,
whether Dorpfeld's or Blegen's, certainly existed on the
spot where Schliemann had dug, it is nothing like the
great city that Homer pictures for us. Walking around
the ruins of Troy itself, my first impression was how
small the place is. On average it is little more than 500
yards in diameter and you can stroll around the circuit

of the ancient walls in less than ten minutes. Troy was
no larger than a village and yet in Homer's epic story
there is the impression of an enormous metropolis
teeming with people where the Trojan king and each of
his sons had their own palaces and there was ample
space for town squares, assembly places, temples to the
various gods and presumably shops, homes, store-
houses, stables and barracks. One scholar has taken the
trouble to calculate that if Homer is to be believed, his
city was big enough to contain 50,000 people. Yet Troy
VI is far too small and Troy VIIa is even worse, a mean,
cramped settlement, a makeshift place barely large
enough to hold a few hundred inhabitants in squalid
conditions. Troy VIIa was a feeble target which any
determined force should have been able to capture and
sack in a trice. There was no need for a ten-year siege,
nor for a thousand ships, all of which was very improbable given the resources of the day in men and material.

Nor, I found, is Troy quite as 'sheer' or 'beetling'
as Homer claims. The hill on which it stands is an
unimpressive 100 feet above the level of the plain, no
more than a low bluff. Even in the days when the bay
came close to the walls it would have been only a minor
elevation. Yet here, in the mind's eye, stood an awe-
inspiring city with soaring battlements dominating the
plain. Homer and the bards were not deliberate liars,
they were describing the place as poets. The magic of
their words took a minor citadel and turned it into a
stupendous stronghold immortalized by their descriptions. This is a credit to poetic imagination, but it was
another warning. If Homer could treat Troy like this,
would he not also have done the same for the places in
the *Odyssey*? Might he not have similarly inflated the
locations that Ulysses visited in their size and grandeur
to embellish his tale?

Surely here was a basic rule of epic writing: the epic

poet does not take large sites and major personalities and make them smaller by reducing them in size and importance. His method is quite the opposite. He takes human figures and transmutes them into heroes. He inflates ordinary places so as to make them seem vast and impressive. As I walked around the ruins of Troy I realized that we would have to apply the same law of the epic while we were searching for the locations of the adventures of the *Odyssey*. If we were not to be fooled as the early searchers for Troy had been deceived by the hot springs and the impressive citadel on the crag above Bunarbashi, we would need to be very suspicious of those places we found which were as grand or awe-inspiring as the poet's vision of them. Conversely we would have to keep a very sharp look-out for insignificant places, perhaps overlooked previously because they were on a small scale like Troy itself. Our task was to try to judge them through the magnifying imagination of the poet. Moreover, the lesson of the discovery of Troy directly beneath Novum Ilium on 'Spratt's Map' was that we might very well find the sites of the *Odyssey* right under our noses.

The three archaeologists – Schliemann, Dorpfeld and Blegen – attacked Troy far longer and even more aggressively than the Greek army. Over a span of sixty-nine years they dug, exhumed, examined, argued over the finds, and re-dug so that modern Troy is now one great spoilheap. There are trenches and holes, tips and ravines clothed under a merciful shroud of grass and brightened by the cheerful red splotches of poppies and the occasional wild fig tree growing out of the ancient stones. Battered metal signs attempt to explain the confusion, telling the visitor which heap of overgrown earth or tumbled wall is from which level of Troy. The site is like the layers of a wedding cake after the marriage feast with the crumbs and broken fragments jumbled together. By far the most impressive ruins still belong to the city of Troy VI, Dorpfeld's Troy, and even if they are not the 'real' Troy, they come closest to doing justice to the Homeric image of the city.

That image is still needed to set the scene for the ill-omened voyage that was to achieve immortality. The Great Siege is finally over. Smoke rising from the tumbled and scorched ruins tells that the foreign city has finally been put to the sack. Its defenders are either dead or waiting in chains as human plunder. Each victor receives his share according to his rank. Defeated males will be brought home as slaves, their women put to work as household drudges or, if they are pleasing, kept as concubines. Paradoxically the single most important woman in the sacked city, the one whose infidelity had been the cause of the war and the bloodshed, is coming home in style and comfort. Faithless Queen Helen, whose abduction by the foreigners had sparked the conflict, is reunited with her husband and preparing to return to her own palace in Sparta. The alleged ten years of bitter campaigning had produced the result that the invaders had crossed the sea to achieve. The entire Greek expeditionary force is getting ready to go home from Troy.

The Greeks – or rather the Achaeans as Homer usually calls them – planned to return as they had come, aboard the great armada of ships which had assembled a decade earlier to transport their elaborate amphibious raid. The armada included contingents from every part of mainland Greece and the islands, each squadron led by its own war chief. The largest contingents had been mustered by the joint expedition commanders: by Queen Helen's husband, King Menelaus of Sparta, whose territory lay in the south-east Peloponnese, Greece's southern peninsula, and by his brother King Agamemnon whose imposing capital at Mycenae – also

in the Peloponnese – was to give the Mycenaean civilization its name. If anyone could be considered to be the
High King of the alliance, it was Agamemnon with his
contribution of a hundred ships. At the other end of
the scale the very smallest units numbered only a dozen
or so vessels. They had been provided by the poorer
minor principalities, yet their war leaders also had a
voice in the general council that now convened to
discuss the arrangements for the departure for home. It
was an angry debate. Inevitably there were squabbles
over the division of the booty. Some men were resentful
and felt cheated of their rightful share of the spoils.
There were worries too about the unseaworthy
condition of the ships. Hulls and ropes had rotted from
age and disuse, and there was an argument about the
safest sea route to take home. One faction wanted to go
directly across the Aegean Sea, taking the more exposed
route from Troy on the coast of Asia Minor towards
the islands off the Greek coast. Others favoured a more
cautious track, coast-hugging southward until a shorter
crossing point was reached. Nothing was decided. The
Greek alliance had always been quarrelsome and dispu-
tatious during the siege. Now victory was having its
usual centrifugal effect: the winners were bickering
among themselves and the alliance was breaking up.

Eventually, for lack of agreement, the armada split
into two main divisions. Those most eager to get home
left with King Menelaus and set off down the seaboard
of Asia Minor, sailing from island to island with the
intention of keeping to the inshore passage. The second
group, under King Agamemnon, dawdled on the Trojan
shore. One small squadron, a mere twelve ships,
behaved very oddly. First it set out with Menelaus but,
after scarcely a day's sail which brought them as far as
the island of Tenedos, turned round and doubled back
to join Agamemnon. Then the same squadron abruptly

changed its plans again and switched direction. It broke away from Agamemnon's group and sailed off independently, heading north-west.

Any observer in the Greek fleet who watched the twelve ships vanish over the horizon and who knew the squadron commander was Ulysses would have guessed his plan. Renowned among all the Greek troops for his ability to seek the main chance, he boastfully dubbed himself 'Sacker of Cities'. Obviously he was sailing off to seek what later generations would call targets of opportunity – a little trading here, a coastal raid there if the potential victim was unprepared or frail. His little squadron would have to travel further than any other contingent in the fleet to reach their homes. What was more natural than to try to wrest an extra profit on the way, to top up their Trojan booty.

But that was not to happen. Not a single vessel of that ambitious little squadron was to survive. Of perhaps 600 fighting men and sailors, not including captives and supernumeraries, all perished except the squadron commander himself. He was the only one to see his home again and to bring home a strange description of the lands he had seen. Now, 3,000 years later, we would see if any physical clues remained to what was true and what was false in his report. We would take up Ulysses' story and follow in the possible wake of his twelve-ship squadron as it set out on its own, heading north-west. Somewhere on the waters of the Mediterranean might lie reflections of the world that a genuine Ulysses had described.

3
Sacker of Cities

'Olive oil! More olive oil for the steering oars!' The crew took up the cry jubilantly, shouting forward to Nazem. He was cook of the day, much to everyone's satisfaction, for though Nazem was officially the on-board photographer he had shown himself to be even more of an artist in the kitchen area. Recipes from his native Syria turned rice, green vegetables and lentils into a series of mouthwatering dishes that had the crew members queueing up to help him scrub, slice and peel. Five feet two inches tall, delicately boned, and with enormous dark, mournful eyes under heavy black eyebrows, Nazem was now looking like a miniature Barbary pirate with five days' stubble of beard and a bandanna tied rakishly round his head. Rolling his eyes for dramatic effect, Nazem flashed us a grin beneath his moustache and bobbed down under the forward oar-bench where the kitchen provisions were stored. A moment later a greasy flagon of olive oil was being passed hand to hand down the length of the ship. 'Here,' said John the ship's doctor, 'a present for Ulysses.'

As I poured a liberal dollop of oil to lubricate the leather strap that held one of the galley's twin steering oars in place, I reflected that we were indeed a motley crew. Nazem I had met in Bahrain where he worked as a photographer for the Ministry of Information. Doc John had been recommended to me as an avid sailing enthusiast by the doctor who had sailed on *Argo* the previous summer, and was proving to be an able second-in-command. Rick, the American on the team, had tracked me down the previous autumn while I was visiting the offices of the National Geographic Society in Washington and offered to be the handyman aboard. Rick was an ex-helicopter pilot so I was puzzled quite how his skills might be applied aboard the replica of a Bronze Age galley. But I need not have worried. Rick was one of those very competent and practical people who could turn his hand to carpentry or ropework as well as handle the rubber dinghy we used for our photography sessions, with Nazem crouched inside it and peeking over the rubber hull like some inquisitive squirrel as he clicked away with his cameras.

My plan was to sail, not row, *Argo* in the wake of Ulysses. Reading the *Odyssey* I had been struck by the fact that it was chiefly by sailing – not under oar – that Ulysses and his men had tried to come home. Like all sensible sailors they infinitely preferred to use the wind to their advantage, sitting on the thwarts and controlling the sails rather than raising blisters and getting aching backs and arms from pulling at the heavy sea oars. Their ships were galleys like *Argo*, probably larger – for fifty rather than twenty oars – and designed for rowing as well as sailing. But on long passages they needed a favourable wind to help them. For such a wind they were prepared to wait weeks on end. King Menelaus patiently waited twenty days on one small sandy island during his homeward voyage until he had the wind he needed because in all those twenty days of idle waiting, as Homer stated simply, 'there was never a sign on the water of the steady breeze that ships require for a cruise across the open sea'.

This need for a favourable wind helps us define when Ulysses left from Troy, homeward bound. Homer does not state in what month of the year Ulysses and the eleven other ship captains of the Ionian squadron set sail, but we can make a reasonable guess that it had to have been in the summer sailing season when there is least risk of severe storms. We also have to remember that the entire Greek fleet was also on the move, ships old and new, burdened down with booty and supernumerary captives and slave women, and very vulnerable to bad weather. Their sailing could only have been in the safest months of all, between June and October, which would also have allowed them time for a spring offensive against Troy. The poet Hesiod, a near-contemporary of Homer's, advised a prudent mariner not to launch his boat until late June and fifty days later to pull his vessel ashore and batten her down with a solid heap of shingle to fend off the howling winter gales.

Perhaps Ulysses' captains were not quite as excessively cautious as Hesiod, who was by trade a farmer and had a deep distrust of the sea. But it would be reasonable to imagine Ulysses' twelve ships rowing out from the great bay before Troy at first light on an early morning in June or early July. They would have started at dawn because a galley sailor's working day has its logical routine. The ideal passage is to rouse at the first glimmer of light and leave a safe beach before sunrise, rowing out in the cool of the early morning before the heat becomes oppressive, and then hoist the cross-spar with its gathered bunch of sail as the first breeze ripples the surface of the sea. With the spar as masthead, the lines holding aloft the sail are eased. The rectangular sail drops like a window blind, catches the puff of air, flaps a couple of times, then billows out in a full curve. The sheet-handlers quickly adjust the sail lines to distribute the pressure of the wind and make fast the ropes to their wooden belaying pins. Now the rowers thankfully haul inboard their long oars and arrange them down the length of the vessel, then shift their own positions on the benches to act as human ballasts so that the vessel rides sweet and level. They are free to relax and chat with one another as the helmsman counts off the landmarks sliding by, always alert to the first sign of a shift in the wind, scrutinizing the moving clouds and the distant whitecaps to warn him of changing weather. By early afternoon the helmsman is already eyeing the shore for suitable anchorage to spend the night because sailing after dark, though possible, is unpredictable and dangerous. Once the sun has gone down, there are no shore lights to mark the run of the coast, no tell-tale swirl of breaking foam to warn of the lurking reefs, and only dim and obscured clouds as harbingers of a gale or, almost as worrying, the strong off-shore wind that pummels a fleet and sends it helter skelter out to sea, the long, slim open boats running for their lives, the men bailing desperately and wondering if they can stay afloat. If the wind does abate, they do not know if they will have the strength to row back to land or, when they come ashore, whether they will find friendly and helpful inhabitants, or hostile and cruel people who treat the exhausted mariner as legitimate prey delivered to them by the sea.

We must never forget that Bronze Age sailing was a high-risk business, and the galleys proceeded very cautiously. They stayed near the coast and dashed from anchorage to anchorage or used the Aegean's myriad islands as stepping stones. Space on these heavily manned vessels was so limited that it was awkward to sleep. With barely room to lie down on their narrow benches, the crews needed to come ashore to get proper rest as well as to prepare their meals, for it seems that they did not like to cook aboard, perhaps because of the risk of fire or the limited space to prepare a cooked meal for so many men. The ships were victualled with leather sacks of grain to be pounded into flour and baked for bread, and well-stoppered jars of wine and water which were blended together before they were drunk. At every landing place the crews foraged enthusiastically and it was an unlucky shepherd or cowherd whose flocks or cattle were near the beach when the sailors landed. They stole whatever they could, butchered and ate the best animals on the spot, and carried off as many of the remainder as they could truss up and stow beneath the oar benches.

As they rowed out at the start of their journey, Ulysses' ships left behind them the low hill of Troy barely distinguishable as a dark line against the larger indistinct land mass of the interior plateau. To the oarsmen's right stood the headland later called Kumkale. Scholars still argue whether any of the tumuli, the burial mounds which now rise in distinctive humps along that ridge, were there in Ulysses' time. Today they are far more visible than Troy itself. The mound called 'Achilles' Tomb' (its neighbour is 'Patroclus' Grave') is the most obvious, and Alexander the Great visited it to pay homage to the heroes of Troy. More cautious modern scholarship believes that the earth is heaped over the corpse of some dead king who lived several centuries later than the Trojan War.

Standing beside the twin steering oars in the stern of each galley, the helmsman would have been calculating his course for the crucial moment when his vessel entered the main run of the Dardanelles current. He had to judge from the wave caps just where the strongest current ran that morning in the strait, and choose the moment to let loose the sail and call out the order for the crew to trim the boat to starboard as she heeled to the north wind. Then suddenly his galley was into the current and being swept rapidly out into the Aegean. The wind thrust her forward through the dark blue water and the waves began to slap crisply against the thin planking of the wooden hull. The squadron had cleared Troy's bay, and they were going home.

A skilful course would have brought the twelve little ships slanting across the mouth of the strait and close around the opposite point where a low cliff and two small beaches mark the tip of the Chersonese, the long whale-backed finger of land which a later generation knew as Gallipoli. From here northward runs a gentle coast of low bluffs and rolling hills, opening out to the quiet bay of Saros, known for its calm weather, and then curving back again to the yellow cliffs of Grimae. The cliffs mark the approach to the shoals of the Evros river, now the border between Greece and Turkey and famous for the white-fleshed flounders which breed on the long sandy shallows. On the Chersonese occurred an event typical of the later embellishments that tradition added to Homer's version of the story. It is claimed that Queen Hecuba, widow of King Priam of Troy, had been allotted to Ulysses as a concubine, part of his share of the Trojan loot. As Ulysses' squadron passed along the coast of the Chersonese, he stopped in the realm of King Polymestor, a former ally of the Trojans. There Hecuba learned that the king had treacherously murdered one of her sons. In revenge she lured the unsuspecting king to her tent, blinded him and killed his children. Then, as the squadron sailed on, she transformed into a fiery-eyed black hell-hound and flung herself into the sea. In later years her grave was pointed out by sailors passing along that shore.

There is little to be extracted from this tale except to confirm that an examination of the lists of allies who came to the aid of Troy in the face of the Greek invasion shows that many arrived from Thrace, the land on the north seaboard of the Aegean. So it was no accident that his squadron was heading in this direction. It was a small pack of wolves hunting for an easy prey, a small town perhaps that had unwisely stripped its garrison when it sent its contingent to help with the defence of Troy.

'Look at Ulysses' route in this sector,' I commented to Theodor, our Bulgarian crew-master who joined us at the Greek island of Thasos. I had first met Theodor in Soviet Georgia where he had sailed with a Bulgarian yacht to greet *Argo* at the conclusion of the Jason Voyage, and I had invited him to participate in our quest for Ulysses. Now we were six days into our journey and I wanted to explain to him the significance of the route *Argo* had taken from Troy. The first stage of the *Odyssey* was the only sector we could be absolutely sure about, and Ulysses' route was entirely in character. He was a cautious man but also an opportunist. His northward path took him away from the main fleet, making him independent of the rest of the Greeks and leaving him free to go roving on his own so that he didn't have to share any plunder with them. But Ulysses was also a careful seaman. This northerly route was as safe as the southerly path the main fleet took because it was a coasting route, westabout around the Aegean, and would eventually bring Ulysses down

to the Peloponnese, the southern peninsula of mainland Greece. 'In seaman's terms,' I told Theodor, 'the way Ulysses chose to go home is less risky, if anything, than the route Agamemnon and Menelaus selected.'

Theodor grinned. 'There are all sorts of legends and stories about the warriors returning from Troy who settled in this area. In fact my own family surname – Troev – is supposed to mean we came from Troy. Probably it's just a family myth, but to celebrate *Argo*'s arrival in Thrace, I've brought with me some good Thracian wine – just in case we meet the Cyclops later on.'

The wine Theodor referred to was the most important item of plunder Ulysses took from what was otherwise a disastrous raid on Ismarus, the city of the Cicones people of the Thracian cost. In the *Odyssey* Ulysses makes no bones about the piratical motive for the attack:

☐ The same wind as wafted me from Ilium brought me to Ismarus, the city of the Cicones. I sacked this place and destroyed the men who held it. Their wives and the rich plunder that we took from the town we divided so that no one, as far as I could help it, should go short of his proper share. And then I said we should be off and show a clean pair of heels. But my fools of men refused. There was plenty of wine, plenty of livestock; and they kept on drinking and butchering sheep and fatted cattle by the shore. Meanwhile the Cicones went and raised a cry for help among other Cicones, their up-country neighbours, who are both more numerous and better men, trained in fighting from the chariot and on foot as well, as the occasion requires. At dawn they were on us, thick as leaves and flowers in their season, and it certainly looked as though Zeus meant the worst for my unhappy following and we were in for a very bad time. A pitched battle by the ships ensued, and volleys of bronze spears were interchanged. Right through the morning and while the blessed light of day grew stronger we held our ground and kept their greater force at bay; but when the sun began to drop, towards the time when the ploughman unyokes his ox, the Cicones gained the upper hand and broke the Achaean ranks. Six of my warriors from each ship were killed. the rest of us contrived to dodge our fate and got away alive. □

Ulysses' raid on the Cicones was a text-book case of the hit-and-run tactics of the era: the sudden attack on a peaceful city by raiders from the sea, the massacre of the menfolk followed by looting which degenerated into a drunken victory feast that gave the defenders time to rally, gather their reinforcements and counter-attack in strength, driving off the invaders with losses. Ulysses had been well-advised to beg his men to take to their heels as soon as they had their plunder, but it is revealing how very little control he really had over them. Time and again, as we shall see, the unruly, often mutinous behaviour of his men was to lead to grief. In the *Odyssey* Ulysses will turn out not at all the successful war leader that the *Iliad* had portrayed. On his voyage home he was to be notably ineffectual. Unable to impose any degree of discipline, he begged and pleaded with his men, ccajoled and threatened. But either they disregarded him or they flagrantly disobeyed him. They distrusted him, and in turn his bungling led them into ambushes and dangerous impasses where they paid the price with their lives. The impression is of a rabble, a band of freebooters with each captain and soldier behaving as he saw fit, and only loosely under the control of a rather inept war chief. This impression, although not 'heroic', may be realistic enough to prove to be the true story.

As luck would have it, Ulysses protected the lives of Maron, a priest of Apollo, and his wife during the sack of Ismarus. To show his gratitude Maron gave Ulysses many gifts including a quantity of the fine wine for which the area was famous. This wine, noted for its strength, was stowed in Ulysses' ship and carried away safely from the raid. As Theodor said, the wine of Ismarus was to feature in the forthcoming encounter with the cannibal Cyclops, save Ulysses' life and, temporarily at least, save the lives of several of his men.

'Where exactly was Ismarus, the city of the Cicones?' I asked Theodor. 'Have the archaeologists been able to locate the site?'

Before joining us Theodor had consulted Bulgarian and Greek scholars about the Bronze Age settlement on the Thracian coast. 'The Cicones lived in the area between the Evros and Nestos rivers, and are mentioned by writers later than Homer. But no one is sure about the precise location of their city of Ismarus. The best estimate is that it could have been near the place still called Maronia after the priest Maron, though other historians say that the site of Ismarus may lie a little inland today, partly because the coastline has changed, and also because many of the cities of the time were sited a little distance from the shore due to the threat of sea raiders like Ulysses.'

Argo received her own gift of Thracian wine on the nearby island of Thasos where the islanders arranged a reception for the galley and crew. We rowed into harbour to find tables had been carried to the quay and loaded with food and drink. For each crew member there was a little gift, wrapped up in a scrap of fishing net. The package contained a selection of the island's main products – a tiny bottle of aniseed flavoured ouzo, a small clay jug, a jar of local honey, and a bottle of the famous black Thasos wine. 'After the heroic Jason, how does it feel to be following the wily Ulysses?' asked the Mayor. 'Let's hope you are shrewder than Ulysses and that it won't take you ten years of voyaging to get home!'

And that is one of the popular misconceptions about the *Odyssey*, and a very misleading one. Homer says that Ulysses was nineteen years away from home in 'sea girt Ithaca' and got home in the twentieth year. But when you ransack the *Odyssey* and add up the actual sea time in the story and then make allowances for the unspecified sectors, the total time spent at sea barely adds up to a single sailing season. The vast majority of the *Odyssey* Ulysses spent ashore and usually very comfortably – seven years of it with the beautiful and amorous nymph Calypso and a whole year in the adoring company of the beguiling witch Circe. In working out Ulysses' route, one is not dealing with nineteen years of voyage, nor even nine years' wanderings after subtracting the ten-year siege of Troy, but with a very few months, perhaps no more than a dozen weeks of actual galley sailing. Far from destroying the credibility of Homer's tale, *Argo*'s voyage was to reveal that this time span neatly fits the geography of the Mycenaean world.

Thasos was a logical port-of-call for us, as it would have been on the ancient sea lanes of this part of the Aegean. Often described as a lump of solid marble, Thasos rises boldly from the sea and makes an obvious landmark for any squadron passing along the rather featureless Thracian coast. Bronze Age sailors navigated by line-of-sight. They used good sea-marks such as bold headlands, tall mountain peaks and distinctively shaped islands to serve as their signposts across the sea. The great mass of Thasos was an excellent turning point on

Ulysses' route, for it led directly to the greatest land-mark of the entire northern Aegean – the 6,670-foot peak of Mount Athos, a day's run southward. Mount Athos dominates the horizon of any sailor. With a fair wind he can keep Mount Athos in view for a full day's sail, whether proceeding south from Thasos, east towards the island of Lemnos on the shortest route to the Dardanelles, or west around the three prongs of the Chalkidiki peninsula. Here he exchanges the beacon of Athos for the snows of Mount Olympus and steers towards that white peak until he comes to the mainland of Greece.

In late May we had the prevailing north wind in our favour as we ran south from Thasos. *Argo*'s sail pulled the galley along easily, and the great mountain loomed over the horizon first to our right hand and then almost dead astern. We passed close under the steep cliffs where the flank of the mountain falls steeply to the water, and isolated, half-abandoned monasteries gaze out to sea with row upon row of empty windows. We could both feel and see the sea current flowing past the rocky penin-sula, again in our favour, drawing out slicks of dirty foam and bobbing bits of plastic flotsam on the grey surface of the sea. Ahead and as yet unseen lay the islands of the Northern Sporades archipelago, and all we had to do to reach them was keep the steady north wind full aft and the tall head of Athos in line with the curved scorpion tail of the galley.

That day Mount Athos stood with its foot in a thick grey-brown layer of polluted haze, and the mountain peak was blurred at ten miles' distance. How much more useful and more spectacular, I thought to myself, Mount Athos must have been 3,000 years earlier when the atmosphere was so much clearer without the dense mass of modern man-made pollution to obscure it. Then the potential of line-of-sight navigation would have been far beyond anything which we can experience today. We can only guess the tremendous distances at which men could have recognized the far-off land features through the clarity of unpolluted air. Very occasionally today, when a mass of cold stable air is established over the Aegean, we can have some inkling of the limpid quality of the view when objects thirty or forty miles away appear distinctly above the horizon. In Ulysses' time a helmsman could see his next seamark appearing out of the Aegean even as his previous beacon sank in his galley's wake.

Crossing the northern Aegean Ulysses did not share *Argo*'s weather luck. After pausing long enough near Ismarus to hold a funeral honouring the seventy-two men who died in the thwarted attack, the men of Ithaca had put to sea when their twelve ships were hit by heavy weather:

☐ Zeus, who marshals the clouds, now sent my fleet a terrible gale from the north. He covered the land and sea alike with a canopy of cloud; and darkness swept down on us from the sky. Our ships were driven sidelong by the wind, and the force of the gusts tore their sails to rags and tatters. With the fear of death upon us, we lowered these onto the decks, and rowed the bare ships landward with all our might. Thus we lay for two days and nights on end, with exhaustion and anxiety gnawing at our hearts. ☐

This description of a gale at sea rings true. It was the situation that every experienced Bronze Age helmsman feared: the wind strengthening to a full gale rips the flimsy sails and creates mayhem aboard the lightly built ships. The cross-yard makes a galley dangerously unstable and must be lowered. First the spar has to be swung fore and aft along the length of the vessel, then the halyard eased away gently so that the lungeing mass of wood and ruined sail can be caught and held by crew members, the scraps of torn cloth smothered under coils of light rope, and finally the spar laid down on deck and secured so that the pitch and roll of the ship does not send it crashing lethally from side to side. The shriek of the wind, the rumble of the waves, the lurch of the galley as each wave crest thumps the hull would indeed strike 'the fear of death' into the sailors. Their helmsman, the most important man in the ship in the crisis, struggles to keep enough movement on the ship to control her attitude to the waves. She must lie slant-wise to their onslaught if she is not to be capsized. Once the spar and probably also the stubby mast have been struck down, the men get out the oars and try to row in that heaving, pitching sea, desperately attempting to get a grip with the oarblades on the broken water.

We had survived similar conditions on *Argo* in the Black Sea the previous year, and knew what it felt like to be thrown about, struggling and bruised, with loose items clattering from side to side, the bilge water swirling higher and higher as spray broke across the vessel or solid water slopped in. The only difference between us and Ulysses' unlucky sailors was that in the Black Sea my decision as captain had been to head further and further away from land, to get as far as possible from ship-smashing rocks and then wait for the wind to ease and allow us to take stock, make temporary repairs and finally limp back. By contrast Ulysses' shipmasters opted to row for land and try to anchor in shelter before the gale sank them. They chose a risky landfall in preference to the long sick-making ordeal of a storm-tossed sea. Perhaps their vessels were in a truly dilapidated condition after long neglect during the siege itself and incapable of enduring a lengthy

The Ulysses Voyage

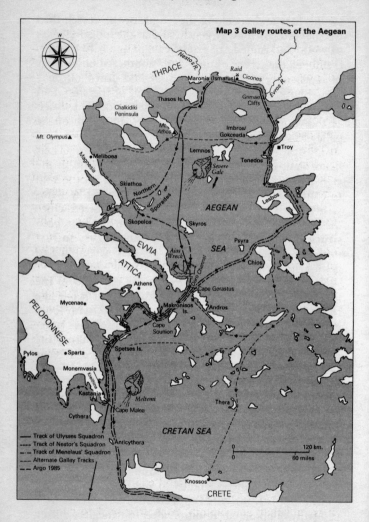

Map 3 Galley routes of the Aegean

N

THRACE

Nestos R.

Raid
Maronia (Ismarus) ✕ Cicones

Evros R.

Thasos Is.

Grimae Cliffs

Chalkidiki Peninsula

Imbros/ Gokceada

Mt. Olympus ▲

Mt. Athos

Lemnos

■ Troy

Magnesia

Severe Gale

Tenedos

Meliboea

Skiathos

Northern Sporades

AEGEAN

Lesbos

Skopelos

Skyros

SEA

Psyra

EWIA

Aias Wreck

Chios

ATTICA

Doro Channel

Athens

Cape Gerastus

PELOPONNESE

Mycenae ●

Makronisos Is.

Andros

Pylos

● Sparta

Cape Sounion

Monemvasia

Spetses Is.

Kastania

Kythira

Meltemi

Thera

Cythera

Cape Malea

CRETAN SEA

—— Track of Ulysses Squadron
······ Track of Nestor's Squadron
—··— Track of Menelaus' Squadron
----- Alternate Galley Tracks
—·— Argo 1985

Anticythera

0   120 km.
0   60 miles

Knossos

CRETE

battering from the waves. Perhaps their oarsmen were more expert than *Argo*'s crew who had found it almost impossible to row in heavy weather, with the water lapping at the top plank one moment, and the next instant so far away it was impossible to bury the oarblade. Whatever the reason for the choice, Homer's account of this Aegean storm establishes the genuine seafaring nature of the *Odyssey:* the danger, the fears of the crew, the ship-handling in a crisis, and the description of the storm itself. They are true to life and take the story out of the realm of fantasy and place it aboard real ships manned by real, suffering mariners.

Just where the battered and frightened squadron found shelter and the crews lay for two days and nights 'with exhaustion and anxiety gnawing at our hearts' is not stated. The mainland coast here, ancient Magnesia, offers no safe harbour in a northerly gale, nor does the bleak coast of the island of Evvia, often treated as part of the mainland because of its great size. The best shelter would have been in the Sporades directly on the squadron's course, and in particular behind Skyros whose anchorages Ulysses may have known from his earlier visits there to fetch Achilles and Neoptolemus. Certainly his twelve crews had been lucky. The fleet they had left behind at Troy, the mass of shipping led by King Agamemnon, came to grief in very similar conditions. Taking a more exposed and direct route diagonally across the Aegean, this fleet was also hit by a gale. Their vessels were driven down on the rock-bound coast of Evvia. Some of them managed to escape destruction, but many were dashed upon the rocks of Cape Gerastus on the southern tip of the island of Evvia. These vessels were smashed to smithereens and their crews drowned. It is said that one captain, Aias, managed to cling on to the rocks and his life seemed to be saved. Indeed, so the story runs, he loudly exulted he had escaped his fate. But the angry god Poseidon heard his boast and struck the rock so that it shattered. Aias fell back into the raging sea and perished.

The partial destruction of Agamemnon's fleet underlines a brutal fact of Bronze Age seafaring: if the early galleys were caught in a full-blooded Mediterranean gale, their crews did not have the strength to row their way out of trouble. They were as helpless as scraps of wind-blown chaff blown by the gale on to whatever shore lay in their lee. If they were lucky, galley oarsmen might frantically row their vessel round a headland into a patch of shelter — as Ulysses' squadron would have done — or they could edge their vessels across the main path of the wind and so take a safer course. But that was the limit of their capacity. They could neither row against the wind nor even hold their vessel steady in the same spot. Aboard *Argo* we learned by hard example that even a moderate wind is master over a crew of oarsmen, and a galley is the wind's plaything.

Ulysses' Aegean gale blew itself out after two days: 'on the third morning, which a beautiful dawn had ushered in, we stepped the masts, hauled up the white sails, and sat down, leaving the wind and the helmsmen between them to keep our vessels straight'. Once again it is under sail and not by rowing that the little squadron resumes its course, and the route it chose is doubtless the one that has remained the same to this day for the southbound sailor.

The key is the Doro Channel, the place where Agamemnon's surviving ships tried to swerve to avoid Cape Gerastus. The channel divides the islands of Evvia and Andros, and all the natural conditions favour the southbound sailing vessel. Here is deep water, good landmarks on either side, and — best of all — a strong current to push the vessel onward even when the wind is slack. For *Argo* the prevailing north wind grew even stronger as it funnelled between the islands and we skimmed through the gap in a tearing rush. Our little twenty-oar galley was at her best, close to the safe limit of speed, swooping boldly over the long march of waves heaping into the gullet of the strait. On each wave crest she gave a wilful lurch and roll, and the full weight of mast, spar and sail brought up hard against the tabernacle of the mast with an alarming thump that sent a shudder quivering down the length of her hull. That was when I called for the olive oil, because the strain on the twin steering oars was terrific. Peering over the side I could see the water rushing past the blades so fiercely that they thrummed under the pressure. The pull was so great that previous anointments of oil were being squeezed from the leather straps like beads of greasy sweat. Unless the straps were kept well lubricated, the steering oars would not turn smoothly and then, in a sudden swerve, they would snap.

The failure of their gear was the true limit to how fast the early ships could be sailed. They had to operate with suspect ropes of leather or loosely woven fibre, and sails of cotton and flax. Metal was so expensive that it could only be used sparingly if at all in the structures. Their captains needed to be constantly alert to a sudden breakage that would cripple the vessel. When sailing conditions were perfect – a moderate following or quartering wind with the waves not yet too steep – the galleys could spin off six or seven miles in every hour as *Argo* was doing through the Doro Channel. But as soon as weather and sea conditions exceeded the limits of the strength of the vessel's ropes, sail and spars, then it was time to duck into shelter and wait, maybe for days on end, maybe for weeks. It did not matter. A single ideal day's passage at maximum speed was preferable to the same distance nibbled away in short stages. So the early galley voyages proceeded by fits and starts, the occasional spectacular passages of over a hundred miles in a day interspersed with long periods of waiting. Just such a stop-and-start regime would have dictated the progress of Ulysses and his squadron, not the steady day-after-day speeds which many commentators tend to award them.

Poor Nazem was made agonizingly seasick by the swooping, swaying motion of the running galley as we sped through the Doro Channel. He lay curled up on a crumpled sail bag like a small, unhappy dormouse, his eyes closed in misery. We felt particularly sorry for him because the previous evening, with *Argo* moored in a bay off Skyros, he had cooked for us a memorable meal of vegetables, rice and fish served with a lemon sauce. But he nibbled only a tiny amount himself, knowing he would not hold it down.

Derry, the youngest of our regular crew, had netted the fish. With his open countenance, innocent blue eyes and soft Limerick accent, Derry was the butt of much of the shipboard teasing which he absorbed with limitless good humour and a huge slow smile. In Istanbul I had bought a light fishing net to add to *Argo*'s equipment because I wanted to test whether a galley crew could have fished for their food during a long journey. Derry made the mistake of mentioning he had once helped set salmon nets in the Shannon estuary, and so was promptly designated our official fisherman and instructed in the use of the net by a Turkish expert. Derry's meagre luck with the net soon explained why the early tests rarely tell of fishing for the pot. Each night when *Argo* came to rest, Derry would set his net in a likely spot near the anchorage. At dawn he gathered up the catch before the trapped fish were mauled by predators. The results were always skimpy – a few small fish, perhaps an eel or two. Derry would have to spend a couple of hours patiently untangling the little fish from the mesh, detaching the tiny crayfish whose pincers had seized the netting in their final agonies, picking out seaweed, battering to death with a rock the poisonous scorpion fish before he cautiously extracted and threw away the bits. Even allowing for the gross depletion of fish stocks in the Mediterranean, which must be partly balanced by the more efficient modern nylon net we used, it was clear from Derry's scanty catches that fishing would rarely have supplied the needs of a ravenous galley crew. All Nazem's skill as a cook was needed to stretch the miserable catch far enough to add even a fishy flavour to our meal.

Once through the Doro Channel our next seamark was the most famous in all of Greece – the bold headland of Cape Sounion at the tip of the Attic peninsula, only twenty-five miles south of Athens. Today the headland is crowned by the ruins of a great temple to Poseidon, whose marble columns turn into shafts of lustrous honey yellow as the coastline of the Attic peninsula darkens against the red path of the sinking sun. Built in the fifth century BC, the temple to Poseidon stands on a spot already considered sacred when King Menelaus' fleet passed Cape Sounion, on that same well-rehearsed route, to bring it home from Troy. Here Phrontis, the king's chief helmsman, died as they passed the cape, and in the *Odyssey* old King Nestor recalls his sudden death at sea:

☐ When we were abreast of the sacred cape of Sounion, where Attica juts out into the sea, Phoebus Apollo let fly his gentle darts at Menelaus' helmsman and struck him dead, with the steering-oar of the running ship in his hands. This man Phrontis son of Onetor had been the world's best steersman in a gale, and Menelaus, though anxious to proceed, was detained at Sunium [Sounion] till he could bury his comrade with the proper rites. □

Few places can be more fitting for the last resting place of a great sailor. Cape Sounion is the final turning point for all the ships homeward bound for Attica out of the east and north. Until they round the tip of dagger-shaped Makronisos Island, Sounion is hidden. Then suddenly the vessel turns the corner and the crew look up and see the cape, and realize that they are nearly home. Every sailor familiar with the lore of the coast would also have remembered Phrontis, the master mariner.

As *Argo* approached Sounion the wind died away to a mere whisper of breeze, and a venerable patrol boat of the Greek Navy, chugging past on the opposite track, gave us a cheer. 'Look, Theodor,' I said, handing him the binoculars as the next vessel approached, 'isn't that a Bulgarian flag she's flying?' He peered ahead. 'Yes, I expect she's headed home for Varna.' 'I wonder what her crew think,' I said, 'suddenly coming across a Bronze Age galley sailing round Cape Sounion. They must wonder if they're dreaming.' 'I'll wake them up!' Theodor chuckled, 'Please can I use the walkie-talkie?' I handed him the little handset, switched to the international ship-to-ship channel. By now the Bulgarian ship had altered course to come closer to us and take a good look. We could imagine the shock in the wheel house when suddenly their radio burst into life and a voice spoke to them in Bulgarian. There was a long pause as the ship's radio operator recovered from his surprise. Theodor repeated his call. Again, there was a long pause. Then, hesitantly, the radio man replied. Theodor, grinning mischievously, spoke with slow deliberation. When the conversation finally ended and he handed back the walkie-talkie he laughed. 'What a puzzle for them! The radio man was so stunned I had to repeat everything twice for him. He couldn't understand how there came to be a Bulgarian aboard an ancient Greek galley. But he did say he'll relay to my family the news that all is well aboard *Argo*.'

Some sort of bush telegraph of the Aegean had also been at work. When we reached the island of Spetses on 11 June we were expected. Vasilis had been tracking our progress – Vasilis Delimitros, the gruff taciturn genius of a shipwright who had built *Argo* two winters earlier at his ramshackle workshed on the shore of Spetses' Old Harbour. As I steered the galley round the lighthouse and into the well-remembered approach, it was as though *Argo* was coming home. Nothing had changed: there was still the same traffic jam of modern cruising yachts tied up to the quay; the higgledy-piggledy of slipways with boats hauled out for repairs; the spare ferry tied up bow first to the quay with her ramp let down; the line of moorings. Nobody seemed to be paying much attention to *Argo* slipping quietly through the water as the crew got ready to berth. Then a small motor boat shot out of the moorings and came racing straight towards us. 'Everything alright, Mr Tim? Vasilis waiting!' called a yellow-jerseyed figure in the boat. It was Mimas, Vasilis' assistant, waving enthusiastically.

Argo glided the last hundred metres. There was the little boatshed, perched on the rocks. I smiled to myself. Hanging from one end of the shed was a large Greek flag, at the other gable was a large Irish ensign. Vasilis had arranged his own private welcome signal. And there he was, a short upright figure with curly grey hair, wearing old jeans and a worn blue sweater, standing on the end of the rickety pier, with his arms folded and his head tilted back and cocked slightly to one side as he regarded his creation swimming in gracefully. I knew he would be taking note of the trim of the galley, the way she steered, every tiny detail of his masterpiece. He was seeing the boat for the first time since she had sailed away fifteen months earlier, bound for the Black Sea.

'Let go stern anchor!' Derry tossed over the anchor with a splash. Mimas had already taken a bow line and was fastening it to the jetty. We hauled in and secured *Argo* to the jetty, and I hurried ashore to greet Vasilis. 'Hello, Vasilis. How are you? Do you like the way she looks?' I gestured at the galley. 'There are no problems. She's in fine condition.'

He pumped my hand, so choked with emotion that he was finding it difficult to get his words out. 'Welcome, Captain. Tonight you stay my home!'

But of course it was *Argo* that Vasilis really wanted to see. He had put his heart into the building of the galley, using the same techniques that the ancient craftsmen had employed, joining the planks with hundreds of mortise and tenon joints. He had laboured with such dedication and confidence, and the skills acquired from a lifetime of building wooden boats by hand, that he had finished *Argo* in less than six months when experts had warned it would require several years to do the job. What is more, the experts had imagined a team of shipwrights, but Vasilis had worked single-handed on the hull with only Mimas to fetch and carry. Now, as soon as the greetings were over and he felt it tactful, Vasilis scrambled on board to inspect the boat. He shouted to Mimas and the latter ran to fetch a light hammer. Vasilis strode from rowing bench to rowing bench down the length of the galley, pausing only to rap his hammer on each rib of the ship. Thump, thump, thump, came the hammer blows. He reached the end of the galley, turned, and came back towards me. 'This, this, this!' he announced, touching the hammer on three of the ribs. 'These ones have been changed.' He was

Vasilis' Boatyard, Spetses, 16 June

right. Instantly he had identified the ribs that Hakki the Turkish shipwright in Istanbul had repaired, judging simply by the sound of the ribs responding to the hammer blow.

Next morning I asked the crew to empty out all the stores so that *Argo* was swept clean for Vasilis to examine the ship right down to her keel. 'She's fine, Vasilis,' I had to keep reassuring him. 'Everything's fine. Only the mast is loose in the mast-step and if you could find some way to hold it more steady it could be better. But there's nothing important to be done. The boat is in splendid condition.' Vasilis sniffed. 'Why did the Turkish carpenter repair the ribs this way?' he demanded accusingly. He was as protective of his creation as a mother of her favourite child. 'The ribs were cracked on the slipway in Volos before the Jason Voyage, not at sea,' I hastened to reassure him. 'The timber was bad.' 'I know,' he replied darkly. 'If the timber supplier had sent me the material that I asked for, *that* would not have happened,' and he left me to guess at the dispute he must have had with the timber merchant. 'I wouldn't have made the repairs the same way as that Turkish carpenter' he added. Luckily I knew

Vasilis of old, and his fierce pride and independence. 'It's fine Vasilis, it really is. I'm sure that the repairs will hold up as we follow Odysseus. Please don't worry.' He grunted. 'Well, if anything does go wrong, you send me a telegram, and wherever you are, I'll come there and fix the problem. And next winter,' he added for effect, 'when you lay up the boat, just check with me before you select who looks after her.'

4

The Lotus-eaters

'I should have reached my own land safe and sound, had not the swell, the current, and the North Wind combined, as I was doubling Malea, to drive me off my course and send me drifting past Cythera.' With these few phrases Homer casually sweeps Ulysses and his little squadron off the edge of the known map. Where did the squadron go? Where did Ulysses wander until the time he reappeared unexpectedly at his home in Ithaca, telling his yarns of one-eyed monsters, a witch turning his men into pigs, and the peaceful Lotus-eaters who lived on a narcotic? Cape Malea is the last known point on Ulysses' route, the last 'fix' that we can put on his position. Yet by applying our knowledge of galley sailing, acquired firsthand aboard *Argo*, we can take the first step towards solving a mystery which has perplexed commentators since well before the time of Julius Caesar.

Cape Malea was, and still is, notorious for strong winds and the rough seas they stir up. The Peloponnese has the shape of a molar tooth pulled from its socket, and Cape Malea lies at the extreme end of one of its roots. Ancient ships accustomed to hugging the coast found Malea a perilous turning point on their route. Here the under-powered galleys were obliged to alter their course through almost 300 degrees as they crept around the point so that a favourable wind bringing them down from the Aegean was abruptly turned into a headwind against which they would have to row as they came back up the other side. Worse, if the wind increased in strength while they were rounding the cape, they would be blown down towards the island of Cythera and then out into the open sea. Cape Malea became a psychological as well as a physical boundary. 'When you double Malea, forget your home' was an early Greek adage for the notion of passing a point of no return, and in the *Odyssey* two of the homeward-bound Greek squadrons got into difficulties there – Ulysses' twelve ships which we shall now try to track, and Menelaus' squadron which was also blown out to sea at the Cape by northerly winds as it tried to get back to Sparta. According to Homer, Menelaus was forced down on the coast of Crete where the heavy weather drove several of his ships ashore.

Today we know why Cape Malea has so much bad weather. Many of the gales arrive as Atlantic depressions which enter the western Mediterranean and sweep down its lengths, bringing strong winds in their wake. These depressions follow regular tracks, and approaching Cape Malea several tracks converge in the Cythera channel just off the headland. The chances of meeting cyclonic winds are highest just at the dangerous point where a coasting galley is turning the corner and most vulnerable.

Argo approached Cape Malea in the early afternoon of 24 June and I could see that the region was living up to its malevolent reputation. A jumble of white caps was breaking beyond the headland where a fresh north-west wind was whipping up the surface of the sea. *Argo* was in prime condition after a week in Spetses. Vasilis had shooed away her crew so that he could get on unhindered with the job of checking over the boat. He had found no faults and devised a clever way to strengthen the mast tabernacle so that the mast no longer thumped and swayed in its fitting, threatening to tear its way out of the hull. Refreshed and confident, we

were following the coast route down towards Malea, a
task made simple by the high mountains of the Peloponnese which could be seen as our guide from a long way
off. Yet I had already noticed how much more fickle
the weather was in this area compared to the northern
Aegean. We had left Spetses in a virtual calm the
previous morning, and at noon a fresh south-easterly
breeze had sprung up so rapidly that I was very glad
we were still far enough off the coast to be able to select
a safe course and slant into the narrow creek of Ieraka
where we had sheltered for the night.

Now the weather was behaving in the same unpredictable fashion. We cleared the creek at dawn and
proceeded cautiously down the coast towards Malea
which appeared in the distance as a grey hump with a
prominent boss on its summit. To our right the remarkable peninsula of Monemvasia projected from the coastline like a miniature Rock of Gibraltar. This was the
last proper shelter before the Cape and in the Bronze
Age had been the site of an important settlement probably founded by Minoans from Crete. Apart from the
huddle of the modern town and a scattering of houses
further inland the scenery could scarcely have changed
in millennia. High to our right on the grey flank of the
mountainous Krithina peninsula a white patch clung
like a fungus – the houses of Kastania, the last village
in this bleak and windswept land. Beyond it there was
only grey, jagged rock, sterile and forbidding except
where small patches of ochre marked a thin smear of
topsoil. The only other colour was a ragged mantle of
dark green scrub, mostly thorn, which scarcely did more
than highlight the hostile grey terrain. There were no
fields, no walls, nor any sign of habitation beyond
Kastania except for the occasional stark outline of a
ruined watchtower where sentries had once kept watch
for raiders from the sea. This was a hostile land, and

Cape Malea, 24 June

to a galley arriving from the north Malea presented a long unfriendly face. Even at five miles' distance the sea was already confused, with steep short waves running in several directions at once. There were local currents and eddies, and sea birds were wheeling and swooping close to the waves, watching for fish in the upwelling water. A slick, dark-grey shape broke the surface as a dolphin surfaced to breathe while he hunted the same prey as the seabirds.

I was sailing *Argo* very cautiously now. She was rolling uncomfortably, and I could feel the steering oars bumping and groaning in their notches. I was extremely conscious of the risk of taking the galley out into the Cythera channel. Certainly I did not want to follow the example of either Menelaus or Ulysses and have my galley swept away across the Cretan Sea. So we had already unlashed the bonnet, the mainsail's extra foot panel, and stowed it. The sail itself was at quarter brail, hoisted partially up to the spar to lessen the effect of any sudden gust of wind catching us wrong-footed. As we came closer to the point, Malea took on a bizarre silhouette. From the north, the profile of the cape looked like the head of a hump-shouldered, bad-tempered baboon crouching with its chin on its forepaws, the swell of powerful shoulder muscle behind the neck, eyes staring south under pronounced eyebrows; at the very promontory was the upturned tip of a baboon's snout.

From across the far side of the peninsula a stream of clouds came hurtling out, a sure sign that a fierce wind was blowing on the opposite flank of the cape. The clouds came streaming over the crest of the ridge like banners, twisting and turning and then ripping into shreds. I was watching the surface of the sea between the cape and the distant shape of Cythera Island. The water was increasingly flecked with breaking waves. Clearly the gale was working up strength. Abruptly I called on the crew for a change of course. I had reached my decision. Conditions were too dangerous for a galley to proceed out into the channel, and we should try to seek shelter under the cape, even though the Sailing Directions offered no shelter. Derry got out an oar and began to pull *Argo*'s head round, rowing with difficulty in the choppy water. We tried three times to turn the galley, and each time the wind was too much for us. As we faltered, the galley lay uncomfortably across the wind, wallowing from side to side, losing ground as she was swept towards the open sea. We were only nine men aboard – not nearly enough to row five tons of laden galley – and it was becoming increasingly urgent to get to shelter. Doc John and Rick hauled in the rubber dinghy which had been trailing astern. We lashed two oars as outriggers to hold the dinghy away from the side of the galley. John jumped the gap and started the outboard, and with a combination of sail- and dinghy-power we edged *Argo* towards the land, watching anxiously as the waves threatened to tumble the little rubber boat upside down.

I had caught a glimpse of what looked like a tiny chapel near the water's edge a mile to the north of the cape. On a hunch I headed *Argo* towards that spot, and found what I had hoped for: a small shallow cove where other storm-bound mariners must have found refuge in similar conditions because they had erected a chapel in thanksgiving on the spot. The cove gave us protection only when the wind was in the west, otherwise it would have been a treacherous spot. A similar inlet 400 yards away was directly in the path of the wind chute. There the gale sweeping down the flank of the peninsula occasionally struck the sea in a whirlwind. The surface of the water would suddenly smoke white as the spume was skimmed away. Spinning devils of spray went gyrating out to sea, tossing spiteful little rainbows in the air that collapsed abruptly as their parent whirlwind tripped on the breaking water over a reef.

We tethered *Argo* firmly with three anchors astern fan-wise, plus two strong lines fastened to rocks ashore. Even so, the sideswipe of the spent gusts sent the boat skittering and slithering across the water, tugging in all directions at her lines as she was buffeted by the wind. The gusts rattled the dry branches of the thorns and ripped leaves from a line of oleander bushes that had taken root in the shelter of a narrow gully that led down to the cove. At the foot of the low cliff where the gully met the beach, we found a small pool of fresh water oozing into a tiny cave. Disturbing a fine fat frog which could have seen few human visitors, we brushed aside the dead twigs from the pool and prudently filled our water containers, aware that if a mishap did blow *Argo* out to sea, shortage of drinking water would be the greatest problem.

Ulysses' squadron *had* been blown out to sea by that baleful north wind: 'the swell, the current and the North Wind combined, as I was doubling Malea, to drive me off my course and send me drifting past Cythera'. Ulysses' description is matter-of-fact, and where the squadron went ought to be a matter of common sea-sense. Ulysses tells us his initial course was 'past

Cythera'. The island of Cythera lies just west of south from Malea and so it seems that the twelve ships were blown down its eastern shore. Very likely the vessels tried to claw into anchorage on Cythera, but failed. After that there was only the open sea before them.

☐ For nine days I was chased by those accursed winds across the fish-infested seas. But on the tenth we made the country of the Lotus-eaters, a race who live on vegetable foods. We disembarked to draw water, and my crews quickly set to on their midday meal by the ships. ☐

Where was this 'country of the Lotus-eaters', the first of Ulysses' cryptic landfalls? To address the mystery we have to apply the practical realities of sailing a squadron of Late Bronze Age ships. The first point to be made is that this was not a gale that drove Ulysses' ships out to sea, nothing as bad as the 'terrible gale' which nearly sunk them in the northern Aegean, tore their sails and forced them to row for shelter. This time off Cape Malea, says the *Odyssey*, it was a combination of wind, current and sea state which overpowered the galleys. From what we had already learned about handling *Argo*, *any* wind above force four is more than a galley crew can cope with if it blows directly against the ship's course. The choppy seas off Malea would have meant that Ulysses' oarsmen were unable to row for shelter, or get close enough to land to put down their anchors.

So what then did a galley captain do in these conditions? If the wind continued to blow, his oarsmen were soon out of action, increasingly weary and probably suffering seasickness as well. A galley commander then had no choice: he was forced to adopt defensive tactics against the sea and wind to ensure the survival of his vessel and the minimum disruption to his plans.

He set his ship at the safest angle to the wind, diagonally across the waves, then lowered the spar far enough down the mast to steady the ship's rolling and reduce the pressure of the wind, but still high enough to give him sufficient steerage way to maintain the ship's attitude. With the sail brailled partway to spill the worst force of the wind gusts, his ship would lie to the waves in a controlled drift, riding them as safely as possible, keeping station with the other ships in the squadron just as a small flock of seagulls can be seen poised on the surface of the sea in bad weather. For hour after hour, day after day, a squadron could lie like this just so long as the ships were not being blown down on a lee shore. Fortunately, as Ulysses said, the ships were blown 'past Cythera' and into the open sea. After that, all that was needed was patience to ride out the strong headwind, wait for a change in the weather, and then try to regain the original course.

But Ulysses had rotten weather luck. The ill-fated squadron endured no less than *nine days* of these hostile winds. In getting to grips with the truth of the *Odyssey* all numbers cited by the poet have to be treated with great caution. Numbers are notoriously unreliable. More than any other detail, they are likely to be changed or distorted from the original epic perhaps by deliberate exaggeration or maybe by something as innocent as a mistake by a copyist or a slip by a bard as he recites the tale. Often, too, we have to be suspicious of a symbolic significance. It's curious how often Homer's numbers in the *Odyssey* are multiples of three – the twelve ships of the squadron, the six men from each ship killed at Ismarus, the nine days drifting across the Mediterranean after Cape Malea, and so on repeatedly throughout the tale as we shall discover.

But whether the nine days is a true figure or not, we have to calculate the squadron's pace *at drift speed*, not as if they were sailing helter-skelter before a gale. There are three good reasons for this. First, Ulysses and his captains knew they were being driven away from their intended track. If they hoisted sail, any increase in speed meant that they were only going further and faster away from Malea. Their purpose was to go home as quickly as possible, and the best way to minimize their bad luck was to slow the ships right down and reduce the amount they were blown away from land. There was no advantage whatever in spreading sail and hurrying away from their intended destination. Second, the only circumstance under which it might be necessary to hoist sail was if the wind rose to gale force and the ships were then forced to turn and run directly downwind to avoid being swamped or capsized by massive waves. These tactics are well-known to all small-boat sailors, but are only employed for survival in gale conditions. Homer does not write of any gale. Rather, we can infer that these downwind tactics were never employed, for the squadron *stayed together* and reached landfall in the country of the Lotus-eaters as a unit. If there had been a full gale, it is extremely improbable that twelve ships, running for survival across the open sea for nine days on end with a gale behind them, would have stayed together as a group. They would have been scattered, lost touch with one another, and there is a good chance that several of them would have foundered. Instead, according to Homer's account, the complete squadron, all ships intact and grouped together, made a safe landfall. The men went ashore, replenished their water supplies which was the natural reaction after a long passage at sea, cooked a proper meal, and three of them went inland to explore.

The third reason for imagining Ulysses' squadron *drifting* is that there is a particular north wind which provides exactly the conditions Homer describes. The *meltemi*, a seasonal wind of the summer, arises suddenly and can blow for days on end from the north, disturbing the sea. Captain Spratt, the cartographer of the Trojan plain, must have experienced dozens of *meltemi* during his time with the Mediterranean Survey and he observed that the wind

> generally rises very suddenly, without any clouds to warn the navigator, some few mountains only being capped by them as monitors of its coming to the experienced local mariner. It is especially dreaded for the violence of its squalls on the leeward side of all high land; for they have the character of what nautical men call 'white squalls' from giving little or no warning until felt, and are truly 'typhonic' in effect, from the whirling columns of wind and spray that they lift from the surface of the sea.

Even modern yachts scurry for shelter before a *meltemi*, and the Port Police will ban any small boat departures until the worst of the wind has abated. The strength of the *meltemi* varies between force five and six rising sometimes to near gale in the afternoon and easing away at night, only to pick up strength again the following morning. Perversely the *meltemi* can sometimes blow with undiminished force for days at a time, and if this is what happened to Ulysses then his squadron would have been blown clear across the Mediterranean Sea. Once again, it must be stressed, the *meltemi* produces conditions for a galley to adopt a controlled drift downwind.

Ulysses' track from Malea is not guess-work. In heavy weather aboard *Argo* in the Black Sea I had calculated the direction and speed of the galley's drift in off-shore winds varying between force four and seven. In twenty-four hours *Argo* had been blown approximately thirty miles off the land, an average of little more than a knot. It was a safe, defensive speed, a survivor's pace, and *Argo* had come through unscathed. There is no reason to suppose that Ulysses' squadron would have reacted any differently. Nine days – if we accept the suspect nine – would have brought them about 270 miles southward, and on the eighth or ninth day they would have been very relieved to see high land on the horizon. Towards that high land the exhausted sailors would have set their course, anxious to replenish their water jars. The coast on which they set foot had to be North Africa, the mountains the Jebel Akhdar or Green Mountains. Most probably they were on the northward bulge of modern Libya between Benghazi and Bomba, in the region now called Cyrenaica.

Virtually every scholar who has studied the geography of the *Odyssey* down through the centuries agrees that the wind-blown squadron arrived on the North African coast and found there the Lotus-eaters. But the majority propose a landfall not in Cyrenaica but at least 500 miles further west across the Gulf of Sirte, on or near the island of Jerba in what is now Tunisia. Their reasoning is thus: Ulysses' squadron was nine days at sea in strong winds, and in strong winds a galley can run anything from seventy to well over a hundred miles a day. *Ergo*, Ulysses' squadron travelled at least 600 miles. Since the Mediterranean is only 250 miles north to south at Cape Malea, the squadron must have been sailing diagonally across the sea and fetched up in Jerba in order to have travelled at least 600 miles. This theory is flawed not only because, as we have seen, Ulysses and his men had no reason whatever to go sailing off at high speed further and further away from the homeward route, but also because no sensible galley commander would take such a dangerous line in strong winds. The course that is suggested by these commentators would have laid the Late Bronze Age galleys almost broadside to the wind and waves. For a light galley without a keel to steady her, rolling abominably from side to side, such an attitude would be extremely uncomfortable if not downright hazardous, for it greatly increases the risks of capsize or, more likely, of a very large wave breaking into the open shell of the boat and swamping her. Multiply this risk by the presence of twelve booty-laden galleys, and it is against all logic that the squadron would have travelled 600 miles on such a foolhardy, slanting course.

Another point which is overlooked is that the Jerba landfall makes no sense to a Bronze Age navigator. The coast is low and featureless, sand-bars and shoals extend as much as twelve miles out to sea, lagoons and mud flats fringe the coast, all making any landing very treacherous. Jason and the Argonauts in their great galley did get entangled on this very coast according to the tale of the Golden Fleece. Their ship was so stranded in the shallows that the men had to hunt inland for water and nearly died of thirst, and a sea god had to intervene to pull their vessel clear via a hidden channel. This contrasts totally with Ulysses' easy landfall, where the Ithacan squadron makes a straightforward arrival, there is no mention of shoals or sand-bars, the men apparently come ashore without difficulty, and they have no trouble finding fresh water. The area for accessible moorings and streams of fresh water is the coast of Cyrenaica, and it cannot be by chance that this is exactly where the first Greek colonies were later to be established.

Imagine the squadron drifting downwind with the galley captains worrying about the dwindling store of fresh water as the days slip by, and scanning the horizon for sight of land. Suddenly the coast of Cyrenaica is *visible*. Once again it must be stressed that the Bronze

Age ships navigated by line-of-sight, and the first high ground they would have seen along the North African coast would have been the 2,000-feet tall range of the Green Mountains of Cyrenaica. Towards this welcome sight they would have steered their course, landed on the unknown shore, immediately replenished their fresh water and, as Ulysses says, prepared themselves a decent meal on dry land. Then, ever curious and probably hoping to find easy plunder, their scouts went inland and encountered the strange local inhabitants that Ulysses dubbed the Lotus-eaters:

□ as soon as we had a mouthful and a drink, I sent some of my followers inland to find out what sort of human beings might be there, detailing two men for the duty with a third as messenger. Off they went, and it was not long before they were in touch with the Lotus-eaters. Now it never entered the heads of these natives to kill my friends; what they did was to give them some lotus to taste, and as soon as each had eaten the honeyed fruit of the plant, all thoughts of reporting to us or escaping were banished from his mind. All they now wished for was to stay where they were with the Lotus-eaters, to browse on the lotus, and to forget that they had a home to return to. I had to use force to bring them back to the ships, and they wept on the way, but once on board I dragged them under the benches and left them in irons. □

Who were these Lotus-eaters? And what was this remarkable fruit, the 'lotus', which induced in the Greek envoys such a trance that they wouldn't carry messages back to the ships but wanted to stay and not go home, until eventually they had to be trussed up like chickens on the way to market and be put under the rowing benches of the galleys and carried away by force? All sorts of likely plants have been suggested. One obvious candidate is North African hashish, whose narcotic effect may well have caused men 'to forget their homes' and weep from the after-effects. But hashish is not a 'flowery plant' in the sense that Homer writes, and it is unlikely that the local inhabitants, men who eat bread, lived on hashish as a staple food. The lotus lily has been proposed. Some forms of lotus were indeed eaten by the people of Egypt. But the lotus does not produce a 'honeyed fruit', any more than does the hashish plant. The date palm, another suggestion for the 'lotus', has sweet fruit but later Greek writers distinguished between the date and the lotus. The *Odyssey* itself (though the reference is a late addition to the text) mentions a palm tree without suggesting that it was the same as the 'lotus'.

The plant with the best claim to being the real lotus is the one which now bears the botanical name *Zizyphus lotus*. Native to North Africa, it is a tree about twenty-five feet high covered with rough brown bark, and its thorny branches put out small pale yellow flowers. The fruit is a blood-red berry roughly the size and shape of an olive, and with a similar pointed, oblong stone. The berry tastes sweet yet astringent, and its flesh is soft and sticky. The Arab name for it is *sidr* and it is claimed to be 'worthy of the heaven of the archangel Gabriel'. Dried, *sidr* was an important source of food among the semi-nomadic North African tribes, and in Arabia was used for preparing a sort of sweet gingerbread by drying the fruit in the sun, pounding the berries to remove the stones and then mixing the paste with water. Why it was supposed to make men lose their memories is not clear. Perhaps it was because a type of cider can be made of it, and Ulysses' three scouts over-indulged when they visited the peaceful and vegetarian Lotus-eaters.

I had planned to visit Libya with *Argo* if only to track down and taste the 'lotus'. But the complications of obtaining visas baffled our best-intentioned efforts. Months of writing and telephoning a selection of Libyan People's Bureaux in various European capitals produced no reply whatever. Finally, while *Argo* was being over-hauled in Spetses, a Greek friend managed to obtain a personal introduction to the senior Libyan diplomat at the People's Bureau in Athens. Taking Nazem with me in case an Arabic interpreter was needed, I duly presented myself at the armoured gate. A sentry let us in, and we were led through the lobby past an unlikely portrait of Colonel Gadaffi romantically depicted as a Hollywood Arab sheikh, riding a white steed across a biliously bright green field, with a cloak fluttering from his shoulders.

Upstairs we were ushered into the office of the diplomat. Hopefully I presented our multi-coloured heap of passports: Irish, British, American, Bulgarian, Greek, even Nazem's Syrian passport, although he was the only member of the crew not to require a visa because Syria and Libya were in fraternal partnership. I also handed over a thick deck of all the necessary visa application cards, in triplicate and complete with the usual obscure details about the applicant's father's father's first name, and date and place of birth. Nazem had filled out every card in immaculate Arabic script. They made, I thought, an impressive bundle and certainly demonstrated that we were serious in our application. 'Who is this person with you?' rudely inquired the Libyan official waving his hand towards Nazem. 'He's a member of my crew, Nazem Choufeh, from Syria.' 'He must wait downstairs.' He pressed a buzzer, and an assistant appeared at the door. 'Take this man away,' was the blunt instruction, and to my astonishment Nazem was curtly escorted out. So much for fraternal Arab partnership, I thought. The rest of our conversation was not encouraging. The Libyan People's Bureau in Athens had no authority to issue visas. He would have to send a telex to Tripoli for instructions. Of course there was a public holiday in Tripoli. Telexes were seldom answered quickly and often not at all. The coastal area was a closed military zone. I would have to specify the exact date of arrival. There would have to be a Libyan on board *Argo* (that I could imagine!) and so on and so on. I realized that we could find ourselves waiting for months without a reply from Tripoli while the summer sailing season ebbed away. I had no intention of arriving unheralded in Cyrenaica and *Argo*'s visa-less crew being treated as illegal entrants, so I mentally deleted Libya from our route plan.

The disappointment was somewhat moderated by the fact that I had never expected to be able to define the exact point of the Libyan coast on which Ulysses set foot. The details in the *Odyssey* are simply too vague. We are given no physical description to let us pinpoint the spot. Nor, until now, have any Mycenaean objects been found in Libya which would help us to identify a locality known to the Greeks at that time. Several Late Bronze Age items of Cretan origin have been found on the Cyrenaican coast and their discovery caused a considerable stir among archaeologists until it was pointed out that the objects were probably imported much later into Libya. To be fair to the archaeologists, however, very little attempt has yet been made to dig down to the Late Bronze Age layers in the major sites in Cyrenaica, and it is still possible that Mycenaean artefacts will be found there one day. For the present the earliest evidence of Greek contact with Cyrenaica dates to the colonial settlements of the sixth century BC, so the *Odyssey*'s information on North Africa seems to derive from the sort of casual visit that Homer describes.

What little we do know about the Late Bronze Age Libyans supports Homer's picture of the gentle Lotus-eaters who live on vegetable food and offer no violence to strangers. Egyptian monuments of the time have pictures of the Libyan natives wearing only scanty loin-cloths and sandals and carrying water skins. The inscriptions make no mention of cities, armies, or houses, and the impression is of a simple and unsophisti-cated nomadic people, so the reception given to Ulysses' scouting party accords with the hospitality of a semi-nomadic group living off wild fruit including lotus berries.

Whether the galleys landed in Cyrenaica or further west, they did not linger. Clearly there was little of value there to hold them and the object of the voyage was to get home. With the lotus-drugged messengers tucked under the oar-benches, Ulysses tells how he

☐ then commanded the rest of my loyal band to embark with all speed on their fast ships, for fear that others of them might eat the lotus and think no more of home. They came aboard at once, went to the benches, sat down in their proper places, and struck the white surf with their oars. ☐

At this stage it is vital to realize that Ulysses and his captains were not lost. Homer does not say they were, nor does he even hint that they hesitated about which direction to go. Any experienced Bronze Age mariner knew very well how to calculate his return track after adverse weather. During the nine days when they were being pushed off-course the ship captains had the sun by day, the pole star by night, together with the wave patterns and the wind direction to tell them in which

general direction they were drifting. To regain Malea they had to reverse this course and back-track until they picked up a recognizable feature such as a mountain or headland. Any notion that Ulysses and his experienced ship captains, who had already satisfactorily sailed more than 1,000 miles outward-bound from Ithaca to Troy and halfway home again, were lost on the North African coast does little justice to the fundamentals of early navigational techniques. Ships were frequently blown off course, and their captains were accustomed to finding their way back on track by observing the general direction they were being driven and then returning the way they had come. Even less plausible is the notion that Ulysses now persuaded his chronically disobedient squadron to continue even further away from Malea into the western Mediterranean on a voyage of exploration. After ten years of siege, a costly raid on Ismarus, a storm in the Aegean, and prolonged bad weather off

Malea they had surely had enough of adventuring. They wanted to go home.

So they would have headed north, and it is logical that the track they used was the same path that galleys and merchant ships took to return from North Africa to Greek waters in later classical times. Naturally this was the shortest, safest crossing point. The sailing directions were simple: you followed the North African coast until you reached a cape with a great bay where the land fell away. There you struck out to sea. Your point of departure from the Libyan coast was at the cape now called Ras el Hilal or, more likely, Ras et Tin, north of Bomba, and you had only 190 miles before you came to land again, arriving on the south coast of Crete. It was here that I now intended to take *Argo* in search of an explanation of the most famous and bizarre adventure in the entire *Odyssey* – the grisly encounter with the cannibal Cyclops in his cave.

5

The Cyclops

Tantalizingly Ulysses omits to tell us how far his twelve
ships sailed to go from the country of the Lotus-eaters
to the country of the cave-dwelling Cyclops people. It
is one of the most exasperating gaps in the entire narrative as we are left with no impression of time or distance
apart from the fact that nothing of interest happened
during this sector — which may perhaps indicate that
this was an open-water and not a coasting passage —
and that as usual the sailors did not enjoy their lot.
Ulysses recounts how

> □ we left that country and sailed on sick at heart. And
> came to the land of the Cyclopes, a fierce, uncivilized
> people who never lift a hand to plant or plough but
> put their trust in Providence. All the crops they
> require spring up unsown and untilled, wheat and
> barley and the vines whose generous clusters give
> them wine when ripened for them by the timely rains.
> The Cyclopes have no assemblies for the making of
> laws, nor any settled customs, but live in hollow
> caverns in the mountain heights, where each man is
> lawgiver to his children and his wives, and nobody
> cares a jot for his neighbours. □

The first puzzle is why Ulysses' Cyclopes are nothing
whatever like any Cyclopes previously known to Greek
mythology. Traditionally the Cyclopes were skilled
master-technicians, and there were only three of them
— Arges, Brontes and Steropes (or Pyracmon). They

were the sons of Earth and Sky and worked in subterranean forges hammering out the thunderbolts which Zeus hurled when the Olympian Gods fought for control of the Universe against the Old Gods. Greek writers later credited these same technician-Cyclopes with constructing the massive walls of the ruined Mycenaean fortresses because the stones seemed so huge – the largest weigh as much as 120 tons – and so intricately put together that only the giant Cyclopes brothers could have shifted them and fitted them together so cunningly. To this day a 'Cyclopean' wall remains a descriptive term used by archaeologists.

By contrast the people Homer describes are as unsophisticated as the Lotus-eaters. They live in caves in the mountains and have no political structures but are organized as family groups. The oddest thing about them, which has to be explained, is that they benefit from crops of wheat and barley and grapes without the need to cultivate them.

How are we to reconcile Homer's simple – and, as it turned out, cannibal – cave-dwellers with the metal-working Cyclopes of mythology? The problem, ignored by many commentaries on the *Odyssey*, may find an eventual solution if we imagine Ulysses' squadron coming back up from Cyrenaica and closing the south coast of Crete.

The twelve ships made their landfall on a misty night. According to Ulysses, the visibility was so poor that the lookouts never even saw the breakers rolling in on the shore. By an extraordinary stroke of luck the entire squadron ran right into a natural harbour and grounded on the beach. There the seamen took down the sails, went ashore, and lay down to sleep. Daybreak revealed that they had not landed on the main coast but on a nearby, uninhabited island swarming with wild goats:

□ there lies a luxuriant island, covered with woods, which is the home of innumerable goats. The goats are wild, for man has made no pathways that might frighten them off, nor do hunters visit the island with their hounds to rough it in the forests and to range the mountain-tops. Used neither for grazing nor for ploughing, it lies forever unsown and untilled; and this land where no man goes makes a happy pasture for the bleating goats. □

The wild goats are the key to the squadron's whereabouts. From the Bronze Age until the present day one place in the Mediterranean above all others has been associated with the wild goat – the great island of Crete which is the home of the true European wild goat or ibex, *Capra aegagrus cretensis*. Zoologists now consider that the wild goat populations on most other Mediterranean islands are feral, that is, domestic goats run wild. But *Capra aegagrus cretensis* is a genuine native species.

The male is utterly unmistakable, whether depicted in Bronze Age paintings or glimpsed today in the fastnesses of the White Mountains of Crete where a handful survive. The male gri-gri, as it is popularly called, carries the most spectacular set of horns. They curve back in such a tremendous arc that it seems that the creature would spike itself in the back if it threw up its head too quickly. It is a marvel how they manage to convey this extravagant headgear so lightly among the crags and screes of the high mountains. Plump and comfortable at first sight, the animal is like a hard rubber ball of solid muscle that ricochets from the rock-faces at impossible angles as it goes leaping and bouncing from crag to gulley making it the most elusive target even for modern high-powered rifles. Though a protected species, the wild goat retains such status for the Cretans that men still illegally hunt it in the remote areas of the White Mountains. Fortunately several off-shore islands around Crete have also been turned into sanctuaries for the wild goats, and there they survive without being disturbed.

The gri-gri was already famous in Crete when the island was the heartland of the sophisticated Minoan civilization which preceded, and slightly overlapped, the Mycenaean Golden Age on the mainland. Minoan artists painted, sculpted, carved and cast in metal their island's most distinctive wild animal. The Minoan galleries of the museum at Iraklion, the island's capital, contain images of wild goats painted on murals, goats modelled in clay, goats cast in bronze, goats leaping, goats feeding, goats being hunted, goats resting, goats mating, goats with their kids, goats carved on gemstone seals. The gri-gri was as much the symbol of Minoan art on land as the octopus motif was its symbol by sea. Not just a source of food, its horns provided the raw material for the curved bows of the celebrated Cretan archers, and the goat is so frequently represented in art that the animal must also have had a cult. So when Homer brought Ulysses to the land swarming with wild goats, the first place his contemporary audience would have thought of would have been Crete.

The sailors found that because the wild goats on the small off-shore island had never been hunted previously, they made an easy target for the hungry travellers.

☐ We were delighted with what we saw of the island and set out to explore it. Presently, in order that my company might have something to eat, the Nymphs, those Children of Zeus, set the mountain goats on the move. Directly we saw them we fetched our curved bows and our long spears from the ships, separated into three parties, and let fly at the game; and in a short time Providence had sent us a satisfac-

tory bag. There were twelve ships in my squadron: nine goats fell to each, while to me they made a special allotment of ten. So the whole day long till the sun set we sat and enjoyed this rich supply of meat, which we washed down by mellow wine, since the ships had not yet run dry of our red vintage. There was still some in the holds, for when we took the sacred citadel of the Cicones, every member of the company had drawn off a generous supply in jars.
□

There they sat, this marauding band of corsairs from Ithaca, swilling the wine they had looted from Ismarus and eating the flesh of the splendid bag of wild goats they had hunted down on the small island. But where was this island? Homer only says that it was 'not very far from the harbour on their coast, and not so near either', a singularly unhelpful and self-contradictory clue to the real geography.

Initially the problem does not seem too difficult. There are only four sizeable islands or island groups off the south coast of Crete where the squadron would naturally have arrived, coming up from Cyrenaica. The two islands of Gaidoronisi (Donkey Island) and Kouphonisi lie too far to the east. The island of Gavdos can also be ruled out as it is so far off-shore that the main coast of Crete is only just visible, whereas Ulysses was to claim that he could see the smoke from the fires of the Cyclopes people and hear the bleating of their sheep and goats. The fourth island, or rather cluster of islands, seems more promising: the Paximada, the 'dried bread' islands, lie close inside the Gulf of Messaras, midway along the south coast of Crete. Unfortunately the Dried Bread Islands do not possess a natural south-facing harbour into which the squadron could have sailed for their lucky landfall. On the other hand, only eight miles away in caves on the mainland cliffs once lived man-eating giants. Or so I was informed.

'Be sure to ask about giants in the village of Pitsidia!' The advice had come from Professor Paul Faure, the acknowledged authority on the caves of Crete. During nine expeditions this indefatigable French scholar had tramped the limestone hills of Crete to make an inventory of caves and grottoes and record the history, archaeology and folktales associated with them. In south-central Crete he had heard folktales about man-eating ogres strikingly similar to Homer's puzzling version of the Cyclopes. These Cretan ogres were giants. They too lived in simple family groups – usually father, mother and child – in the deep recesses of caves, and they were cannibals. There was only one major difference from Homer's Cyclopes, and in a curious way that difference only served to strengthen the possible connection between the two monstrous legendary races. The cannibal giant that Ulysses was to encounter had a single eye placed in the middle of his forehead. The cannibal giant of Cretan folklore had not one, but three eyes. The extra eye was all-seeing and situated in the back of the ogre's head. These ogres, Professor Faure wrote to tell me, were called *triamates*.

We sailed *Argo* to the south coast of Crete and anchored her in the Gulf of Messaras so that I could follow up Professor Faure's advice. The townsfolk of Pitsidia, a smal community a mile or so inland from the eastern shore of the gulf, told me that the schoolmaster Michaeli Fasoulanis was the most knowledgeable man in the community, the proper person to give me any information. I wondered if an educated schoolmaster would be embarrassed to talk about such unlikely creatures as three-eyed giants. Not at all. We settled down at a small café and the schoolmaster took my question very seriously. When he began to tell me about the *triamates*,

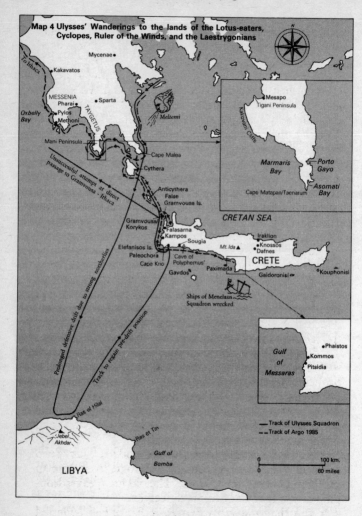

a very old man wearing the traditional all-black Cretan costume of loose shirt, breeches and tall boots edged his chair closer to the café table, and sat expectantly. It was obvious that an oft-told story was about to begin.

'Two men who lived near Pitsidia,' said the schoolmaster, 'went on a journey to Iraklion. As they travelled they came to a village called Choraskilio [Dog Town]. Entering the village they noticed that outside every house was a large dog. Being tired, they knocked on the door of one house, and when a woman came to answer, they asked if they might stay for the night. She invited them into the house, and said that she would go to fetch her husband. While they waited, the young son of the house came into the room. One of the travellers happened to touch the boy's head and noticed to his horror that the child had a third eye, hidden under the hair at the back of his head. He was a *triamates!* The boy told the travellers that his mother had gone to fetch the other *triamates* who would come to kill and eat the strangers. They could not escape as the huge dog guarded the door to the house. So the two travellers thought up a plan. They caught the boy and killed him. Then they cut his body into pieces and fed the pieces to the dog so that they could escape. They came back to their own village, and raised the alarm. The villagers armed themselves and went back to Choraskilio with the two travellers as their guides, and they attacked the village and killed every one of the *triamates* and destroyed the village.'

The schoolmaster finished his tale and sat back. Then he added, 'Choraskilio was on the road from here to Iraklion, not far from Dafnes.' The old man, eavesdropping at the tale, nodded his agreement.

It was the same story Professor Faure had collected more than ten years earlier and it was still recited not as a quaint anachronism but as a genuine local folktale.

I could not tell whether the schoolmaster himself believed in *triamates* but Faure had found that the country people certainly did. Cretan shepherds living in isolation in the mountains had a genuine dread of meeting cannibal *triamates*, particularly at night and in caves. It was said that a young *triamates* might appear in the back of the cave and ask to share the shepherd's meal. One of the encounters recorded by Faure concerned a thief who, returning from a raid on a nearby village with a stolen sheep, took cover for the night in a lonely cave. He had killed the stolen sheep and was roasting it over the fire when a young naked stranger appeared. The stranger demanded a piece of the meat. 'Wait till it is cooked,' replied the robber. When his visitor insisted on gobbling the meat raw, the thief was alerted to the real identity of the stranger and seized the red-hot spit and attacked the young *triamates* who ran off howling for help, allowing the sheep-stealer to make his escape.

The similarities between the tales about the *triamates* and the story of Ulysses' encounter with the Cyclops are striking. Yet there are enough differences of detail – such as the matter of the third eye – to indicate that the Cretan stories are not merely copies from the *Odyssey* but stories of genuine Cretan origin.

After their feast of wild goat meat, the men of the Ithacan squadron spent a second night on the beach of the small island. The next day Ulysses announced that he was curious to find out what sort of people lived on the neighbouring coast. Taking only his flagship, Ulysses and his crew rowed across to the mainland where they noticed a large cave close to the water's edge. The cave's entrance was fenced off with a high wall of grubbed-out boulders, and oak and pine trees so tall that it was clearly the home of a giant. Leaving his galley out of sight with most of the crew, Ulysses led a picked band of twelve men to the cave. Acting on a premonition, he says, he took with him a goatskin bottle of the sweet black wine which he had been given at Ismarus by the priest Maron. This wine was so strong in alcohol that normally it had to be diluted one part with twenty parts of water and still the mixture was very heady. Maron kept it stored secretly, and only the priest himself, his wife and one old servant knew of its existence.

Coming to the great cave, continues Ulysses, they found it deserted as its owner was off in the hills looking after his flocks.

☐ So we went inside and had a good look round. There were baskets laden with cheeses, and the folds were thronged with lambs and kids, each class, the firstlings, the summer lambs, and the little ones, being separately penned. All his well-made vessels, the pails and bowls he used for milking were swimming with whey. ☐

Ulysses' crew reacted with their customary rapacity. They begged their leader to let them steal some of the cheeses, carry them to the waiting galley, come back quickly to the cave and drive off the lambs and kids from the pens, getting everything aboard and making their escape before the owner of the cave returned. Ulysses refused. He wanted to wait to see what the owner of the cave was like. Perhaps, he said, 'he would give me presents'. His curiosity was to be fatal for six of his companions.

So the little group of men lingered in the cave. They built themselves a fire and ate some of the cheese and in the evening the owner of the cave duly returned from his herding. The entry of the Cyclops, Polyphemus, into his cave recalls the traditional return of the ogre to his castle in dozens of children's fairytales.

□ At last he came up, shepherding his flocks and carrying a huge bundle of dry wood to burn at supper-time. With a great din he cast this down inside the cavern, giving us such a fright that we hastily retreated to an inner recess. Meanwhile he drove his fat sheep into the wider part of the cave – I mean all the ewes that he milked: the rams and he-goats he left out of doors in the walled yard. He then picked up a huge stone with which he closed the entrance. It was a mighty slab, such as you couldn't have budged from the ground, not with a score of heavy four-wheeled waggons to help you. That will give you some idea of the monstrous size of the rock with which he closed the cave. □

With the doorway to the cave securely blocked, the Cyclops began to milk his sheep and goats, carefully putting half the milk aside for making cheese and saving the rest to drink with his supper. Only when he had finished his chores and lit his fire did he notice Ulysses and his men cowering in the recesses of the cave. In a great booming voice he demanded

□ 'Strangers! . . . and who may you be? and where do you hail from over the highways of the sea? Is yours a trading venture; or are you cruising the main on chance, like roving pirates, who risk their lives to ruin other people?' □

This summary of the two categories of seafarers – legitimate traders or pirates – is a fair appraisal of contemporary seafaring. Ulysses of course hastily explained that he and his men were Greeks returning from Troy. They had been beaten off-course by contrary winds. As visitors under the protection of Zeus, he suggested, he was hoping that the Cyclops might give them the

presents of hospitality. The Cyclops answered him piti-
lessly. He cared nothing for such customs, he told them,
and he did not fear the gods. Where had Ulysses left
his ship?

Ulysses the wily dissembled. He claimed that his ship
had been wrecked on the coast and that his men were
the sole survivors. The Cyclops then

☐ jumped up, and reaching out towards my men,
seized a couple and dashed their heads against the
floor as though they had been puppies. Their brains
ran out and soaked the earth. Limb by limb he tore
them to pieces to make his meal, which he devoured
like a mountain lion, never pausing till entrails and
flesh, marrow and bone, were all consumed . . . ☐

Helpless to intervene, Ulysses and his remaining
companions looked on aghast. Even when the Cyclops
had finished his human meal washed down with
draughts of milk, and lain down to sleep sprawled
amongst his sheep, Ulysses realized the hopelessness of
their plight. He thought of creeping up to the giant and
stabbing him to death as he slept, but realized that with
the Cyclops dead there would be no way to roll back
the immense boulder sealing the cave mouth.

So Ulysses devised the second classic strategy for
which, with the Trojan Horse, he is so famous. The
Cyclops got up next morning, milked his flocks, break-
fasted on two more of Ulysses' men, rolled back the
boulder and drove out his sheep and goats. Replacing
the vast doorstone 'as easily as though he was putting
the lid on a quiver' in order to keep his captives imprisoned, he went off to watch over his flocks for the day.
Ulysses saw that he had left behind a tremendous staff
of olive wood, still green and waiting to be seasoned.
This massive piece of timber 'looked more like the mast

of some black ship of twenty oars'. Ulysses cut off about a fathom's length, and while his men smoothed it down, he sharpened the end to a point which was then hardened in the fire. Hiding the stake by burying it under the thick layer of sheep dung which carpeted the cave floor, the captives waited for the Cyclops to return and drew lots to see which four men would assist Ulysses in attacking their captor.

The second evening went as before. The Cyclops returned, drove in his flocks, replaced the great stone, milked the animals, seized and ate two more of Ulysses' men and then settled down at his ease. Then Ulysses approached the Cyclops with a wooden bowl filled with the powerful undiluted black wine from Ismarus, and offered it to him. The Cyclops appreciated the wine so much that he drained three bowls of it, and became quite fuddled.

In a twist to the story which is a favourite among the world's folktales, the giant now asked Ulysses his name. If he would tell his name, he could have his hospitality present. Ulysses answered that his name was 'Nobody'. Then his present, the Cyclops replied in a cruel jest, would be that Nobody would be eaten last of all. With that, the ogre

☐ toppled over, and fell face upwards on the floor, where he lay with his great neck twisted to one side, conquered as all men are, by sleep. His drunkenness made him vomit, and a stream of wine mixed with morsels of men's flesh poured from his throat. ☐

Ulysses now retrieved the hidden stake and placed it among the cinders of the fire to heat until it glowed incandescent. He carried it forward to where his four picked companions stood ready, and they

☐ drove its sharpened end into the Cyclops' eye, while I used my weight from above to twist it home, like a man boring a ship's timber with a drill while his mates below him twirl with a strap they hold at either end, so that it spins continuously. In much the same way we handled our pole with its red-hot point and twisted it in his eye till the blood boiled up around the burning wood. The fiery smoke from the blazing eyeball singed his lids and brow all round, and the very roots of his eye crackled in the heat. I was reminded of the loud hiss that comes from a great axe or adze when a smith plunges it into cold water – to temper it and give strength to the iron. That is how the Cyclops' eye hissed round the olive stake. He gave a dreadful shriek, which echoed round the rocky walls, and we backed away from him in terror, while he pulled the stake from his eye, streaming with blood. ☐

This is the first time that Homer implies that the Cyclops had only a single eye. Otherwise the fact is never stated, presumably because the story was so well-known.

When the Cyclops had pulled the stake from his burning eye, he bellowed aloud in pain and his neighbours, the other Cyclopes, came running from their caves to ask what was the matter.

☐ 'What on earth is wrong with you, Polyphemus? Why must you disturb the peaceful night and spoil our sleep with all this shouting? Is a robber driving off your sheep, or is somebody trying by treachery or violence to kill you?'

Out of the cave came Polyphemus' great voice in reply: 'O my friends, it's Nobody's treachery, no violence, that is doing me to death.'

'Well then,' they answered, in a way that settled

the matter, 'if nobody is assaulting you in your solitude, you must be sick. Sickness comes from almighty Zeus and cannot be helped. All you can do is pray to your father, the Lord Poseidon.' And off they went ... □

The trick of the false name 'Nobody' is faithfully echoed in several Cretan stories about the *triamates* that Professor Faure collected. But the ruse is so common to folktales in many different countries that the comparison cannot be taken too far. More striking is the likeness between Ulysses' fire-hardened stake and the red-hot spit used by the Cretan sheep-stealer to wound and drive off a hungry cannibal *triamates* in a cave. Yet even this parallel will have to be treated cautiously, as the sequel to Ulysses' adventure with the Cyclops shows.

Cooped up in the cave with the groaning, blinded and enraged Cyclops, Ulysses engineered the escape of his six surviving companions. He rounded up the rams in the Cyclops' flock and tied them together in threes with willow withes. The flocks began to bleat at dawn to be let out from the cave. Blind Polyphemus rolled back the great boulder and sat there by the entrance as the animals walked out, feeling over their backs to check that the sailors were not taking their chance to escape. Ulysses' men avoided detection by clinging on underneath the lashed-together rams and so got out of the cave. Finally Ulysses himself escaped by hanging on underneath the big lead ram in the flock, grasping the animal's thick wool. Polyphemus was puzzled why the great ram, usually so eager to leave the cave, was last to leave that morning.

□ As he felt him with his hands the great Polyphemus broke into speech: 'Sweet ram,' he said, 'what does

this mean? Why are you the last of the flock to pass
out of the cave, you who have lagged behind the
sheep, you who always step so proudly out and are
the first of them to crop the lush shoots of the grass,
first to make your way to the flowing stream, and
first to turn your head homewards to the sheepfold
when evening falls? Yet today you are the last of all.
Are you grieved for your master's eye, blinded by a
wicked man and his accursed friends, when he had
robbed me of my wits with wine? Nobody was his
name; and I swear that he has not yet saved his skin!
Ah, if only you could feel as I do and find a voice to
tell me where he's hiding from my fury! Wouldn't I
hammer him and splash his brains all over the floor
of the cave, till that miserable Nobody had eased my
heart of the suffering that I owe to him!' □

Undetected by fumbling Polyphemus, Ulysses was
carried out of the cave by the great ram. As soon as he
was clear, he dropped down and ran to release his
companions. Then, like the sea robbers they were, they
drove the flock to where the galley and the rest of her
crew were waiting. The sailors would have raised their
voices to mourn the loss of their companions killed
and eaten by the Cyclops, but Ulysses kept them silent,
gesturing for them to load the sheep as fast as possible
into the galley. They tumbled their booty aboard,
pushed off the galley and began to row away. Now
Ulysses, in Homer's plot, showed his fatal failing of
pride that was eventually to bring him lasting grief and
destroy his entire crew. Judging he was safely clear
of the shore, Ulysses shouted back his triumph at the
Cyclops, taunting him.

□ 'Cyclops! . . . so he was not such a weakling after
all, the man whose friends you meant to overpower

and eat in that snug cave of yours! And your crimes came home to roost, you brute, who have not even the decency to refrain from devouring your own guests. Now Zeus and all his fellow-gods have paid you out.' □

Hearing Ulysses' mocking voice, the blinded Cyclops broke off a piece of the mountain and threw it at the sound. The huge rock barely missed the vessel, grazing the edge of the steering oar, and the backwash picked up the galley and flung it back ashore. Seizing a long pole, Ulysses used it as a quant to push the galley off again, and his men grimly rowed further out. Over their terrified protests, Ulysses once again mocked the Cyclops: 'Cyclops, if anyone ever asks you how you came by your unsightly blindness, tell him your eye was put out by Odysseus, Sacker of Cities, the son of Laertes, who lives in Ithaca.'

Polyphemus gave a great groan and answered him. A seer by the name of Telemus, son of Eurymus, who had lived among the Cyclopes, had foretold that Polyphemus would one day be blinded by a man called Odysseus. But the giant had expected 'some big and handsome fellow of tremendous strength to come along' not a 'puny, good for nothing, little runt' who resorted to the underhand trick of making him helpless with wine. Polyphemus beseeched Ulysses to return so that he could give him a proper gift. Ulysses only taunted him the more, telling him that if he had his way, he would make sure that Polyphemus died. Then the Cyclops reached up his arms and called down a curse. He asked his father the sea god Poseidon to make sure that

□ 'Odysseus, who styles himself Sacker of Cities and son of Laertes, may never reach his home in Ithaca.

But if he is destined to reach his native land, to come once more to his own house and see his friends again, let him come late, in evil plight, with all his comrades dead, and when he is landed, by a foreign ship, let him find trouble in his home.' □

Then the Cyclops picked up an even larger rock and despairingly threw it at the departing galley. Again the huge missile only just missed its target. It splashed into the sea astern of the galley and the tidal wave it caused drove the ship forward so that it reached the island of wild goats where the rest of the squadron was waiting.

The story of rock-casting Polyphemus is now so popular and widespread that in literally dozens of places in the Mediterranean, and in the Black Sea too, local fishermen have pointed out to me rocks and reefs, just awash, and said 'Those are the rocks that the Cyclops threw'. So I was not in the least surprised to be told in Pitsidia that if I went to the cliffs at Drakotes two miles away I would see lying in the water the missiles that Polyphemus had hurled. The caves along the cliff top were once the home of monsters and there Ulysses had met the Cyclops. Was it not proof that Drakotes means 'something monstrous' – like a Cyclops?

Standing on the heights of the Drakotes cliffs, I could see the scatter of submerged boulders that had fallen away from the cliff. The outline of the Paximada islands was away to my left, eight miles off-shore, and the cliff top was pockmarked with caves and rock shelters, a few closed with walls of stones to make sheep pens. It all looked very suitable as Polyphemus' home, particularly with the black silhouette of *Argo* anchored in the shallows beside a long sandy beach where the bones of ancient walls could be seen, poking up from the dunes. I could just make out tiny human figures working among them, clearing debris. They were members of a

Canadian archaeological team in their tenth year of excavating an ancient port, whose newly uncovered story has some bearing on the historical background to the *Odyssey*.

Kommos is the port's name and Homer must have known – at least by reputation – this part of the south coast of Crete. He mentions the Minoan city of Phaistos four miles inland, and says that here Menelaus lost several ships on a headland after his fleet, like Ulysses', was driven down from Cape Malea by adverse winds. Phaistos was a palace city, and Kommos was either its port or a substantial Minoan harbour in its own right. The Canadian archaeologists had uncovered impressive buildings by the beach, monumental structures with generous colonnades and courtyards and a broad paved road running inland towards Phaistos. The archaeologists did not yet understand the function of the great buildings, whether they had been palaces, huge warehouses, perhaps hangers for storing ships. But it was clear that Kommos had engaged in international trade. Pieces of pottery imported from Cyprus and the coast of Syria had been found, and there was a forge for working metal, perhaps to smelt copper brought in from the east.

Kommos was established in the great days of the Minoan empire about 1600 BC and flourished for three centuries. Then something had gone wrong. The city had died. Its buildings had been abandoned and fallen into decay. The modest houses up on the knoll where the ordinary townsfolk and labourers of Kommos had lived with a fine view over the beach, had been deserted. The people went away. The archaeologists couldn't say why the evacuation had taken place, but they knew when: in the middle of the thirteenth century BC, around the time of the Trojan War. That, as Dr Shaw their leader put it succinctly, was 'when the lights went out'.

Was it, I wondered, a coincidence that this happened shortly before the time ascribed to Ulysses' wanderings? Could there be a connection? The excavations at Kommos revealed that after the abandonment of the port occasional visitors passed that way. Were they men like Ulysses and Menelaus who had brought back a mixture of tales which confused the heyday of Minoan prosperity with the primitive life that survived the collapse? What had happened to the survivors of Kommos and the other Minoan settlements along this coast? Could they have fallen back to the barest subsistence level, living in caves and practising the sort of simple pastoral farming that Ulysses found with the Cyclopes people? If so, the puzzling reference to the untended fields of the Cyclopes which still grew crops and vines, could then be a reference to the abandoned field systems of the old Minoan civilization.

All this was conjecture but it fitted very neatly with the details of the *Odyssey*, even down to the abandoned forge of Kommos which was a link with the metal-working Cyclopes of normal mythology.

Crete has an excellent claim to being the home of Arges, Brontes and Steropes, the three original metal-working Cyclopes. The infant Zeus grew up in a mountain cavern in Crete, aided by the three Cyclopes brothers working at their subterranean forges. Presumably the three brothers were still located in Crete when the Olympian god Hephaestus assumed the role of chief artificer to the gods and they became his assistants. There is a faint echo of Polyphemus in Talus, the legendary Cretan giant whom Hephaestus fashioned of bronze to protect the island from strangers. Talus was a colossal articulated figure of bronze who marched around the coast of Crete and threw great rocks at any ship which dared approach. Was this rock-throwing Cretan giant another parallel of the Cyclops story? And what about the clever wall-building Cyclopes who were supposed to have constructed the 'Cyclopean' walls of Mycenae? Could they be a memory of the Cretan engineers? The Minoan and Mycenaean civilizations were closely intertwined, and historians still argue fiercely about which was the dominant influence. The traditional view is that the Mycenaeans derived their culture from the Minoans, so it could be argued that Cretans introduced city engineering to the Mycenaeans.

An ex-partisan called Kosti Paterakis had another candidate to show me for the cave where Ulysses met the Cyclops. During the guerrilla war against the German occupation, Kosti and his fellow partisans had often brought Allied agents to a place actually called the Cave of Polyphemus or the Cave of Cyclops. The agents were usually landed by submarine or small craft on the south coast, and the cave made an ideal place to hide them and their supplies of weapons and explosives. Kosti himself had a reputation as a spectacular sharp-shooter. In his translation of *The Cretan Runner*, a Cretan shepherd's account of the partisan war, Patrick Leigh Fermor adds a footnote to the story of how a German patrol had surrounded a mountain village suspected of helping the guerrillas. The women and children had been herded to the edge of the village where the German execution squad was setting up its weapons when the partisans counter-attacked from an ambush outside the German circle. Kosti fired the first shot and picked off the German machine gunner with a single bullet from a distance of over 400 yards. It was, commented Leigh Fermor, one of the most spectacular moments of his war.

Kosti now looked more like a kindly bank manager than a crack shot with an army rifle as he led me at ankle-turning pace over the hillside behind the little town of Sougia, ninety kilometres west of Kommos.

Before the Second World War, Kosti explained, it had been customary to put up to a thousand sheep in the great 'cave of Polyphemus', and when we got there, it fulfilled my every expectation.

The cave was *exactly* as Homer described. A great slab of a boulder was tilted against the entrance like a massive door. A sheep pen had been made behind the boulder by heaping rough stones together so that a shepherd could hold and milk his ewes just like Polyphemus. The high roof was streaked with the smoke of cooking fires. A hollow log was balanced on top of a rock to catch the drip of ground water from the cave roof and serve as a reservoir. The floor was thickly carpeted with pungent sheep dung, and there was no difficulty in imagining Ulysses concealing the sharpened stake in the dirt.

If a carpentry crew from a film studio had been asked to dress a set for the Cave of Polyphemus, it could not have done a better job. The place was perfect. Where the floor sloped upward at one side of the cave was a curiously shaped boulder, dank and slightly green with moss. It looked like a rude throne. I walked over to it, sat down, and looked back towards the cave entrance. The sunlight was shining through the crack between the great boulder and the rock wall and cast a slant of light across the surface of a large boulder below and slightly in front of the 'throne'. I saw it glint off a repulsive jelly-like blob. A steady drip of water falling from the roof was raising an eight-inch diameter ring of lime deposit on the top of the round boulder where the splash was flung in a circle and then evaporated. At the point of impact, in the centre of the raised ring, the drip was forming the foot of a stalagmite. The smooth dome of this embryo stalagmite looked like a grotesque round eyeball, the surrounding ring its monstrous eyelid. With the light reflecting off its surface, the rock seemed to be staring wetly at the ceiling with a single Cyclopean eye.

It was, of course, altogether *too* perfect. The Cave of Polyphemus is so romantically like Homer's cave that it requires very little imagination to see the resemblance and draw the conclusion that this is the very place Homer wrote about. The adventure in Polyphemus' lair is so famous that a village schoolmaster or any educated man could have entered the cave at Sougia, been reminded of Homer's description, and dubbed the spot 'Polyphemus' Cave', just as the fishermen so often speak of the 'rocks that the Cyclops threw.' Unfortunately the cave near Sougia is not close to the shore, like Homer's cave, but high up on a scree. Nor can it be seen from the sea but is so well hidden that it was never found by German search parties when it was used by the guerrillas. Nor is there a suitable island nearby where Ulysses' men hunted the wild goats and waited for their leader to return.

So where does that leave us? One is forced back to the *combination* of details – the juxtaposition of wild-goat island and cave – to indicate which of the various caves along the coast might have been the original one of the Polyphemus story. Aboard *Argo* we scoured the length of the coast, sailing close inshore, inspecting even the smallest islet and climbing up to visit every cave we noticed from the sea. There was no shortage of them. Crete is made largely of limestone and riddled with caves. Professor Faure had gathered information about 747 of them and calculated there must be well over 1,400 in total. The Island of Wild Goats was the problem. As we have seen, the only suitably placed islands, the Dried Bread Islands, lack the south-facing harbour into which Ulysses' squadron sailed that dark night. Was there any alternative?

Then I remembered the indispensable Captain

Thomas Abel Brimage Spratt. The creator of 'Spratt's Map', which had led the successful archaeologists to Troy, had also carried out a painstaking survey of the coast of Crete. He had become so interested in the island that he had written the two-volume *Travels and Researches in Crete*. In his book Spratt noted that sections of the coastline of Crete showed clear evidence of cataclysmic changes. Some places, he reported, had been heaved up out of the sea. He had searched for an ancient galley harbour called Falasarna on the west coast which had been described by the geographer Strabo, but could find no trace of harbour-works, not even a beach fit for landing small boats. Then Spratt realized that Falasarna was high and dry. The harbour basin was sixteen feet above sea level and 100 yards inland, stranded by a massive alteration in the shoreline. Spratt judged that in some places the coast had been lifted as much as twenty-six feet by some major upheaval of the earth, and he pointed out a groove running round the base of the cliffs of the west end of Crete. The groove was a wave notch cut at the ancient sea level.

We noticed the same wave notch from *Argo* as we crept round the coast. It was as if some titanic glass cutter had scored a groove around the island ready to snap it off a few metres above sea level. Modern studies of the history of Crete's sea level have shown that the position was much more complex than Captain Spratt had imagined. Parts of Crete's coast have been elevated, particularly in the west, while other sections in the east have sunk. Kommos, for example, seems to have gone down by perhaps three or four feet. But on the whole the observant Captain Spratt had been right. The west end of Crete was now much higher out of the sea.

I turned back to the charts to see if perhaps there was another possibility for the 'Wild Goat Island'. Was there a place which would have been an island 3,000 years ago when the shoreline was at the level of the wave notch? Immediately I saw the natural candidate: the peninsula of Paleochora or 'Old Town' which lies close to the south-west corner of Crete. It is in exactly the right position for a landfall by a squadron coming up from Cyrenaica. We sailed *Argo* back to Paleochora, and while the crew were filling our fresh water containers I walked to the southern end of the peninsula. Sure enough, there was the tell-tale wave notch marking the ancient sea level; and there too was the outline of a natural harbour which faced southwards when the water level had been higher. The neck of the Paleochora peninsula is merely a low ridge of sand, scarcely above the modern sea level. Even a change of a few feet would turn Paleochora into an island. Spratt had calculated that the intervening channel would be 'from half to three quarters of a mile wide, and from three to four fathoms deep'. That seemed to fit the *Odyssey*'s description. Later I was to learn that a British archaeologist some twenty years ago found, four kilometres away from Paleochora, the remains of a small Minoan settlement which had originally been on the sea shore. Now it lies 150 metres inland. Paleochora's peninsula, he wrote, 'would have been a low exposed islet off the coast' but he could find no signs of ancient habitation there. This, I thought, was fully in keeping with Ulysses' uninhabited Island of Wild Goats.

So could the Cyclopes people have been living in the cliffs between Paleochora and Cape Krio, the south-west corner of Crete? Certainly there are caves in the area and, significantly, the owner of one of them, digging building clay from the cave floor, reported unearthing an outsize bone. He was to be believed, I was told, because he was the local policeman. Probably the bone was a fossil from a large mammal – elephants and hippopotami once lived on Crete – but if there had been earlier finds of massive fossil bones in these caves surely they would have provided the necessary element to sustain a story of local giants to supplement the folktales of the *triamates* with their uncanny resemblance to the Cyclopes.

A final answer to the precise whereabouts of Polyphemus' cave will probably never be possible. But the *region* of Ulysses' landfall as he came back from the country of the Lotus-eaters now seemed to comply with the basic rules of Bronze Age navigation. Coming north from Cyrenaica, the squadron met the coast of Crete, most likely close to its south-western corner. There the sailors hunted the *agrimi*, perhaps on Paleochora island, and encountered simple shepherd people living in their caves. By then, the Minoan settlements had been abandoned though their fields may have still been producing a few residual plants and fruits which 'sprang up unsown and untilled' and were gathered by the cave-dwellers. Crete, however, was still familiar as the home of the metal-working Cyclopes. Homer or the earlier bards from whom he took his story further elaborated the visit with a tale from local folklore about the *triamates* but confused them with the more traditional Cyclopes technicians of Greek mythology.

If my interpretation of the tale of Cretan Cyclopes/*triamates* was correct, then I was beginning to suspect something else: the key to understanding the wanderings of Ulysses might lie in the link between practical seafaring and regional folklore. The *Odyssey* was a chain of tales – further along his voyage Ulysses was to meet such legendary beings at the Sirens, Scylla the man-snatcher, and Charybdis the swallower – and perhaps each story might turn out to be associated with a particular coastal locality. If we could identify the places the folklore came from, then we might have a shrewd idea of the places Ulysses visited. That suspicion was to take a very much more definite shape as the result of a very unexpected discovery concerning our next port-of-call – the Island of Aeolus, Ruler of the Winds.

6

Ruler of the Winds

Cape Ram's Forehead is another of Nature's remarkable animal sculptures. The headland looks exactly like its namesake: a long-nosed boney muzzle dips to the sea as if about to drink from the brine. There is the scoop of a nostril and a flaring eye, and the rock strata curl round to give the distinctive spiral of a ram's horn. It is a key turning point on a coasting galley's route around Crete, just as Cape Malea with its profile of an irate baboon had marked the end of the Peloponnese. *Argo* crept round Cape Krio, 'the Ram's Forehead', on 12 July, no more than ten yards from the stone tip of the ram's nose, and I wished that the scholars who had deciphered the Linear B tablets, the writings of Mycenaeans, could have been aboard. They would have appreciated why 'the Ram's Forehead' is a place-name scratched on a wet clay tablet by some forgotten scribe in King Nestor's palace 3,000 years ago. It is unmistakable.

Capes and headlands seemed to be playing a major role in the geographical perception of the *Odyssey*. In the six weeks since we had sailed from Troy in Ulysses' wake and begun to establish the framework of the natural galley routes of the eastern Mediterranean, we had noted Cape Gerastus where Agamemnon's fleet was damaged, Cape Sounion where the royal helmsman had been buried, the unnamed southern headland of Crete where Menelaus lost his ships, and the crucial role played by Cape Malea. I was beginning to wonder if this was another pattern which was beginning to emerge from our search. If the country of the Lotus-eaters was situated in Cyrenaica near the most northerly cape of Libya, and the land of the Cyclopes was the south-west corner of Crete, then it was beginning to look as if the *Odyssey* had set the scenes of Ulysses' adventures at the pivots or turning points of a known sea route. If so, then the place for Ulysses' next adventure ought to be the next turning point on the logical way home to Ithaca, and in theory that spot should be the north-west corner of Crete. Here was the jumping-off point for the open-water crossing back to Cape Malea where Ulysses would try to rejoin the original route home. Here, if my hypothesis was correct, we ought to find an explanation for the next episode in the *Odyssey* – Ulysses' visit to the home of Aeolus, the Ruler of the Winds.

Aeolus is something of an exception among the grotesque or semi-divine beings who populate the verses of the *Odyssey*. Compared with them he is really very human. He lives comfortably on an island with his family of six sons and six daughters who are married to one another. They have plenty to eat and drink and prove to be most hospitable to the visiting Ithacans, entertaining them for a whole month with feasting and music. The most striking feature of their island home is that it is said to be surrounded by a great wall of bronze, and the only peculiar or outlandish point about Aeolus is that the gods had given him control over the winds. Very kindly he used this faculty to help his guest. Leaving free only the favourable west wind to blow his guest on his way, Aeolus imprisoned all the boisterous winds in a leather bag which he then gave to Ulysses. This was the target of Eratosthenes' sceptical epigram that there was as much likelihood of finding the places of Ulysses' wanderings as locating the cobbler who sewed up the winds in a leather bag.

Now it seemed to me that there could well be a link

between the north-west corner of Crete and the winds. When Ulysses' squadron headed back north from Libya to Crete and on around Cape Krio, they were travelling uphill. That is, the galleys were going against the prevailing northerly winds of the summer sailing season. To advance along the coast of Crete was not too difficult. It can be done by using the dawn calm to make a few miles' progress, then anchoring during the strong daytime winds, and with a little luck adding a few more miles by rowing in the evening lull. But eventually when you have crept your way all around the coast and reached the north-west corner of Crete, the system breaks down. You are faced with an open-water crossing back to Cape Malea, with only the islands of Anticythera and Cythera to use as stepping stones. If you are caught in the open crossing by another strong north wind, say a *meltemi*, then you risk being blown away to Africa once more. If this had happened to Ulysses once already, he would have taken every precaution against a similar mishap a second time. Logically he would wait at the north-west corner of Crete until he had perfect conditions, spread sail and make a dash for Malea hoping that the favourable breeze would hold until he reached the Peloponnese. Small boats, leaving Crete to cross to the mainland, behaved in precisely this way up to the present century. They would get themselves into the best position on the extreme north-west corner of Crete and wait for a fair wind. Just one anchorage was suitable for this tactic. The only safe shelter on that dangerous and rocky corner was the small island of Gramvousa or Grabousa, once notorious as a pirate's lair. So towards Gramvousa I now steered *Argo*, wondering if we would find any trace of Aeolus who had sewed the winds into a leather bag.

We nearly came to grief on the way. We turned Cape Krio and ventured out on the exposed west coast of

Crete when we were stopped in our tracks by exactly the sort of north wind that the ancient galleymen had dreaded. Like them we had no way of knowing that this foul wind would develop into a maverick of such unseasonal ferocity that it blew like a winter gale for a full week. All normal activity on the Aegean was disrupted. Ferry services were cancelled, charter flotillas went into harbour and their charter parties returned home by air, beaches were cleared of swimmers as it was foolhardy to venture out into the heavy surf. Of all this we knew nothing, for *Argo* was completely cut off, clinging on for survival in an uninhabited cove on the west coast of Crete.

I knew we were in trouble five minutes after we rounded Elefanisos, Deer Island, just beyond Cape Krio. *Argo* began to fall thunderously off each wave crest as we lurched past the reef at Elefanisos that is an ominous graveyard of ships. The sea was too much for her and the galley was almost unmanageable in the breaking waves that were heaping the reef. We reverted to our emergency system of trying to coax the galley forward with the help of the rubber dinghy, and rigged the spare outboard engine on its bar. But it was not enough. No sooner were we past the long tongue of reefs than the rising wind began to force us ashore inside the curved line of breakers so that we could no longer even turn back without being driven on the rocks behind us. There was nowhere to cast anchor in that bleak and windy spot and we had no choice but to keep grinding forward as I anxiously looked for the slightest recess in the rocky shore that might give a scrap of shelter. There was nothing. For six hours we struggled on at a snail's pace. The crests of the waves were swamping the spare motor which spluttered and gagged in protest at the maltreatment and only the most experienced seamen in our crew were able to operate the rubber dinghy in the choppy seas. Soon they were grey with exhaustion.

Finally, at five o'clock in the afternoon, we lost the struggle. The wind speed was still rising, and as we laboured past yet another bleak stretch of cliffs, *Argo* definitely began to slide backwards. Close under one stretch of cliff there seemed to be a quieter patch among the turmoil of wind and spray, a wind shadow. For the first time in *Argo*'s journeying, whether in the Aegean or the Black Sea or the Sea of Marmara, I ordered the storm anchor to be made ready. It was a heavy, old-fashioned fisherman's anchor of iron stowed low in the bilge of the ship as ballast. We grovelled in the bowels of the ship, shifting the stores to get at the anchor, cut the lashings that held it, and manhandled the unwieldy affair onto the foredeck. We knew that if the storm anchor did not catch and hold, then *Argo* had little chance. It was a plain lesson on why early sailors almost worshipped their ships' anchors. They carried not one but dozens of them, and when they came ashore at the end of a voyage they often dedicated their crude stone anchors at a temple to give thanks for their survival. They knew, like us aboard *Argo* that ugly afternoon, that when a galley is being blown down on a hostile shoreline, only the anchor stands between the ship and destruction.

The spot where *Argo* was headed was no sensible place to drop that anchor. The water was perhaps twenty-five feet deep and the sea bed a jumbled mass of foul ground, rocks and boulders, with nowhere for the flukes of the anchor to bite. Our only chance was that the iron anchor or its chain would snag in the rocks. Cormac had charge of the anchor. He was a professional fisherman from Ireland, six feet three inches tall, who had sailed on the Jason Voyage. Of splendid value in a crisis at sea, his Dublin wit was a constant fillip to the crew's morale.

'Let go the anchor!' Cormac threw it over as if it were a toy. The chain rattled out, checked, and we felt *Argo* stagger to a halt. I had to admit that we were better equipped than a Bronze Age ship. Ulysses and his squadron may have used chain attached to their anchors, but more likely they had to rely on fragile leather rope, easily cut by the sharp edges of rocks. They would not have had *Argo*'s metal anchor, but only a poor thing made of stone, perhaps with wooden prongs sticking out of it, or maybe a pyramid-shaped weight on the end of a rope. I pointed out to Cormac that in a similar situation Ulysses would probably have ordered one of his men to jump overboard clutching a stone anchor, sink to the bottom with it, and jam it between a couple of rocks. I got back a look that plainly showed what Cormac thought of that idea.

For six tedious and empty days *Argo* clung on grimly to that spot while I fretted that we had failed by only thirteen miles to reach the proper anchorage at Gramvousa. It was no consolation to know that we were proving beyond all doubt that a galley is totally dependent on a break in the north wind and that on the west coast of Crete the homebound sailors had to wait patiently, whether at Gramvousa or in that drab little cove. We amused ourselves as best we could. The nearest settlement was the hamlet of Kampos, an hour's stiff climb up a very steep and rough road that led to the saddle of a pass. The wind came roaring through the gap, kicking up the dust so you had to turn your back and protect your eyes against the flying grit. Kampos was only half a dozen houses, two of which did duty as small shops where we could buy basic provisions. The gale had brought down the telephone and electricity lines so the place was out of touch with

news from the north coast, but the people of Kampos
did not seem to care and they were hospitable enough.
Weather-bound mariners must have been a novelty in
a place so high up on the mountainside with no port
within miles. When we came trudging each day up the
mountain, the shopkeepers let us linger over our cups
of coffee and saucers of local cheese and honey. Day
after day we took it in turns to keep an emergency
watch aboard the galley, while the shoregoers visited
the hamlet or went on long walks across the deserted
mountain slopes. On one of these hikes Derry was bitten
in the leg by a two-foot-long silver and grey snake. It
took three hours to find a local doctor who pronounced
that if Derry had not suffered any ill-effects by that time,
then the snake was harmless. Naturally when Derry
returned to *Argo*, he had to endure the inevitable jokes
about St Patrick banning snakes from his homeland so
that he couldn't recognize a snake when he saw one.
Next morning he was shaken awake by Cormac loudly
demanding 'Wake up Derry! Wake up. Are you
hungry?' Derry, who was perpetually hungry, nodded
eagerly. 'Then how about coming ashore for a bite?'
chortled Cormac.

Argo was stuck as helplessly as if she had been nailed
to the spot. Luckily there was drinking water from a
little stream which plunged down a glen and also
provided a natural shower under a small waterfall
where one could wash while the gale lashed through
the trees overhead. Every morning a peasant family
arrived by mule, carefully picking their way down the
winding track, then tethering the animals by the stream
while they spent the day stooped over their tiny patch
of market garden on the flat land behind the beach. The
reward for their labour was desperately meagre, a few
tomatoes, beans and melons which they carefully loaded
into panniers on their beasts and plodded off back up

the track before dark. The pitted track looked too treacherous to negotiate once the sun went down, but Doc John, Rick and Derry managed it after a prolonged drinking session with new-found acquaintances in the settlement up in the pass. Far too much home-distilled alcohol was consumed, and at three in the morning I thought I heard raucous singing over the crash of the waves and took the rubber dinghy to investigate. I found the three members of the shore party flat on their backs on the shingle beach, howling at the sky, with no memory of how they had managed to descend the breakneck track. To my astonishment they were neither injured nor bruised, though they must have fallen most of the distance down the mountain because their clothes were literally in tatters. Reflecting that Ulysses probably had similar experiences with his inebriated crew when they over-indulged at Aeolus' home, I philosophically lugged the miscreants into the rubber dinghy, stacked them on the floorboards, and transported the trio back to *Argo*.

On the seventh day the gale relented, and we continued up the Cretan coast towards Gramvousa. From a long way off the peak on the west end of the island is unmistakable, its crown as flat as if lopped off by a cleaver. As we drew closer, we noted that a line of sheer cliffs extended around the island, rising to a dizzy height on the west. There was a single landing place on a south-facing beach protected by twin reefs but even here the cliff line had only receded fifty yards so that the beach was backed by a bluff that was part of the encircling rampart.

☐ Our next landfall was the floating island of Aeolia, the home of Aeolus son of Hippotas, who is a favourite of the immortal gods. All around this island there runs an unbroken wall of bronze and below it the cliffs rise sheer from the sea. □

Gramvousa's extraordinary ring of cliffs fitted the description so admirably that I asked Will, the expedition artist, to sketch the shape of the island. Will was away all day, making working sketches from a vantage point on the neighbouring island. When he returned in the evening, he made a revealing comment. 'It's strange,' he remarked, 'how draftsmanship makes you notice details that you wouldn't normally observe. When I was doing the preliminary studies of the great cliff face, I began to realize how regular are the cracks in the rocks, horizontal as well as vertical. They're so evenly spaced that they look like square-cut blocks as though the whole cliff face is an enormous man-made wall.'

Will did not need to point out the other phenomenon which all of us had been watching as the sun went down. By some trick of light, the entire rock wall of Gramvousa which faced west was changing colour — Gramvousa's rampart turned a rich red, the colour of new bronze, the metal of Aeolus' island.

All this could have been mere wishful thinking, but they were facts which we were able to sketch and photograph. Dozens of islands in the Aegean are totally surrounded by spectacular cliffs but very rarely do they have safe harbours. The island of False Gramvousa, for example, lies just north of Gramvousa and has sheer cliffs, but there is no way to come ashore and even less chance to shelter a squadron of galleys. By contrast Gramvousa made a superb site for precisely the sort of Bronze Age settlement where Aeolus lived with his family:

□ Aeolus shares his house with his family of twelve, six daughters and six grown-up sons; and I must tell you that he has given his daughters to his sons in marriage. With their father and their estimable mother they spend their days in feasting. Of luxuries they have a never-failing store. All day long the house is fragrant with the roasting of meat, and the courtyard echoes to the sounds of banqueting within. At night they sleep in blankets by their loving wives on well-made wooden beds. □

The summit of that great flat-topped hill is an ideal place to build a Bronze Age acropolis. Its natural defences are unmatched and there is ample space for houses and storerooms. Lower down, the shoulder of the island widens to a plateau of heather and shrub excellent for the raising of flocks of sheep and goats to provide meat for the lavish feasts of Aeolus. The pasturage is still famous for the special flavour that the salty grazing gives the flesh of the half-wild Gramvousa sheep that are left on the island to grow fat without the need for a shepherd in this remote yet favoured hideaway. The only weakness of the acropolis is lack of fresh water, but this can be solved by the construction of cisterns. In times of peace there is an excellent well of sweet water for the entire settlement, down by the beach at the anchorage.

□ To this domain of theirs and this palatial home, we found our way. For a whole month Aeolus was my kind host and I was able to satisfy his thirst for news by giving him a full account of the Argive expedition to Ilium and the Achaeans' start for home. □

For a month, then, Ulysses and the Ithacans waited with this generous host on his bronze-walled island. Why would a dozen ships' captains have delayed so long when the squadron was eager to get home? They were, I believe, biding their time for the favourable wind they needed to get back across to the Peloponnese, and they were waiting on the island which has always been the departure point for open-sea crossing. Gramvousa is ideal for a stop-over. The anchorage is sheltered from winds from all directions but particularly from the hostile north wind. Self-sufficient and virtually impregnable, the island is a strategically vital corner of Crete. Gramvousa has been the key to navigation in this area throughout recorded history. You can still see the foundations of the guardhouses for the German lookout post established there in the Second World War. The crest of the acropolis is crowned by the ruins of a tremendous castle the Venetians built there to protect their trade routes, and which they eventually sold to the Turks, it is claimed, for a barrel of sequins. In the eighteenth century the island fell into the hands of Cretan pirates who preyed on passing shipping and became such a thorn in the flesh of the mercantile nations that a major expedition was launched by the Royal Navy to eradicate them. The rampart cliffs defended the island so effectively that it proved impossible to take Gramvousa by direct assault. The island had to be besieged for the entire summer; the well at the beach was seized to deny it to the defenders in the acropolis, who were forced to drink rainwater from cisterns. Only when the cisterns finally ran dry did the pirate stronghold surrender. The surviving men, women and children were found to be suffering from terrible privation, and local legend has it that the only person not to be rounded up was the wife of the pirate chief, named Vousa, who hid in a cave, and the island was subsequently named in her honour. The classical Greek name for the island had been 'Korykos', but it meant nothing to me when *Argo* visited the island.

As luck would have it, we arrived at Gramvousa on the one day of the year when people come by fishing boat from the mainland to re-dedicate the little Church of the Twelve Apostles by the landing beach. Otherwise Gramvousa is uninhabited except when fishermen choose to stay the night in the ancient anchorage and perhaps take water from the well. That afternoon, however, a dozen boats streamed into the anchorage, all crammed with Cretan families carrying baskets of food and large plastic flagons of wine. They settled themselves comfortably on the beach and arranged their picnics under the stunted trees by the well. Young men went off in twos and threes with hunting dogs, rifles and coils of rope to capture the half-wild sheep. Half a dozen were hunted down and, bleating with piteous cries appallingly like a human infant, they were carried down slung across the shoulders of the men and thrown into pits to await execution. A young priest held a ceremony outside the chapel. Fires of brushwood were lit on the beach, the sheep were killed and skinned and thrown into cauldrons, and while the stew cooked, the Cretan families sang and danced, first to their own music on fiddles and guitars but, as the players tired, to the sounds of the ubiquitous cassette players. The revelry continued long past midnight. A few boats left, but the majority stayed on, and for hour after hour the celebration continued, punctuated by volleys of rifle shots as the hunters fired off their weapons. Finally only the diehards were awake, hoarsely chanting drunken refrains that eventually petered out to be replaced by a strange, anxious, high-pitched twittering. Seabirds, disturbed from their ledges in those stupendous cliffs by the human racket, hovered over the anchorage until dawn broke.

*

Ruler of the Winds

When the time came for Ulysses to leave Aeolus' island he went to the Ruler of the Winds and asked

□ whether I might now continue my journey and count on his help. He gave it willingly and presented me with a leather bag, made from the flayed skin of a full grown ox, in which he had imprisoned the boisterous energies of all the winds. For you must know that Zeus has made him Warden of the Gales, with power to lay or rouse them each at his will. This pouch he stowed in the hold of my ship, securing it tightly with a burnished silver wire so as to prevent the slightest leakage. Then, for my present purpose, he called up a breeze from the west to blow my ships and their crews across the sea. But his measures were doomed to failure, for we came to grief, through our own criminal folly.

For the next nine days we sailed on, day and night; and on the tenth we were already in sight of our homeland, and had actually come near enough to see the people tending their fires, when I fell fast asleep. I was utterly exhausted, for in my anxiety to make a quick run home I had refused to let any of my men handle the sheet of my ship and had managed it myself without a break. □

How does this sector of his journey which Ulysses described match up with the reality of trying to sail onward from Gramvousa to Ithaca? Once again we have the very suspicious repetition of nine days' sailing and a landfall on the tenth day. It is exactly the same length of time as the voyage from Cape Malea to the country of the Lotus-eaters, and could just be a meaningless poetic formula. At *Argo's* normal pace, a nine-day passage from Gramvousa to Ithaca would be leisurely but not unduly long if overnight halts were made in the normal manner of Bronze Age sailing. To use the west wind for the trip would require careful sailhandling but clearly that is what Ulysses describes when he says that he refused to let anyone else touch the sheet controlling the sail. *Argo* had demonstrated that a galley can sail broadside to the wind and, well handled and shrewdly ballasted, can make a course a few degrees upwind, but little more. To lay the course from Gramvousa up the west coast of the Peloponnese to Ithaca the wind would need to be south-west, and Zephyr, the West Wind which Aeolus gave the squadron, can come anywhere from a north-west to south-west direction. Homer, like his successors in classical times, did not employ strict compass points. Winter west for example lay further south than summer west as it was determined by the point where the sun rose and set on the horizon. The names of North, South, East and West were often no more than the names of the winds themselves, so that the direction was general rather than precise.

So there is nothing physically impossible in the events that Ulysses describes, though it does sound like a poetic exaggeration to claim that he had not slept for nine days and the squadron was actually in sight of the fires of their homeland when disaster struck. The cause was the crew's suspicion about the bag of winds and their doubts about their leader's honesty. They thought that Ulysses was cheating them and this tells us a good deal about the greed and ill-discipline of the Ithacans and their leader's failure to win their trust. Quite simply, the crew believed the leather bag that Aeolus had stowed in the ship contained treasure that Ulysses was taking back home without sharing with his men.

☐ The crew seized this chance to discuss matters among themselves, and word went round that I was bringing home a fortune in gold and silver which the generous Aeolus son of Hippotas had given me. You can imagine the glances and the comments that were exchanged: 'What a captain we have, welcomed wherever he goes and popular in every port! Back he comes from Troy with a splendid haul of plunder, though we who have gone every bit as far come home with empty hands – and what must Aeolus do but give him all this into the bargain, just for friendship's sake! Come on; let's find out all about it and see what gold and silver is hidden in that bag.'

A few speeches in this vein – and evil counsels carried the day. They undid the bag, the Winds all rushed out, and in an instant the tempest was upon them, carrying them headlong out to sea. They had good reason for their tears: Ithaca was vanishing astern. As for myself, when I awoke to this, my spirit failed me and I had half a mind to jump overboard and drown myself in the sea rather than stay alive and quietly accept such a calamity. However, I steeled myself to bear it, and covering my head with my cloak I lay where I was in the ship. So the whole fleet was driven back again to the Aeolian Isle by that accursed storm, and in it my repentant crews.

Once there, we disembarked and watered. The men fell to and took a quick meal by the ships. But as soon as we had had something to eat and drink I detailed a messenger and one sailor to accompany me and set out for the palace of Aeolus . . . ☐

If Ulysses the unfortunate, dogged by bad weather-luck, had been driven back to Gramvousa, one can almost see him trudging up the path from the landing beach, then clambering up the track up the bluff, and finally reaching Aeolus' mansion on the flat top of the acropolis to tell him that the south-west wind had not held, and that the squadron had overreached itself by trying to make a direct run to Ithaca. Once more the *meltemi* had sprung up and they had been swept back to Gramvousa where they were lucky to find shelter. This time, says Ulysses, the Ruler of the Winds refused to help him. It was obvious that Ulysses was cursed, said Aeolus. He should leave the island at once. More prosaically, one suspects, Aeolus did not relish the idea of entertaining the entire squadron for yet another month.

Most of those Greek and Roman writers who believed that there was real geography in Homer identified the island of Aeolus elsewhere. Their theory places the bronze-walled home of the Ruler of the Winds 500 miles from Gramvousa in quite another part of the Mediterranean. The Lipari Islands, a group of volcanic islands off the north coast of Sicily, are still sometimes called the Aeolian Islands as a result of that theory. There are seven of these islands, but there was never any agreement among the early authorities which of them was supposed to be the home of Aeolus. Some said it was the island of Strongyle, which was an active volcano; others that it was Lipara, the largest island of the group, and that Aeolus foretold the winds by watching the direction of the smoke plumes rising from the neighbouring volcanoes. Yet Homer says nothing whatsoever about active volcanoes, a feature which would be hard to overlook in an epic. But the real flaw in placing Aeolus off the north coast of Sicily is that to sail home from there to Ithaca takes Ulysses on an unbelievable track. He and his squadron would have had to pass through the Straits of Messina between Sicily and the toe of Italy, cross the entire breadth of the Ionian Sea and arrive off Ithaca. There they would encounter the storm, alleged to have been caused by opening the bag of winds, and been blown all the way back across the Ionian Sea, again through the Straits of Messina (a dog-leg course that is very unlikely) and finally to land once more on the Lipari Islands. This feat, by accident or navigation, is totally improbable. Moreover, the same authorities who place Aeolus in the Lipari Islands also claim that Ulysses met the legendary monsters Scylla and Charybdis in the Straits of Messina at a later stage in his journey. If so, it is difficult to see how twice before he could have missed Scylla and Charybdis as he shuttled back and forth through the Straits. But then, as we shall see, even the traditional and apparently secure locations of Scylla and Charybdis in the Straits of Messina, confidently identified by commentators from the fifth century BC until the present day, do not stand up to close scrutiny.

By contrast, after *Argo*'s visit to Gramvousa I found the island had so many features to match Homer's story that it seemed a far better qualified candidate for Aeolus' island. There was its key position on the homeward route, its remarkable bronze-coloured rock wall, the ideal terrain for a Bronze Age settlement, the anchorage where vessels waited for a favourable wind going back up to Cape Malea. Geography and practical navigation therefore supported the identification, but I would have preferred some additional evidence that Gramvousa was associated long ago with a fable or a tale, which connected the Ruler of the Winds with the island. I would have liked to have uncovered a similar link to the one we had found between the *triamates* and the Cyclopes, but I seemed to have come to a dead end.

Three months after my return home, I wrote to a historical geographer who taught at the University of Sheffield, asking for information on the classical history of Gramvousa. She consulted a colleague expert in both classical and modern Greek. In her letter she told me that Gramvousa's early name had been Korykos or Corycus – a fact I already knew – but the next sentence in her letter was a revelation. 'Korykos (= a leather bag) is a Greek placename.'

Korykos was a leather bag. The link was obvious. The most memorable detail of the entire Aeolus story is how the Ruler of the Winds bottled up the winds *in a leather bag.* Why would anyone have called Gramvousa the Island of the Leather Bag unless there was some reason? It was a bizarre name and surely the most likely cause was that this island was associated with the folktale of the Leather Bag of Winds. Eratosthenes the sceptic, I felt, had his answer after more than 2,000 years. *Argo* and her crew hadn't found the cobbler. But we had located the bag.

7

The Harbour of the Massacre

Like a beagle picking up the strengthening scent of his quarry, *Argo* hunted forward. Now we were searching for a place that might be the sombre harbour where eleven ships of the homecoming squadron were trapped by hostile natives and smashed to pieces. All their crews were butchered, possibly 480 men not counting their Trojan captives as they floundered in the water. Only Ulysses and his crew aboard the flagship escaped the bloodbath. The corpses of the rest were eaten by the cannibal natives.

It took the squadron six days to get to the ill-fated spot from Aeolus' island. 'We resumed our journey in a state of gloom', Ulysses reported,

□ and the heart was taken out of my men by the wearisome rowing, though it was certainly through our own folly that the friendly breeze that we had before enjoyed now failed us. For six days we forged ahead, never lying up even at night, and on the seventh day we came to Telepylus, Lamus' stronghold in the Laestrygonian land . . . □

In the classical literature there was no other reference either to Lamus or to Telepylus, so the best clue we had to go on to find 'the Laestrygonian land' was the description of the harbour where the massacre took place. Ulysses said that he and his companions

□ found an excellent harbour, closed in on all sides

by an unbroken ring of precipitous cliffs, with two bold headlands facing each other at the mouth so as to leave only a narrow channel in between. The captains of my squadron all steered their craft straight into the cove and tied up in the sheltered waters within. They remained close together, for it was obvious that the spot was never exposed to a heavy or even a moderate sea ... □

What we were seeking, therefore, was a distinctive harbour like a cul-de-sac, surrounded by tall cliffs and entered through a very narrow opening pinched almost shut by two opposing points of rock. Inside the haven there should be enough room for eleven galleys to be moored up 'close together', and their situation would have to be like sitting at the bottom of a well shaft because the hostile natives, the Laestrygonians, had lined the cliff top and tossed down boulders that ripped through the hulls of the thin-skinned galleys. There were two other possible clues to the harbour, though these details had perplexed rather than helped earlier commentators. The first and more cryptic clue was that 'in this land nightfall and morning tread so closely on each other's heels that a man who could do without sleep might earn a double set of wages, one as a neat-herd [cowherd] and the other for shepherding white flocks of sheep'. In other words the Laestrygonians were located near the border between day and night. The second scrap of information was more straightforward: a spring called Artacie supplied the city of Telepylus (which means Far Gates) with its water.

Applying the principle that the adventures of Ulysses had, so far, been set on the major turning points of the natural coasting route, I conjectured that our best chance of finding the fatal harbour of the Laestrygon-ians would be near the next major headland after Malea on the logical path towards Ithaca – Cape Matapan, known in ancient times as Taenarum and the most southerly point of the Greek mainland.

To make quite sure that I was not overlooking other possible Laestrygonian harbours, we carefully took *Argo* to check every mile of the coasting route between Gramvousa and Taenarum. As we approached the island of Anticythera eight or nine northbound dolphins crossed paths with the galley and promptly swam over to amuse themselves by leaping and playing around *Argo*'s ram. They came bursting jauntily out of the water before ducking down and racing away with exuberant wriggles of their streamlined bodies. One dolphin was so consumed with curiosity that he lingered for ten minutes about twenty yards ahead of *Argo* with his head poking out of the water to gaze at the galley, occasionally heaving himself vertically into the air for three-quarters of the length of his body to look over the gunnel and get a better view. His curiosity was matched by Nazem's wonderstruck delight. The Syrian had never seen playful dolphins in the wild before and was enraptured. He had a great fondness for all animals and constantly fed scraps from his kitchen to stray cats and dogs at every quayside. Now he rushed forward to the prow and stood there in amazement, with sparkling eyes and uttering gasps of 'La! Voila! Regarde!!' as the dolphins tumbled and curvetted. They were putting on a superb display and their joyous leaps were so like the painted dolphins speeding across the wall frescoes of Minoan palaces that I couldn't help thinking that perhaps the finest context ever to see this aquatic spectacle was from a Bronze Age galley, slipping through the water with a dolphin shape and questing eye, herself another natural sea creature.

Dutifully we searched both sides of Anticythera, circled the shores of Cythera, and found nothing. There were plenty of bays and creeks backed by sheer cliffs, but not a single place that remotely resembled the cul-de-sac of the Laestrygonian harbour. If the bays had cliffs, they were U-shaped and not horseshoe as they should be to fit Ulysses' description. The narrowest creeks could not have contained eleven galleys moored up close together, and the good anchorages were either backed by valleys sloping to the shore or by gulleys carved by winter streams. It became increasingly clear as we proceeded that a harbour like a cul-de-sac and surrounded by tall cliffs, if it existed, was indeed a very rare spot.

Six days and nights under oars, if again we accept the suspicious number of six despite its being a multiple of three, would have brought Ulysses' squadron between 140 and 240 miles from Gramvousa along the coastal route towards Ithaca. The distance can only be very vague because the speed of a galley being rowed at sea varies extravagantly with the number of oarsmen

Anticythera

aboard, the amount of time they are expected to row each day, whether the hull is clean or weed-covered, the heat of the day, the amount of cargo, the enthusiasm of the oarsmen, and the slightest breeze whether favourable or adverse. The great war galleys of the classical age could sustain four or five knots under oars but they were powered by as many as 160 oarsmen, rowing in teams. They recorded some truly remarkable passages of over 150 miles in twenty-four hours. But these were exceptional speeds by single ships on urgent missions and of short duration. The more consistent evidence shows that oared ships (and that included the Mediterranean galleys of the Venetians) averaged something in the region of two knots on long journeys as the constant grind of rowing day after day sapped the energy of the rowers.

Certainly it was out of the question to row without a break for six days and nights as Ulysses claimed, without at least heaving-to to rest the oarsmen. *Argo* on her 1,500-mile coasting voyage to Soviet Georgia had settled down to a daily average of some twenty-five to thirty miles per day, stopping each night on the shore so that the crew could stretch out on the beach and get a decent rest after five to ten hours' hard drudgery on the oars. We quickly learned that getting some sleep on the cramped bench of a galley, each man restricted to a plank 8.5 inches wide and 4 feet long, was only feasible if the crew was sufficiently exhausted. Three or four nights spent under such conditions dulled the most enthusiastic crew, and there is no reason to imagine that Ulysses' Ithacans with 'the heart taken out of my men by wearisome rowing' had much spirit left in them to row night after night.

Rather, they had good cause to be advancing sluggishly. We must remember they were obliged to travel at the speed of the slowest ship in the group of twelve.

The leaders would have to wait for the laggards to catch up. The laggards would then resent the rest periods already enjoyed by the crews of the faster galleys, and demand their turn for a break as well. Then, too, the galleys were heavily laden. Besides food and water for the six-day passage, they were also carrying the booty from Troy, jars of wine, bronze and precious metals, captive women, and all their war paraphernalia from a long campaign. Worse yet, as Ulysses indicates, the crews were utterly demoralized after their series of misadventures and their bad luck with the weather. Nothing corrodes the morale of oarsmen more effectively than the feeling that the weather is always against them, and even without the knowledge that they were now heading for their final disaster, the crew must have been rowing without enthusiasm. Under such conditions an average of twenty-five miles per day would be a generous estimate.

Six days on from Gramvousa, then, they would have been somewhere off the second root of the Peloponnese tooth, the Mani peninsula and its Cape Taenarum. It is a spectacle that would have depressed them still further. The Mani peninsula is among the bleakest, most forbidding parts of Greece, a raw and blasted ridge of rock which protrudes into the Mediterranean. By land it is almost completely isolated from the rest of the Peloponnese behind the sharp ridges of the Taygetus mountains. From the sea the Mani looks grim, a parched dun and grey jumble of steep cliffs, ravines, and the high crest of a central ridge with scarcely a living plant to be seen. The headland itself at Taenarum lacks charm or grandeur. A ragged clutter of rocks runs out into the sea where the swell heaves grumpily. Fittingly, in Greek myth, Taenarum was an entry to Hell. A cave hereabouts led the traveller into the Underworld.

'In this land nightfall and morning tread so closely

on each other's heels', was Ulysses' puzzling phrase. I wondered if perhaps his words had something to do with this entrance to Hades. We have only a hazy understanding of how the Late Bronze Age inhabitants of Greece viewed their world. Judging by the poetry of Homer and his near-contemporary, Hesiod, they saw themselves as living on a landmass surrounded by an endlessly flowing River of Ocean which circled about them. Above their heads the inverted bowl of the sky was held up by pillars. Beneath the ground was a huge void, through which a falling weight would take a year to drop before it reached the Underworld where lived the Shades of the Dead. When the Sun dipped below the horizon at the end of the day, he briefly illuminated this gloomy Underworld. There was also the notion that the Sun, entering a gold cup which served as a celestial boat, somehow sailed round on the River of Ocean and reappeared at dawn in the east to begin his daily transit of the sky.

What if the very early Greek concept of their habitable world ended at the western edge of Greece itself? How would that have affected the geography in the *Odyssey*? Homer mentions many lands to the east, Egypt, Syria and Cyprus, and in Mycenaean times Greeks were settled on the opposite shore of the Aegean on the coast of what is now Turkey. By comparison the *Odyssey* says next to nothing about the west. Sicily is mentioned in what may well be a later addition to the text, but that is all. Even the provinces on the west coast of Greece seem poorly understood, as if they stood on the fringe of the known world. If the western margin of Greece was the limit of common geographical knowledge when the earliest folklore was formed, we would expect to find there the bank of the 'River of Ocean' and the Sun climbing into his golden cup after a brief appearance below ground to light the Underworld. This would be entirely consistent with the view of someone standing at Taenarum on the extreme tip of mainland Greece and watching the sun dip into the sea in the unknown and mysterious west. In this context Taenarum's cave entrance to Hell made sense. It was positioned on the boundary between the habitable land, the River of Ocean, and the gloomy Underworld. This would explain why here, in the *Odyssey*, 'nightfall and morning tread so closely on each other's heels', because as the sun vanished so night emerged from the gloom underground.

Hesiod used this same concept and he certainly linked the end of the Sun's daily path with the limit of the world and the entry to Hades. He even used virtually the same phrase as Homer to describe the place:

There is the yawning mouth of hell, and if
A man should find himself inside the gates
He would not reach the bottom for a year;
Gust after savage gust would carry him
Now here, now there. Even the deathless gods
Find this an awesome mystery. Here, too,
Is found the fearsome home of dismal Night
Hidden in dark blue clouds. Before her house
The son of Iapetos, unshakeable,
Holds up broad heaven with his head and hands
Untiring in the place *where Night and Day*
Approach and greet each other as they cross
The great bronze threshold. When the one comes in
The other leaves; never are both at home,
But always one, outside, crosses the earth,
The other waits at home until her hour
For journeying arrives . . .

Cape Taenarum was a natural end-of-the-world. The place was literally the uttermost place of habitation in mainland Greece, and significantly the headland which in later days was to become sacred to Poseidon had previously been held sacred to Helios the Sun God. Here, according to a hymn attributed to Homer but now believed to be by a slightly later poet, had stood 'the sea girt town of Helios, gladdener of mortal men, Lord Helios whose *fleecy sheep forever feed and multiply*'. Wasn't this the explanation for those mysterious flocks and herds on the borders of day and night where a man could earn double wages 'one as a neatherd and the other for shepherding white flocks of sheep'? In the scheme of the *Odyssey* Cape Taenarum and the tip of the Mani peninsula seemed to be another spot where myth and legend held an echo of the events Homer described. Once again what was needed was some sort of cross-reference to underpin the suspicion that we were still on Ulysses' track.

That confirmation came on 22 July, when we found the harbour of the cul-de-sac. We had sailed that morning from Porto Gayo, a fine sheltered bay on the east side of Taenarum but far too wide ever to be blocked by boulder-tossing Laestrygonians. We hugged the Cape itself, almost grazing the rocks as we watched eagerly for the famous cave entrance to the Underworld. But it must either have been so small that we overlooked it altogether or, according to a recent theory, it was not at sea level but beside the beach of Asomati bay to the east of the headland. The Mani scholar and traveller, Professor Greenhalgh, writes in *Deep into Mani:*

The cave is still to be seen alongside the pebbly beach below the ruined church of Asomati that gives its name to the bay. It is roughly oval in shape, mainly open to the sky but with a few smoke-blackened caverns at the north-west side and a few slabs of masonry inside. It is only about 3 metres deep and perhaps 9 metres long, and with a leafy tree growing out of it – the only tree in the whole neighbourhood – it hardly satisfies the terrifying expectations of Virgil's 'Tenarian jaws' especially as we were able to confirm Pausanias' disappointed observation that 'there is no passage leading down through the floor'. But there is no doubt that this was the famous cave . . .

So for the professor, too, reality had proved to be a miniaturized version of the imagined poetic scene. The Mouth of Hell was only a modest cave, not a gaping hole. Its significance depended entirely on the way that it had been regarded by the ancients, and had then passed down through legend. It was exactly the same lesson that had been driven home by our own visit to Troy, and it also introduced our first glimpse of a man who was to play a key role later in our search. Pausanias, who the professor said was disappointed not to find the steps leading to Hades at Taenarum, was a Greek doctor who had also searched for the traces of Homer's world in Greece, but eighteen centuries ago in the reign of the Roman emperor Hadrian. Further along *Argo*'s route, he made a shrewd observation that was to have a major impact on our latter-day search, because Pausanias had noted a second Mouth of Hell whose importance to the geography of the *Odyssey* has been largely discounted because it seemed to make no sense. Set alongside *Argo*'s discoveries, however, Pausanias' idea was to make a perfect match.

Beyond Taenarum the Mani coastline turns north. The galley followed it faithfully, her crew still watching every inlet for a harbour like a cul-de-sac. Marmaris Bay, two miles from the cape, was a false hope. One arm of the bay did indeed have cliffs on each side, but the cove turned out to be U-shaped and there was a sloping valley at the back where a footpath led to a well on the beach. Ideal for a swim, it was disappointing for our search. Overlooking the bay the houses of a Maniot village were being carefully restored to their former condition, and nothing symbolizes the nature of the Mani more accurately than their domestic architecture. Quite simply the Maniots built their homes as forts. Thick stone walls were pierced by small windows to give good angles of fire and protect massive doors built to resist forcible entry. Overhead watchtowers concealed lookouts, and parapets screened sharpshooters and defenders dropping rocks or pouring hot oil and scalding water on an enemy trying to burn down the door. An entire army would have had the greatest difficulty fighting street by street through a Maniot village, but these miniature castles had little to do with repelling foreign invaders. Indeed the Maniots rarely bothered to build a defensive wall around their settlements because their enemies came not from outside, but from next door. Maniot clan fought Maniot clan, and family feuded against family, like ferrets in a sack. Rarely can a population have been more truculent. They built their homes thinking of murder, violence and ambush from foes just down the street.

Their attitude towards the outside world was not much different. The barren peninsula offered scarcely a scrap of living from the rocky and desiccated land, but it projected like a jagged spike into the main artery of coasting trade. So the Maniots lived by piracy. They harassed passing shipping and acquired a horrendous reputation for rapine. Nothing, it was said, was too inhuman for them. They traded in slaves, selling Christian to Moor or vice versa with equal aplomb. They amassed fortunes by ransom, by banditry or by extracting protection money from sea merchants. They were notoriously brave, seawise, untrustworthy, and bloodthirsty. Even their priests were reputed to have offered prayers that a fat merchant ship would be the next to waddle past the pirate coast. As Patrick Leigh Fermor, the most eloquent of all the writers who have described the Mani (and who built his home there), put it:

> No pirate enterprise of any consequence was complete without a priest. He blessed the expedition at its outset, prayed for fair weather for his pirate ship and foul weather for the enemy and interceded for the souls of his fallen messmates. He absolved the sins of his floating flock, and saw to it that a share of the loot, often wet with blood, was hung beside the ikons on the mainmast as a votive offering. If more than eight days passed and no prize came their way, he would intone a litany on the deck, and when the prospective prize was sighted he would level a matchlock over the bulwarks with the rest and join the boarding party with khanjar and scimitar.

The pirate Maniots of the Middle Ages and the seventeenth and eighteenth centuries could be said to have been worthy heirs to the Laestrygonians who ambushed Ulysses' squadron and cut it to pieces. Whether after the Trojan War or during the Crusades, the Mani was ideally placed as the ambush from which to pounce on the unwary sailor. But it was a remarkable 'hollow harbour' which clinched the identification. We came upon it some fifteen miles beyond Taenarum after a long hot passage beneath the towering cliffs of Kakovani, a great bulge of coast that juts out into the Gulf. In a landscape already remarkable for its bleak hostility, Kakovani would have sent shivers down the spine of any Bronze Age captain. The cliffs go on and on, seemingly for ever, fully exposed to a sudden gale from the west. There is no anchoring depth beneath them, and no protection. A galley caught by a gale would be swatted against those cliffs like a housefly. Yet there is no avoiding this sector. Coasting around the Mani the Kakovani cliffs must be skirted, and for at least five or six hours of rowing a vessel would be entirely exposed to danger. The relief that Ulysses' captains must have felt as they rounded the last turn of the cliff wall, and saw the coast opening into a sheltered bay, must have been enormous. The crews, weary from hour after hour of toil, baked by the heat reflecting off those lofty cliffs, would have quickened their stroke, and headed for the welcoming shelter. Behind the tongue of a small peninsula, today called Tigani, 'the Frying Pan', they would have already been in what the Admiralty Pilot calls the 'best harbour on the west coast of the Mani'. But the Admiralty Pilot refers to the roadstead, suitable for large ships to anchor and send boats ashore. For a Bronze Age galley there was shelter even more attractive. Scooped from the north face of the bay is a remarkable hollow in the hillside. It can be seen from three miles off, and its curious shape beckons the stranger arriving by sea. As you draw closer, it can be seen that the cliff curves round in almost a full circle. At the sides the two arms of rock fall away to low promontories that almost touch. There is just room for a galley to slip in between the promontories, gently rowing without the oars touching the sides. Once inside, the vessel is in a circular pool, the geological phenomenon that is the harbour of Mesapo.

'This place gives me the creeps,' muttered Peter Warren, another veteran of the Jason Voyage, as *Argo* crept in through the pincers of the entrance. It was a strange remark for Peter, a big tough ex-Marine, but we could all sense what he meant. The place was a freak of nature, airless, still and unnatural. It had a dead feel despite the cheerful colours of a handful of

fishing boats moored to take advantage of this total
shelter inside the hollow cliff. We were floating inside
a natural amphitheatre. Long ago in the geological past
there must have been a subterranean cavern hollowed
out by underground water, close to the shoreline. The
sea had gnawed away until it had invaded the cavern
which had fallen in like a bursting bubble. The roof
had collapsed, leaving an almost circular pool some
thirty yards across. In the pool there was just enough
room for eleven galleys to be tied up 'close together',
as Homer had put it, and he was not exaggerating when
he said that 'the spot was never exposed to a heavy or
even a moderate sea'. The surface of the enclosed pool
was absolutely motionless. *Argo* lay on its transparent
surface like a toy boat in a bath tub. Except for the
narrow gap at the entrance the place was totally
enclosed, and it was scarcely necessary to put mooring
lines ashore. The yellow cliff rose upward at the back
of the basin for maybe eighty or a hundred feet, scored
by bands of erosion, and the cliff curled very slightly
inward over the edge of the pool. It was this overhang
which gave the main feeling of claustrophobia and the
sensation of menace, almost as if the lip of the cliff
might break away and come crashing down into the
placid pool. Any foe who chose to line that cliff top,
armed with boulders, could have tossed them down
with terrible results, smashing to splinters the boats
moored below. There would have been no chance of
escape. Two men armed with long pikes could close
the entrance to Mesapo pool, standing on the twin
promontories and spearing the helmsmen. As for the
sailors from the smashed boats, struggling in the water
as they tried to climb ashore, they could be speared like
fish in a barrel, which is exactly how Ulysses described
the massacre by the Laestrygonians:

□ Antiphates [the king of the Laestrygonians] raised a hue and cry throughout the place, which brought the Laestrygonians running up from every side in their thousands – huge fellows, more like giants than men. Standing at the top of the cliffs they began pelting my flotilla with lumps of rock such as a man could scarcely lift; and the din that now rose from the ships, where the groans of dying men could be heard above the splintering of timbers, was appalling. One by one they harpooned their prey like fish and so carried them off to make their loathsome meal. □

Ulysses and his crew escaped only because he had kept his galley outside the death trap, moored to one of the promontories. When the rest of the squadron had ventured right inside, he said: 'I did not follow them. Instead I brought my ship to rest outside the cove and made her fast with a cable to a rock at the end of the point.'

When the Laestrygonians launched their attack, he was able to reach his vessel, and

□ while this massacre was still going on in the depths of the cove, I drew my sword from my hip, slashed through the hawser of my ship, and yelled to the crew to dash in with their oars if they wished to save their skins. With the fear of death upon them they struck the water like one man, and with a sigh of relief we shot out to sea and left those frowning cliffs behind. My ship was safe. But that was the end of all the rest. □

Mesapo pool with its overhanging cliffs fulfils every requirement as the place of the massacre, and the southerly promontory answers equally well for the spot where Ulysses moored his own galley outside the death trap.

Mesapo Harbour – The Laestrygonian Cove, *c.* thirteenth century BC

Here the local fishermen have cut a small landing ramp, for it is the natural place to come ashore when landing the day's catch. The topography fits the *Odyssey*'s description so neatly that I would have been suspicious of the match, as with the cave of the Cyclops on Crete. But whereas the Cyclops story is so well known that a suitable cave can easily be imagined to be a giant's den, Mesapo's pool is unlike anything that I had ever seen in twenty years of sailing, and as far as I was aware no one had even hinted that this could have been the harbour of the Laestrygonians. The evidence was not tainted by artificial tradition: Mesapo is simply the place that fits exactly the description in the *Odyssey*, and it lies at the correct point along the coasting route. Like Gramvousa as the island of Aeolus, this was the logical spot and yet no one had thought to look there.

Many places had been offered as the Laestrygonian harbour, but without much conviction: Strabo suggested a region near Leontine in Sicily but that locality is actually some distance inland. Several Roman commentators preferred a stretch of coast near Latium on the Gulf of Gaete, but there is no suitable port there. The long and spectacular Gulf of Kotor in Yugoslavia, or the harbour of Bonifacio in Corsica, or Port Pozzo in Sardinia have all been offered. All three have the beetling cliffs and well-protected shelter, and in Sardinia there are the remains of tall stone towers from the Bronze Age which would make suitable citadels for the savage Laestrygonians. But what they all lack is the *correct scale* of the *Odyssey*'s harbour. Every one of them is far too large for a squadron of eleven ships ever to be trapped inside. They all have entrances through which any vessel could have escaped, rowing out inhindered by landsmen. The Gulf of Kotor is 300 yards wide at its narrowest point, impossible for a Bronze Age warrior to close with spears or even arrows. Port Pozzo barely resembles the scene described by Homer, and the entrance to Bonifacio is 100 yards across.

If Mesapo fits the description so minutely, who then were the Laestrygonians? And what about the other clue – the spring called the Spring of Artacie where, according to Ulysses, his scouts met the daughter of King Antiphates, drawing water. I asked the people of Mesapo if there was a spring of Artacie nearby, but was met with blank looks. No one had heard of such a name.

One possibility is that the names of the Laestrygonians are symbolic, not real. It has been pointed out that 'the name Laestrygonians connotes devouring, Antiphates killing, and the city Telepylos remoteness'. This could equally be true of the spring of Artacie. The other possibility is that Homer simply imported the name from another famous tale of a voyage – the story of Jason and the Argonauts fetching the Golden Fleece. The Argonauts too were attacked at an anchorage by monstrous men from the mountains who rolled down boulders and tried to blockade their galleys. Led by Hercules the Argonauts successfully killed many of the attackers and drove off the remainder who retreated into the hills. We can safely locate the general area of this attack to the south coast of the Sea of Marmara. The place is still called Erdek, the Turkish form of Artacie, and there is a spring on the edge of town called *Jason's Spring*. Our modern *Argo* had visited Erdek in Jason's wake the previous year and we had found the spring just as described. Homer certainly knew the Jason story and refers to it later in the *Odyssey*. But what made him think of the spring of Artacie when he came to tell the story of Mesapo? Obviously the two ambushes by giants were similar, but was there any further connection? It happens that Artacie was one name of Artemis, the ancient goddess of fertility. In Greek mythology the entire Taygetus range including the Mani was held sacred to Artemis as the favourite hunting ground of the goddess and her attendant nine-year-old girl companions who served her until they were nubile. They were often called the 'arktoi', the she-bears, and Artemis herself sometimes appeared in the form of a bear, often being confused with the Great Artemis, the Mother of the Gods in Asia Minor. At Erdek the mountain overlooking the harbour was sacred to the Great Earth Mother and was called Bear Mountain. A reasonable hypothesis is that Homer, who refers to the Taygetus as sacred to Artemis, overlapped the two traditions – bringing Jason's Artacie to Ulysses' land of Artemis when composing the epic of Ulysses' return. All the same, I have to confess that I hope that one day a spring of Artacie will be identified near Mesapo, in the hunting grounds of Artemis/Artacie, to match the remarkable hollow harbour.

Modern Mesapo lived up to its inhospitable ancestry. *Argo*'s crew walked the few yards to the cheerless and decaying little hamlet which was once the unloading point for steamers bringing supplies to the peninsula. Now its role has been usurped by the modern motor road which runs down the spine of the Mani, bypassing the coastal villages. Today Mesapo has a tumble-down and scruffy appearance which the attitude of its inhabitants did little to dispel. Derry muttered with disappointment at the small size, staleness, and outrageous cost of the miserable and greasy platter of small bony fish offered for his lunch in the bedraggled taverna. 'They're still pirates,' he grumbled in his never-ending hunger. Cormac was equally critical of the beer, overpriced and tepid. 'Costas!' he boomed. 'Tell them to put three dozen bottles on to cool for our supper.' Captain Costas, retired chief pilot for Olympic Airways, was *Argo*'s interpreter. Grey-haired and courteous, he was the sort of man who always impressed his countrymen with his air of well-travelled authority though underneath lurked a schoolboy's love of pranks. That evening the beer was equally warm, the fish as badly cooked, and the bill just as piratical.

'We're only the first galley of many,' Cormac solemnly assured the morose café owner who was totally mystified by the strange visitation from a Bronze Age vessel. 'It's a new tourist venture. From now on you can expect one boat regularly every week, like ours only even bigger, with fifty men aboard, and they'll all be thirsty. If I were you, I'd lay in a good stock of beer and food to sell them. It would make a good investment.' By the brief flash of avarice in the tavern-keeper's eyes as Costas translated with absolute conviction, the Maniot may have half-believed our large and plausible Irishman.

Mycenae, capital of King Agamemnon who led the expedition against Troy

Above: Silhouette   *Below:* Mesapo Harbour

'By some trick of the westering light, the entire rock wall of Gramvousa, which faced west, was changing colour – Gramvousa's rampart turned a rich red, the colour of new bronze, the metal of Aeolus' island'. *Argo* beneath the towering cliffs of Gramvousa Island, which match Homer's 'bronze walls' around Aeolia, the home of the Ruler of the Winds

'Set up your mast, spread the white sail, and sit down in the ship.
The North Wind will blow her on her way...' Circe's
advice to Ulysses on his way to the Halls of Hades

'...drugs may have been used to confuse and befuddle'
The Halls of Hades, entrance to the Underworld on the river
Acheron in Epirus, north-western Greece, lit by flares

The Clashing Rocks: the great sea cleft of Sesola Islet recalls the
ancient tale of the two floating masses of rock that smashed
together too late, allowing Ulysses' galley to slip through

The sky at night

Paleocastritsa on Corfu's west coast, claimed as the site of King Alcinous' fabled palace

The isthmus of Aetos, where the literal-minded Schliemann enthusiastically searched hoping to find Ulysses' bed

Argo surrounded by a charter flotilla in the channel between Ithaca and Cephallonia, where Penelope's suitors laid an ambush for Telemachus on his return from King Nestor's palace

8

King Nestor's Palace

Argo's shadow lay black and sharp upon the white sand, a cleanly defined patch superimposed on the myriad of tiny ripples of the sea floor. The undertow had brushed the floor of the cove so gently that even the broken blades of dead seagrass were laid out in serried dark brown rows, absolutely motionless. The water was so clear that the galley might have been resting on a transparent membrane stretched a metre above the sand. It was an ideal spot to clean the hull of its thin beard of weed and algae, and I had asked the crew to go over the side into the lukewarm water with scrubbing brushes and paint scrapers. They were revelling in the assignment, splashing and joking as they ducked and dived, each to scour his allotted square of hull.

The white sand beneath *Argo*'s hull explains why Homer called this vicinity 'Sandy Pylos', and we now know that it was the home port for old King Nestor, the third most powerful king of the grand alliance which had laid siege to Troy. Here we will take leave for a time of Ulysses on his homeward path because it was to the court of King Nestor that Ulysses' son, Telemachus, came to seek news of his missing father. Scholars have long recognized that the *Odyssey* strings together at least four different tales which at one time existed on their own. It gathers in the story of Telemachus' quest for his father; the tale of King Menelaus' wanderings in Egypt; the saga of the homecoming when Ulysses arrived back in Ithaca; and the events of the sea journey known as the 'Great Wanderings', the true Odyssey. But as I shall seek to show, there is a fifth strand to Homer's epic, which tells of the folklore of the Ionian Islands, and has a special relation to the rest of the tale for it embodies some of the most spectacular of Ulysses' adventures.

All these individual strands Homer linked together in a single narrative, often not bothering to conceal the joints very effectively and apparently unconcerned if there were contradictions within the assembly. Thus Telemachus' visit to Pylos is presented quite separately from Ulysses' wanderings right at the beginning of the *Odyssey*. This explains why there is no reference to Ulysses ever visiting Pylos, though it lay on his home-ward route after the massacre by the Laestrygonians. A visit to Pylos had no part to play in the unfoldings of the saga of the Great Wanderings, which are concerned with adventures at the limits of the Mycenaean horizon.

From 'Sandy Pylos' Nestor had set out with ninety ships to join the Greek armada assembling for the amphibious assault on the Dardanelles, and back to Sandy Pylos he returned at the end of the campaign after a tranquil voyage that must have been the envy of every other returning hero. For King Nestor had weather-luck, like everything else, in abundance. He was wealthy, respected, and long in years. What is more, archaeology was to be very kind to him long after his dynasty had passed away. Ninety minutes' uphill walk from the idyllic crescent bay where *Argo* was anchored are the ruins of his palace, scrupulously excavated in a model exercise of the 'new archaeology', much more charitable to Nestor's memory than the devastating attack which the earlier archaeologists wreaked on Troy itself. But Pylos only just escaped. Schliemann sniffed around this sandy bay looking for Nestor's home before he ever went to Troy, and fourteen years later the energetic German made a second visit still playing the hunch that Nestor's palace had to have been here. If Schliemann had been a little luckier, or spent a few more days in the hunt, perhaps he would have been the excavator of Pylos in the ruinous style of his pioneering days rather than the quiet, courtly American professor whose team eventually did the work with such finesse and discrimination.

Carl Blegen, the third of our trio of outstanding Homeric archaeologists, was utterly different from his two predecessors, Schliemann and Dorpfeld. Where they were didactic and flamboyant, Blegen was calm and unpolemical. Yet he succeeded just as brilliantly in the search for the vanished world that Homer had described when he discovered and described a gem of royal architecture that provides a unique cross-check on the accuracy – or shortcomings – of the *Odyssey*. Blegen's 'Palace of Nestor' lets us compare Homer's picture of courtly life against the physical evidence unearthed by the spade and trowel, and that comparison can help tell us how far we may trust the voyaging record.

Blegen came from a Mid-Western family of modest background and studied classics with his father who taught Latin and Greek at a small Lutheran college. With financial backing from the wealthy Taft family, Blegen, who became a professor in the University of Cincinnati, led the third great examination of the ruins of Troy. Following on the heels of the two Germans, it was Blegen who applied the newly developed systematic techniques to solve the riddle of which level at Troy had been the city reputedly sacked by the Greeks. By the time Blegen got to the site the place was so badly churned up by the earlier digs that he was obliged to sort through the rubble, reassess the voluminous German excavation notes, and supplement his conclusions with the careful analysis of a few spots untouched by the pick-axes, shovels and drag-lines of his predecessors who had considered these places not worth bothering with. Painstaking analysis and, by modern standards, the lavish application of manpower and equipment made possible by the Taft funds enabled Blegen, as we have seen, to refine the work of Dorpfeld and trace a more complex series of cities on the site at Troy. Eventually he announced that it was the rather meagre city known as Troy VIIa which had been the capital of King Priam. This conclusion, meticulously documented and quietly argued, was widely accepted by his profession and disposed of Dorpfeld's more spectacular Troy VI as the city of Homer's tale, and is in vogue to this day.

But even before he was finished with Troy, Blegen had turned his attention to the evergreen problem of Nestor's 'Sandy Pylos'. With Blegen there is a feeling that this was the quest that really attracted him, far more than the work at Troy. His Trojan researches had been a restatement, worthy, challenging and of profound interest to Homeric scholars. But it was digging in other men's trenches. Sandy Pylos – if it could be located – would be a personal triumph, virgin territory archaeologically speaking.

By the mid-1930s two royal establishments, Agamemnon's Mycenae and Menelaus' Sparta, had long been identified and were in the process of being excavated. So 'Sandy Pylos' and Ulysses' home on Ithaca were the two big prizes which remained to be won. Ulysses' home was proving to be something of a disappointment despite persistent attempts to locate it for nearly a century, and there again Blegen would only have been following in other men's tracks. 'Sandy Pylos' however was a chimera. Essentially it had vanished from the Greek map, or rather it had divided itself into three, like a developing cell, and each version was claimed as the 'real' Pylos. Dorpfeld, like Schliemann, had gone on the search for Pylos and identified Nestor's home as some ruins at a place about midway along the western shore of the main Peloponnese near a small town called Kakovatos. He largely based his claim on the existence of three *tholoi* or beehive-shaped tombs nearby. His view agreed with the often-cited opinion of Strabo, whose interpretation of Homer carried such enormous weight with scholars that his 2,000-year-old opinions had virtually become holy writ. A second site for 'Sandy Pylos' had been proposed even further north, near the town of Elis, on the grounds that it lay much closer to Ithaca, but this was really too far inland to be the coastal site that Homer described. The third possibility was the one that Schliemann had already checked. The grassy crown of the southern headland overlooking Oxbelly Bay, as the sand-floored cove where *Argo* now lay is called, appeared to be an ideal site for an ancient town. Moreover local tradition claimed that this was where Nestor had lived, and here was a cave known as 'Nestor's Cave'. Schliemann dug hopefully in it, but found only a few pieces of broken pottery, some of it far too old to be from the time of the Trojan War, and the rest much too modern. So Schliemann in his characteristic haste abandoned the search and rushed back to Troy itself to consolidate his well-deserved fame.

The confusion about Homer's 'Sandy Pylos' had arisen because the *Odyssey*, as so often, contradicts itself. Early in his story Homer tells how Telemachus grew exasperated with the cluster of suitors hanging about the mansion of his father Ulysses in Ithaca and paying court to his mother Penelope who was loyally awaiting the return of her husband after an interval of nineteen years. The suitors had come in from the neighbouring Ionian Islands, hoping to marry the rich widow, and were taking outrageous advantage of the laws of hospitality. They spent most of each day at Ulysses' house, flirting with the serving maids and steadily eating and drinking their way through the royal larder and wine cellar. Hoping to put an end to the depredations of these human locusts, Telemachus decided to sail to Pylos, interview King Nestor, and try to find out what might have happened to Ulysses. The ship Telemachus used to travel from Ithaca to 'Sandy Pylos' was precisely the same size and description as *Argo* – a 'black ship' of twenty oars – and he accomplished the sea journey in less than a single day, slipping away from Ithaca under cover of darkness and reaching Pylos well before dusk the following evening.

Homer says that the goddess Athena, who favoured Telemachus' cause, called up 'a steady following wind and sent it singing over the wine-dark sea' to aid him on his way. Under good sailing conditions this would have brought Telemachus about a hundred miles and close to the place that Dorpfeld favoured. But Homer then says that Telemachus, after his interview with Nestor, went by chariot to the palace of King Menelaus in Sparta. The first sector of this chariot journey from 'Sandy Pylos' to a place called Pharai took only half a day. Pharai is near modern Kalamata, and there is very little chance that the distance between Dorpfeld's Pylos and Pharai could be covered so quickly by chariot. On the other hand the twenty-oared galley would have been travelling exceptionally fast, especially with the dangers of night-time navigation, to have covered the 130 miles to the southern Pylos in less than twenty-four hours. In short, the distances given by the *Odyssey* do not fully match up and there is an awkward gap in the travel times. All that could be taken as certain was that

Nestor's palace lay somewhere on the western rim of the Peloponnese and close to the sea.

Blegen persuaded his sponsors at Troy to fund a search. In 1927 he established the joint Hellenic–American Expedition to look for Mycenaean remains in the Messenia area of the western Peloponnese, surmising that this was the most likely area for Nestor's palace. Blegen based his field research on the very straightforward observation that in the area of Oxbelly Bay, where local tradition claimed the citadel of Nestor, were a remarkable number of the *tholos* tombs. These were usually taken to be the sepulchres of Mycenaean royalty. If there were so many tombs there, Blegen reasoned, then a royal palace ought to be nearby, even though Schliemann and Dorpfeld had both searched the area without success. Blegen and a Greek colleague, Constantine Kourouniotes, visited the area several times in the late 1920s and in 1938, to walk the terrain and interview local antiquarians as well as farmers who reported stumbling across ancient remains. By 1939 their search had been narrowed down to three major possibilities. The most promising was on the brow of a low hill called Epano Englianos, three miles inland from Oxbelly Bay. In a grove of olive trees the searchers noted substantial lumps of ancient rubble poking up through the ground. The main doubt about the site was that it was totally undefended, and in this respect completely different from the palace locations so far known. There was no sign of the massive walls like those protecting Mycenae, no evidence whatsoever of earthworks and defensive lines like those of Troy. Instead the hill top at Epano Englianos was an open, pleasant, rural spot set among modest hills with a fine view over the bay. In fact when Blegen and his team came to begin their formal digging there in the spring of 1939, their first concern was to avoid damaging the olive trees that covered the site in this peaceful agricultural landscape.

The matter of compensation to the landowner had not yet been settled so the archaeologists planned the line of their first exploratory trench in order to miss as many olive trees as possible. As luck would have it, their very first trench sliced not only into Nestor's palace but across what the digging team later called the Archive Room, probably the most important find of their entire programme. On that very first day, 4 April 1939, Blegen and his group gathered the first five examples of ancient palace ledgers, clay tablets scratched with examples of Mycenaean writing known as Linear B. When deciphered, these tablets were to revolutionize knowledge of court life in Ulysses' time. Blegen's discovery had to wait for the conclusion of the Second World War to be investigated systematically, but when the work was done it brought into focus the true fabric of the society which Homer, writing 600 years after the event, had been trying to portray from hearsay. The Linear B tablets of 'Sandy Pylos' proved to be genuine written source-material about Ulysses' world, and in this sense the professor from Cincinnati and his colleagues discovered more about King Nestor than Homer himself would have recognized.

It was remarkable to learn just how honestly the details of the *Odyssey* did match the facts of Blegen's great discovery. The beach of 'Sandy Pylos' where Telemachus arrived in his twenty-oared galley, would either have been the crescent of white sand at Oxbelly Bay as it is now, or on the shores of the silted-up lagoon just behind it. There Telemachus found King Nestor with his entourage and townsfolk already on the strand making a sacrifice of jet-black bulls to Poseidon the sea god. Nine companies (again the suspect figure nine) of 500 men were assembled, each company with nine bulls.

The sacrifice had just concluded, and the entire congregation was sitting down to feast on the flesh of the slaughtered animals when Telemachus' ship came sailing in, brailled up sail, and the crew disembarked. The Pylians waved a greeting to the strangers and beckoned them to join the feast. Nestor's son, Pesistratus, came forward to welcome the newcomers and invite them to a place of honour. Telemachus respectfully explained to Nestor that he was Ulysses' son and he was hoping to have news of his father.

On the beach at Pylos King Nestor told him the story of how the Greek fleet had split in two after Menelaus and Agamemnon quarrelled at the conclusion of the siege of Troy, and how Ulysses had gone off on his own with his squadron of twelve ships and not been seen again. Then, said Nestor, his own ships together with the vessels led by King Menelaus had safely crossed the Aegean by the open-water passage. Nestor had carried straight on for Pylos, wafted there by a fair wind that never dropped from the moment that it began to blow. He had heard, too, that the contingents from Crete, from Meliboea and Thessaly, also got home safely. But King Agamemnon had been murdered by his wife's lover when he returned to Mycenae, and King Menelaus, whom Nestor had last seen off Cape Sounion, ran into bad weather off Cape Malea and had been blown down to Crete. Later Menelaus had gone on to Egypt and the Levant and had only just returned to his palace in Sparta after a long absence. Possibly, Nestor suggested, Menelaus had picked up news of Ulysses during his own wanderings, and it would be a good idea if Telemachus went to see Menelaus as well. To guide and introduce him to the King of Sparta, he would send Pesistratus as his companion and they could travel overland by chariot. Meanwhile Telemachus was invited to spend the night at the palace because 'the son of my friend Odysseus shall not lie down to sleep on his ship's deck so long as I am alive or sons survive me here to entertain all visitors that come to my door'. So saying, King Nestor 'led the way towards his stately home'.

The path they took must have ascended the steep slopes of the foothills to the level ground among the olive trees Blegen was to excavate 3,000 years later. Here Nestor's forebears had built their palace at a safer distance from the sea than the more obvious, but dangerous, headland where Schliemann had drawn a blank in his earlier search. Arrived at his home, Nestor asked his young guest to be seated and offered him vintage wine as refreshment. This wine, said Homer, was drawn from 'a jar that had stood for ten years before the maid undid the cap and broached it'. Then everyone retired for the night. The king went to his room 'at the back of the high building' and Telemachus to sleep on a wooden bedstead placed in the 'echoing portico'. Next morning King Nestor rose and took his seat on a bench of white marble in front of the lofty doors of the palace to hold a levée. Summoning his six sons, he ordered one son to go back to the beach and invite Telemachus' crew members also to attend the palace. Another son was sent to the royal cowherd to arrange for a young heifer to be driven up to the palace. A third son was to contact the goldsmith Laerces and ask him to come to the palace with the tools of his trade so that he could gild the heifer's horns ready for a formal sacrifice. Meanwhile the palace staff was to prepare a feast, heap firewood around the altar, arrange the seating, and bring fresh water.

All this, in Homer's account, was quickly done. The goldsmith arrived bringing his hammer, anvil, and special goldworking tongs. King Nestor issued him with gold from the royal treasury, and Laerces beat the bullion into thin foil which he laid on the heifer's horns. Aretus, one of the royal princes, emerged from the store-rooms with a basket of barley-corns as the heifer was led forward. One prince stood ready with an axe to cut the heifer down, and another held the dish to catch its blood. The barley-corns were sprinkled, prayers offered up, and the heifer killed. Then the animal was butch-ered, part of the meat thrown onto the fire as burnt offerings, and the remainder roasted on spits to be eaten at table. Meanwhile Polycaste, Nestor's youngest daughter, was giving Telemachus his bath. She bathed him and rubbed him with olive oil, gave him a clean tunic to wear and arranged a fine cloak over his shoul-ders. Decorous and resplendent, Telemachus sat next to Nestor during the meal, and when it was over Nestor briskly announced that it was time for Telemachus to be on his way to see Menelaus. A pair of horses was harnessed to a palace chariot. A housekeeper prepared a traveller's meal of bread and wine and dainties, and with Pesistratus at the reins, Telemachus was borne off towards the capital of Menelaus.

This is the picture that Homer gives, and in one particular after another Blegen's finds validate the poet's scenario. The palace on the hill did have a porch or portico outside the main reception hall, where on a hot night Telemachus could have slept comfortably on a wooden bed placed there by the palace staff. The palace was a 'high building' with at least two floors, and although there was no marble bench for the king to sit on and his quarters were to the right rather than behind the main building, the grand reception hall of the complex had an enormous circular hearth easily big enough to roast an ox, and there was a curious groove in the floorstone which appeared to be a channel to carry away sacrificial libations made by the king in ceremonies like the slaughtering of the heifer. A pair of heraldic griffins painted on the far wall as a backdrop and a symbolic octopus on the floor almost certainly marked the place where the royal throne had stood. At the rear of the main building substantial magazines contained olive oil in large quantities, while rows of massive wine jars in a separate building made up the royal wine cellar. Here the researchers picked up clay seals which had been attached to the jars and indicated both the vintage of the wine and the particular vineyard that had supplied the grapes. There was even a decorated bath tub of terracotta, dumbbell shaped and still mostly intact, in a small room adjacent to the portico area where Telemachus would have slept. Beside the bath were the storage jars for the bath water, and in the tub itself the shards of a clay cup which may have been used for anointing oil.

A handful of archaeologists refused to accept that Blegen's discovery was really Nestor's palace. They pointed out that its location still did not conform to the original directions in Homer, and they stubbornly cited Strabo's opinions. Blegen's palace, these sceptics said, was not Nestor's home but had belonged to another Mycenaean king. Characteristically Blegen did not take offence. 'All I know,' he once said, 'is that I have found the capital of a rich kingdom, which is just about where Nestor's capital must have been. If someone else, later on, finds another even finer palace in the same general area, then I'll be ready to agree that I've misplaced Nestor's Pylos.' He was too tactful to point out that the physical evidence far outweighed the literary tradition – when the Linear B script was eventually deciphered, the name Pylos, written *Pu-ro*, was found to occur repeatedly – and it was time to admit that Strabo, so often cited as the arbiter of Homeric geography, had been proved wrong. Blegen's discovery had exposed only minor flaws in Homer's literary tradition but it should have forced a major reassessment of traditional authorities whose long-established ideas had too long been sacrosanct.

Even if Blegen's palace at Epano Englianos was not Nestor's home but another Mycenaean building, the Linear B tablets scattered on the floor of the ruin enhanced the picture of Ulysses' world well up to most scholars' expectations. We cannot say for certain whether Homer was even aware that the Mycenaeans knew how to write, though in the *Iliad* there is mention of a folded tablet with 'baneful signs' which may have been some form of writing. But as far as we can tell the literate Mycenaeans did not use writing for aesthetic purposes as a medium for historians and poets. Writing was a tool for book-keepers. At Pylos there was evidence of a regular system of palace accounts scratched on wet clay in the handwriting of perhaps forty different scribes. So presumably the court bards used their trained memories to retain the great works of literature and recite them in the great hall while upstairs in the offices and in the ground-floor archive room, first on the left as you entered the main vestibule, humble clerks, the civil servants of their day, were busily occupied keeping the royal ledgers. Paradoxically the very ordinariness of their work made their contribution all the more valuable. Like laundry and shopping lists their working notes reveal a quite different but complementary side to life in the royal household as portrayed by the romantic bards.

Here is the wealth of the king – calculations of the number of his cattle and sheep and pigs, the stocks of oil and corn and wine, the obligations of his bondsmen and freemen. The records were compiled a couple of generations after Telemachus' visit, so perhaps the royal cattle listed on the tablets were descendants from the home farm herd which provided the sacrificial heifer killed in his honour. Here is an inventory of the palace's high value goods, chairs inlaid with gold and silver, ivory suitable for carving, stocks of bronze for the smithies. From these reserves gold bullion would have been doled out to Laerces so that he could beat out the gold foil for the heifer's horns. Here are details of the palace staff: the drawers of water and the gatherers of wood whose predecessors arranged the tables and seating for Telemachus' meal, and laid the fire for the roasting of the heifer. Here too is an inventory of the equipment in the royal stables, the number of chariots and the condition of their wheels, just as if they were waiting to be readied for the road to carry Pesistratus and Telemachus rattling off to see Menelaus. Here is the occupation of fuller, the equivalent of the modern drycleaner, whose skill would have prepared the clean tunic that Telemachus put on, and the names of weavers, carders and spinners whose handiwork created the fabric for the glamorous cloak that he wore at the King's high table. There are even the official job descriptions of bath attendant and unguent boiler, the latter a specialist in mixing aromatics and oils to make perfumed body salves for the favoured guest.

Professions, stores, customs, architecture, the evidence that Blegen and his team painstakingly exposed at Epano Englianos in fifteen seasons of digging, corroborated the accuracy of the Homeric picture. There were no contradictions, only omissions. Homer had failed, for example, to mention that the palace was marvellously decorated in rich colours. Returning at the start of one season, the American team found that someone had been trespassing on the site. There were marks of illicit digging. Again their luck was in. The illegal surface scratches led them to a rubbish tip where the palace decorators of the Late Bronze Age had dumped old plaster during a redecoration of the main building.

Where modern workmen strip out the wallpaper and throw it away, the ancient craftsmen had prised off the previous plaster surface with its old frescoes and untidily tossed it down the hillside at the rear of the palace. The dump was an archaeological bonanza and forty-five trays were collected there, each with between thirty and a hundred plaster fragments: a nightmare for anyone but the most dedicated lover of jigsaw puzzles. Carefully pieced together, the 3,000-plus scraps of old plaster still bore the pictures they had carried in the Late Bronze Age: scenes of hunting and warfare, flowers, griffins, horses, panthers, deer, birds and sea creatures, landscapes and patterns, both freestyle and regular. Nestor's palace had dazzled the visitor with a peacock display of red and blue and yellow, black and white. Even the stucco pavement of the great hall was painted in colourful chequerboard.

The life of a major Mycenaean king, it turned out, was far more luxurious and sophisticated than Homer had pictured. If we add to the evidence of Pylos all Homer's references to royal households, scattered throughout the *Odyssey* and the *Iliad*, we arrive at a panorama of an extraordinary society. Serfs, agricultural labourers, weavers, fullers, armourers, headband makers, jewellers, shipwrights, bakers, saddlers, furniture makers, all laboured to support the lifestyle of its ruling élite. The common people were assessed for their contribution to the royal stores and delivered their quota to the palace where it was carefully noted by the palace clerks on the clay tablet-ledgers. In return the commoners were issued with oil and grain and wine for living, and raw material like bronze or wool or flax for their crafts.

Well-regulated, effective and cosy, the system went a long way to explain the economy of Ulysses' politically fragmented world. Greece was ideally suited to exist as a mosaic of principalities and baronies, each ruled by its own royal family. The topography was made of compartments. Fertile valleys were separated by difficult mountain ranges. Peninsulas and islands were isolated from one another and from the mainland. Each region provided a limited area for a petty kingdom to take root and grow. Communication between them was never easy, and while roads fit for chariots could be constructed at great effort on the mainland the farther kingdoms existed in virtual isolation and were scarcely known at all. Even Messenia, where Nestor's dynasty the Neleids flourished, did not come within the Mycenaean orbit until fifty years before the Trojan campaign. The poorer lands towards the periphery remained marginal. In this league Ulysses' realm on Ithaca was very insignificant indeed. Compared to the grandeur of Nestor's home where Telemachus was clearly over-awed by the reputation of his host, life on Ithaca was very simple. Nestor was rich enough to provide ninety ships for the armada; Ulysses could bring along only twelve. In that illustrious company Ulysses and his Ithacans must have seemed rather like a band of Highland clansmen joining a royal army mustering in London to begin an overseas campaign in mainland Europe – good fighters led by a cunning war leader, but few in numbers and rough at the edges.

Blegen deduced that Nestor's palace went up in flames during a great conflagration in about 1200 BC, half a century after the Trojan War. The large stocks of olive oil in the magazines made the palace burn fiercely. Much of the skeleton of the building was built of wood: the great fluted columns were timber, and there was a mass of wooden panelling. To judge by the way that sections of stone wall toppled outwards the big-bellied olive jars may have exploded like bombs. The building seems to have been looted before being put to the torch because barely any of the most valuable items listed in the clay tablets were ever found. A rare exception was the chalice whose medallion decoration we had copied for *Argo*'s sailmark. The chalice may have been dropped by a looter as he ran for the door to escape the blaze. Luckily for posterity, the same heat baked the soft clay writing tablets and preserved them for 3,000 years underground. The palace site was never reoccupied. Its reputation survived in the verses of the *Odyssey* but its location was entirely lost.

That loss was significant for our own search. Homer, as we have seen, knew the local details about Pylos. He knew that it was sandy, that it had a beach where Telemachus sailed in and found Nestor and his assembled company making their sacrifice, and that his 'stately home' lay a little distance away from the beach. But Homer either did not know or did not think it important that Pylos was too far away from Ithaca for a twenty-oar galley like *Argo* to get there in less than twenty-four hours. Either his knowledge of the geography of the west coast of Greece was hazy and he did not know precisely where Nestor lived or, more likely, it was of little concern anyhow. The atmosphere and impression of Pylos mattered, not its geographical coordinates. He was not writing a pilot book or a gazetteer but an epic.

Blegen's 'Palace of Nestor' measures just 163 by 104 feet. It was luxurious, colourful and convenient – it even had plumbing – but it was also small. By modern standards it was more of a mansion than a palace. Once again the modest size of a Homeric location was confirmed but, more important, 'Sandy Pylos' had given us a human dimension for the first time. The royal residence of Pylos with its bath tub and cheerful frescoes, 2,853 wine goblets and 6,000 vases, exactly suited the image of benign King Nestor with his hospitality and good living. Homer's people had come to life and could be matched to the human scale of his locations. Blegen, writing of the gold and enamel medallion found in the burned ruins of Pylos, supposed that it was the picture of 'a well born young man of the Mycenaean *haut monde* – perhaps even a royal prince'. Some claimed it to be a portrait of a Neleid, one of Nestor's immediate family. I hoped so, for it was a perfect symbol for *Argo*'s sail if it commemorated the family of one of the most congenial characters of Ulysses' world.

9

Circe and the Halls of Hades

We left Ulysses, it will be remembered, distraught after
the dreadful massacre of his men by the Laestrygonians
and fleeing from the hollow harbour in his sole
remaining vessel. Without any preamble Homer then
whisks his hero to his next landfall as if by magic, and
this is in keeping with the nature of its ruler – Circe,
the witch goddess 'of the lovely hair', who had the
power to transmute men into animals. 'We travelled on
in utter dejection, thankful to have escaped destruction,'
reports Ulysses, 'but grieving for the good comrades,
we had lost. In due course we came to Aeaea, the home
of the beautiful Circe, a formidable goddess.'

The poet gives us no length of journey time, no direction, no distances, and indeed seems deliberately to
obscure the location of Circe's fey home, so that we are
plunged into the most elaborate mystery of the *Odyssey*
so far without the preliminary clues to help us decide
in which direction to look. Ulysses and his men simply
'approached the coast of this island and brought our
ship into the haven without a sound. Some God must
have guided us in. And when we had disembarked, for
two whole days we lay on the beach, suffering not only
from exhaustion but from the horrors we had been
through.'

At dawn on the third day, Ulysses says, he left his
demoralized companions on the beach and walked
inland to explore. He took his spear and sword and
searched for a vantage point so that he could get an
idea of the lay of the countryside. Climbing a rocky

promontory, he caught sight of smoke, rising through the tree cover. Debating whether to go forward to investigate by himself, Ulysses decided that his first priority was to find food for his crew. On his way back to the ship he was lucky enough to meet a large stag as it came to drink at the river and killed it with a well-aimed spear thrust through the spine. Tying up the carcass with a makeshift rope of twigs and willow withes, Ulysses draped the animal over his shoulder and carried it back to the ship. There he threw his prey down on the ground and spoke to each of his men, trying to raise their spirits. They were not finished yet, he chided them. They should take their minds off their troubles by eating and drinking while food was available. This cheered up the crew considerably, and they spent the rest of the day cooking and eating the venison.

The following morning, the fourth on the island, Ulysses reversed his earlier optimism with a despondent summary of their situation:

☐ 'My friends,' he told his crew, 'East and West mean nothing to us here. Where the Sun is rising from when he comes to light the world, and where he is sinking, we do not know. So the sooner we decide on a sensible plan the better – if one can still be found (which I doubt).' ☐

In short, they were lost and he did not think there was any way out of their desperate situation.

If Ulysses himself admits to being lost, it would seem very unlikely that we can ever deduce where Homer now imagined him to be. The only faint clues to the whereabouts of Circe's island are sparsely scattered throughout the description of the adventure with this goddess. Though circumstantial they will eventually help to lead to an unorthodox hypothesis.

Circe and the Halls of Hades

His reconnaissance, Ulysses told his crew, had shown that they were on an island surrounded by empty sea. The only sign of life was the column of smoke he had observed rising through the undergrowth and the forest. Understandably his crew were terrified. They remembered all too vividly the drastic misfortunes with the cannibal Laestrygonians and the man-eating Cyclops. But Ulysses insisted on following up his discovery. He divided his crew into two groups of twenty-two men, one to be led by himself, the other by a man called Eurylochus. They drew lots to see which group would be the scouting party to investigate the mysterious smoke, and Eurylochus' team lost the draw. Lamenting, they went on their way and in a forest glen came to Circe's house which 'was in an open place', and built of stones 'well polished'. About the house prowled lions and wolves who fawned on the strangers. They huddled in terror in the porch of the house and from within heard a woman's voice singing. They called out to her, and Circe herself opened the doors of the house and invited them to enter. There they were seated on chairs and benches and given food, a mixture of honey and barley and cheese flavoured with wine. But Circe had added a magical drug to the dish, and when they had eaten it she touched them with her wand and the sailors were turned into pigs. They had the heads and voices and bristles of swine, but they kept their human minds. Circe brusquely drove them out of her house and into her sties where she threw down acorns and ilex and cornel buds and other pig foods. Only Eurylochus escaped. Cautiously he had hung back from entering Circe's house, and now ran to the ship bearing the dreadful news of the fate of the scouting party.

This tale of the goddess who used magic potions to turn men into beasts – for the lions and wolves were her former victims – is so much like another traditional fairytale, this time the witch-in-the-glen, that once again there seems little hope of locating the spot where this magical farrago is supposed to have happened. Yet Aeaea is important. The *Odyssey* treats Ulysses' visit to Circe as a major episode in the voyage. It claims Ulysses and his crew spent an entire year with Circe, the second longest stopover of his entire voyage, exceeded only by his seven-year stay with another amorous goddess, Calypso.

What happened was this: when Ulysses heard that half his men had been turned into pigs, he set out for Circe's house by himself to try to rescue them. On the way he encountered the god Hermes in the guise of a young man, who explained Circe's method of using wonder-working drugs to turn men into animals. Hermes provided Ulysses with an antidote, a plant called 'moly', 'black at the root, but with a milky flower', which Hermes plucked from the ground. Protected by this moly Ulysses was to enter Circe's home and eat the drugged food which now could do him no harm. When Circe touched him with her wand to turn him into a pig, he was to rush upon her with a drawn sword. She would be panic-stricken, said Hermes, and her reaction would be to invite him to make love to her. This Ulysses had to do, and then the goddess would no longer try to hurt him but would be willing to change his men back into human form.

Everything turned out as Hermes predicted. The moly guarded Ulysses against Circe's drugs. He became Circe's lover, and thereafter was treated to every comfort. Four nymphs, 'the daughters born of the springs and from the coppices and the sacred rivers' who worked in Circe's palace, prepared lavish hospitality. One spread purple coverlets over the chairs, another laid the silver tables with golden utensils, and a third prepared a wonderful meal. The fourth brought water and, heating it in a great cauldron, bathed Ulysses to 'take the heart-wasting weariness' from his limbs and then anointed him with olive oil. Bathed and dressed in a splendid mantle and fresh tunic, he was invited to the table. But he refused to eat until Circe had restored his men back into human form, and they were released from the sties looking 'like nine-year-old porkers'. Circe smeared another magic ointment on them so that their bristles fell away and they resumed their human shape but younger and more handsome than before.

Now Circe persuaded Ulysses to drag his ship up on land, stow all the tackle in a cave, and bring the rest of his crew to her house. Eurylochus, still waiting by the galley, protested. He pointed out that the recklessness of Ulysses had already cost them dearly at the cave of the Cyclops, and it was extremely rash to venture into Circe's lair. But this time Circe's hospitality was genuine. All the crew were bathed, oiled, given fresh clothes and entertained to a banquet. At Circe's invitation, they remained an entire year on this wondrous island of Aeaea 'feasting on unlimited meat and sweet wine' until finally they became homesick and asked Ulysses to resume the journey homeward.

He consulted privately with Circe and was told that before starting out for Ithaca, he first had to visit the 'Halls of Hades'. There he was to consult with the soul of Teiresias, the blind Theban prophet. Ulysses was appalled.

□ This news broke my heart. I sat down on my bed and wept. I had no further use for life, no wish to see the sunshine any more. But when at last I grew tired of tears and tossing about on the bed, I began to question her: 'But tell me, Circe, who is to guide me on the way? No one has ever sailed a black ship into Hell.' 'Odysseus,' the goddess answered me, 'don't think of lingering on shore for lack of a pilot. Set up your mast, spread the white sail and sit down in the ship. The North Wind will blow her on her way; and when she has brought you across the River of Ocean, you will come to a wild coast and to Persephone's Grove, where the tall poplars grow and the willows that so quickly shed their seeds. Beach your boat there by Ocean's swirling stream and march on into Hades' Kingdom of Decay. There the River of Flaming Fire and the River of Lamentation, which is a branch of the Waters of Styx, unite around a pinnacle of rock to pour their thundering streams into Acheron.' □

Here, at last, is the primary clue to the location of Aeaea. Working back from Circe's directions of how to sail from Aeaea to the 'Halls of Hades', we can calculate where her home was, providing, that is, that we know where to place the Halls of Hades. Fortunately they are the best 'fixed point' in the entire *Odyssey* since Cape Malea was left behind by the wind-blown squadron. The location of the river Acheron, on whose banks stand the Halls of Hades, has been common knowledge for 2,000 years and confirmed by archaeology in the last thirty years. The irony is that its role in the *Odyssey* has been overlooked by all but a few observers for equally long. Today the archaeological evidence, like Blegen's discovery of Nestor's Palace at Epano Englianos, makes a nonsense of the long-established theories about the *Odyssey*'s geography. Instead of despatching Ulysses to the furthest reaches of the Mediterranean as the orthodox theory proposes, his visit to the Halls of Hades brings him to where we should by now expect him to be – on the west coast of Greece.

But – and at first sight this is the oddest paradox in the whole story – Ulysses seems to have sailed straight past his home in Ithaca, where his wife and family were waiting for him. The most spectacular of his remaining adventures, as *Argo* and her crew were about to learn, will all occur *north* of Ithaca. Landfalls here simply do not make sense if they are regarded as part of Ulysses' return from Troy. The solution, as I shall try to substantiate in due course, is that they form a new and distinct strand in the epic poet's assembly of his story.

The river Acheron has suffered only mildly from the confusion of identity that hid the Pylos of King Nestor. In mythology the Acheron was a river linked with the Underworld. It flowed either out of Hades or past its borders, and was usually connected with a lake known as the Acherusian Lake. Sometimes the souls of the dead on their way to the Underworld were ferried across the Acheron and in this respect it was confused with the river Styx. Geographically there were several different rivers of the Underworld just as there were several places alleged to be entrances to Hades such as the cave at Cape Taenarum. One Acheron river flowed into the Black Sea on what is now the coast of Turkey. Another Acheron river was alleged to drain an 'Acherusian Lake' in Italy, about fifty miles south-east of Rome. But if we discard the river Styx (of which there were also several versions) there was only one well-known river Acheron in Greece and it was never 'lost' in the sense that 'Sandy Pylos' had been. The Greek river Acheron is found in the district of Epirus or Thesprotia in north-west Greece and empties into the Ionian Sea. This river has always kept the name Acheron and it mingled with a shallow lake called the Acherusian Lake. The lake has now been drained to provide rich farmland, but five miles upstream of the present mouth of the river is the site of a *nekymanteion*, an Oracle of the Dead. Here in pagan times people came to consult the spirits of the Dead just as Circe had instructed Ulysses to do.

This oracle is situated on top of a rocky outcrop. Where the Acheron winds past the steep side of the rock it is joined by a tributary stream, formerly called the Cocytus. Pausanias, the Homeric enthusiast of Emperor Hadrian's time, drew a simple conclusion: 'Near Kichyros,' he observed, 'lie an Acherusian lake and a river Acheron, and the detestable stream Cocytus. *I think Homer must have seen this region and in his very daring poetry about Hades taken the names of the rivers from the rivers in Thesprotia.*' Pausanias spent fourteen years compiling his *Guide to Greece*, conscientiously visiting the major Greek sites and listing their antiquities. His first-hand testimony as to Homer's 'daring poetry about Hades' ought to have been conclusive.

But Pausanias' suggestion that Ulysses' Oracle of the Dead lay in Greece, in Epirus, clashed head-on with a much better known theory. Strabo and dozens of writers after him asserted that Circe and the Oracle of the Dead were located near the Italian river Acheron, in Campania. A promontory there was (and still is) called Monte Circeo, as it was said to have been the home of the goddess and to contain an ancient cave shrine to Circe herself. The *Odyssey* makes a puzzling reference to a people called the Cimmerians who lived near the Halls of Hades in a perpetual gloomy mist. These, according to the 'Italian School', were the aboriginal attendants of the shrine who lived in underground tunnels and never saw the sun. The Halls of Hades were at some vague spot a little distance inland near some hot springs and here was the lake said to be the Acherusian Lake.

This argument was riddled with flaws. There was no sign of an Oracle perched on a rock beside the river, and Mount Circeo was not an island like Aeaea, Circe's home, but joined to the mainland. This did not matter so much if, as seems probable, the low ground behind

the promontory of Monte Circeo had been covered by
the sea in the Late Bronze Age, although it could never
have taken Ulysses a day to sail to the mainland – as
the *Odyssey* says he did – across a gap which would
have been half a mile wide at most. Much more
damning is the fact that the abrupt stump of Monte
Circeo is too stark and angular to offer the sort of
landscape with a sheltered bay and a house in a glen
which the *Odyssey* describes. Strabo had to admit that,
on investigation, the claims for Monte Circeo turned
out to be mere fable. In his own day the draining of the
marsh and the opening up of the area of Monte Circeo
revealed that there was neither a shrine to Circe nor any
underground tunnels nor troglodyte aborigines living in
them. Nevertheless, the thought that the Halls of Hades
could be on the mainland of Greece, more than 500
miles away by sea, was difficult to accept. If that was
the case, then the whole theory that Ulysses had ever
sailed along the coast of Italy would be thrown back
into the melting pot. For centuries that theory had
offered Italian or Sicilian locations for the Cyclops, the
Island of the Winds, the Laestrygonians, and the later
adventures. An Oracle of the Dead on the river Acheron
in western Greece was an uncomfortable coincidence
that was better ignored.

The nagging presence in Greece of the Oracle of the
Dead and the river Acheron would not go away.
Pausanias was not the only person to draw attention to
a Greek river Acheron and a *nekymanteion* in Epirus.
Before him the same place had been noted by the
historian Herodotus, and the historian Thucydides
mentions how pilgrims came here to cross the 'Acherusian Lake' by boat and visit the Oracle. Supporters
of the 'Italian School' objected that the evidence of
Thucydides, Pausanias and Herodotus was irrelevant as

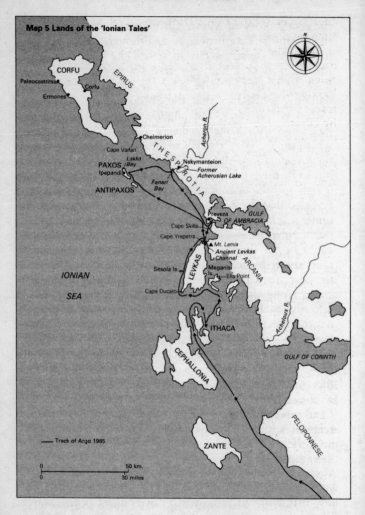

Map 5 Lands of the 'Ionian Tales'

their Greek Oracle of the Dead was much later than the time of Ulysses.

There the matter rested until 1958 when a Greek archaeologist, S. I. Dakaris, led a team to excavate the ruins of the *nekymanteion* on top of the rock over-looking the course of the Acheron. They came across traces of sacrifices made in exactly the manner described by Ulysses. He had dug a pit 'about a cubit long and a cubit in breadth' and into it poured an offering to the dead: honey mixed first with milk, then with wine, and last of all with water. Over this mixture he had sprin-kled white barley, then sacrificed a young ram and a black ewe so that their blood poured into the pit. Exca-vating the Oracle Dakaris found identical sacrificial pits and in them the bones of sheep, cattle and pigs, together with grain and the urns which had once held honey. Here, a thousand years after the Trojan War, visitors to the Oracle had been making offerings to precisely the formula laid down by Homer. But had the site been used in Mycenaean times? Dakaris found pieces of broken Mycenaean pottery, and within the Oracle walls themselves a Mycenaean grave. There was no way of confirming whether the Mycenaeans had practised Underworld rituals there, but if they had buried a corpse there, it seemed likely. Certainly the place was familiar to them because on the crest of the adjacent hill was a Mycenaean fortress.

Dakaris turned his attention to the relationship of the Acheron with its two tributary streams mentioned in the *Odyssey*, the 'River of Flaming Fire and the River of Lamentation which is a branch of the Waters of Styx'. He established that the small tributary stream which joins the Acheron at the base of the rock and is now called the Vouvos was formerly the Cocytus, the 'River of Lamentation'. But there was no sign of the third stream, the 'River of Flaming Fire'. Then the local peasants reported that before the drainage work on the 'Acherusian Lake', there had been a third small tributary which fed into the Acheron. This stream was phosphorescent, and in the months between March and June produced a strange noise of subterranean waters rumbling and echoing. It fitted exactly the description of the River of Flaming Fire.

Argo came to the mouth of the Acheron in Epirus in suitably dramatic circumstances. The last of the evening light was fading and a deep bank of black cloud hung over the western horizon, out of which dropped a blood-red sun to be swallowed up in the sea. A heavy dew settled over the galley as we anchored in the shallow bay and began to cook our evening meal on board. There was a warning spatter of rain and for the first time in a month we rigged the canvas awning. We heard rolls of thunder in the distance, and occasionally lightning flickered inland towards the *nekymanteion*. To complete the theatrical air of menace, the embers of a burnt-out brush fire were still glowing on the hills to the north of the bay. When the gusts of wind ignited them, the smell of scorched brushwood drifted across to the galley.

Daylight revealed a very different atmosphere. The bay turned out to be a jolly place, with dogs, children, bathers, and a trio of noisy motorcyclists disporting themselves on a pleasant sandy beach. It made a bright contrast to Circe's gloomy picture of the river mouth, with 'the groves of Persephone and tall black poplars growing and fruit perishing willows'. In shape, Fanari Bay – its modern name – was somewhat like Nestor's Oxbelly Bay, and I could see how silting had filled in the coastline. Formerly the bay extended further inland, perhaps even made it possible to take a shallow draft galley up-river as far as the Acherusian Lake itself and almost to the foot of the rock of the Oracle. The river mouth would have been a very safe place for Ulysses to leave his galley while he went to make his sacrifices. Fanari Bay is still being used as an overnight harbour by passing yachts despite the swell which comes rolling in between the two headlands and occasionally bursts into white water as it heaps into the constricting shallows.

Greek farmers were irrigating their fields with water drawn from the Acheron itself, and the air was filled with the buzz of the water pumps and plumes of spray sprouted where the sprinklers were drenching growing crops. Black and yellow paint on a bent metal sign pointed to the 'Acheron estuary', and walking round the beach I came to where the river has now been channelled to flow into the side of the bay. The modern equivalent of Persephone's Grove was a glade of imported tall eucalyptus trees alive with hundreds of sparrows busily chirping and scuffling. In a country parched for water the Acheron, though barely twenty-five yards wide, was an unusual sight. Despite losing so much water to irrigation work, the grey-green water of the river ran deep, still sufficient for a small galley to navigate. On the near side small punts were tied under the willows. A herd of goats was grazing on the tender green shoots of the reeds on the far bank, standing hock deep in the shallows like wild deer seen on an African safari. A second herd was traversing the steep hillside of the southern headland. The clanking of the goat bells reflected across the river like a distant call to prayer from the small white chapel with a red tile roof that sat just below the headland. Yellow daisies mingled with the pale violet of a small heather-like flower on the river bank and in the reeds were large bright purple blooms I did not recognize. The mouth of the modern Acheron, far from being sinister, was one of the most pleasant spots of the entire voyage.

Today the approach to the Oracle of the Dead is by a road which leads from the village of Mesopotamon – 'between the rivers' – to the top of the Oracle Rock. The 'Rock' is a spur of hillside thrusting out into the flood-plain of the Acheron, elbowing aside the river's course beneath a steep rocky bluff. As so often happens, a new religion has usurped the prominent holy site of its predecessor. Perched uncomfortably on the cross-walls of the ancient Oracle is the eighteenth century church of St John the Forerunner. The Christian church is actually propped up by the pagan architecture devised by priests of the Underworld cult to impress and confuse supplicants coming to consult the spirits of the dead.

Dakaris worked out that the pagan visitor entered the *nekymanteion* through a gate in the north side of the *temenos*, the sacred enclosure. He was then led down long corridors around three sides of the *nekymanteion*. Drugs and smoke may have been used to confuse and befuddle him and in the final approach to the main sanctuary he had to twist and turn his way through half a dozen sharp corners with the aim of disorienting him still further. Finally the supplicant passed between a pair of bronze doors and came to a short passage. A flight of steps led down into the crypt – the home of Hades, dread god of the Underworld, and his wife Persephone. From there the Oracle's priests summoned up the supposed spirits of the departed. Dakaris found a number of cog wheels, bronze castings and a large spoked wheel that he surmised were parts of an elaborate contraption by which the priests of the shrine could winch up one of their number, as if emerging from the Underworld, to intone his prophecies to his credulous and half-stupefied audience.

This hocus-pocus ended in about 168 BC when the *nekymanteion* was destroyed by fire. But the renown and location of the Thesprotian Oracle to the Dead were always remembered through the writings of Pausanias, Thucydides and their successors. Dakaris' discoveries made Homeric scholars take a second look at the *nekymanteion*'s possible relationship to the *Odyssey*, and G. L. Huxley – a distinguished English classicist who had trekked all over the Epirus compiling a gazetteer of the ancient geography – produced a very satisfactory explanation for Homer's reference to the fog-dwelling Cimmerians, who were to be found near the Halls of Hades. Huxley pointed out that on the coast of Epirus, not far from the *nekymanteion* and only ten miles from *Argo*'s anchorage, had been a place called Cheimerion. The name was applied sometimes to a headland, now Cape Varlan, sometimes to the area, sometimes to the people living there. The name itself implied 'stormy'. Surely, Huxley argued, this explained Homer's puzzling reference to the 'fog bound Cimmerians': they were no more than the misspelt Cheimerieis. It was a simple yet elegant solution to an artificially complicated problem, and fitted very well. The subsequent edition of the *Cambridge Ancient History* tacitly admitted that the *nekymanteion* had emerged as the leading candidate for the 'Halls of Hades':

> The Odyssey, of which ... the background is the northwestern area (of Greece), has rather more information to offer. The river Acheron is mentioned as leading to Hades, which suggests that the famous *nekymanteion* already existed at Ephyra, a place where deadly poisons were sold perhaps by the priests or priestesses of the Oracle of the Dead.

For me the Oracle of the Dead had helped to shape the plan of the 'logical route'. I had read about Dakaris' work at the *nekymanteion* when delving into the background of the *Odyssey* during the preparations for the

Jason Voyage into the Black Sea. The very strong argument in favour of the *nekymanteion* being in north-western Greece raised questions about the whole geography of the *Odyssey*. If the Oracle of the Dead was in Greece, why should the other sites of Ulysses' wanderings still be found in Sicily or Italy and the western Mediterranean? None of the western Mediterranean sites had the same quality of modern archaeological evidence to support them. They were based on tradition, on century after century of repeating the same ideas and quoting the same authorities. I saw the *nekymanteion* as the pivot on which a whole new perception of the *Odyssey* might turn. Maybe the adventures of the *Odyssey* had taken place very close to home, perhaps even in Greek waters. If we sailed *Argo* along Ulysses' logical homeward route from Troy and explored the approach to the Greek *nekymanteion*, we might bring sea-going sense to the *Odyssey*.

So far it had all gone much better than I had dared hope, I thought to myself, as I picked my way through the underbrush to reach the crown of the rocky hill which overlooked the *nekymanteion* from the north-west. It was here that the archaeologists found the outer wall of a Mycenaean settlement on the easily defended summit. Crunching through the scratchy maquis, I could see the heads of hundreds of asphodel plants, spikes of white flowers rising above the scrub on long thin whippy stalks. The asphodels grew out of fat, dark brown bulbs with peeling skins like overripe onions, barely covered by the soil. It seemed suitable that there were so many of them here, for Homer had written that the dead lived among 'the fields of asphodel', and according to ancient belief the buried corpses fed on the bloated bulbs. From the top of the hill I looked down on the course of the ancient Cocytus, the River of Lamentation, where it flowed towards the *nekyman-*

teion rock to join the Acheron. As I had expected, the Cocytus was no more than a thin stream. Like Troy and the hollow harbour at Mesapo, or like Nestor's home which had proved to be more of a mansion than a palace, Homer had described places of a measurable size, and because they were so modest I was finding them all the more believable.

From my vantage point the line of poplars and willows marked the lower course of the Acheron itself, as it flows towards Fanari Bay and *Argo*'s anchorage. There, dimly visible on the horizon, was the island which I now supposed was the best candidate for Circe's island: the green and pleasant island of Paxos.

There is no archaeological evidence to support Paxos as Circe's home, for as far as I am aware no remains have been sought or found on Paxos. But then the sylvan retreat of the 'goddess of the lovely hair' is not likely to have left behind any very noticeable ruins. Paxos' claim must rest largely on the fact that it lies off the mouth of the Acheron in the correct relationship to the Oracle of the Dead. Paxos is the natural departure point for a galley, using the coastal islands as stepping-stones, to turn aside and visit the mouth of the Acheron on the mainland. Certainly Paxos fits the rather vague description of Aeaea in the *Odyssey* as a heavily wooded pleasant island. Paxos is famed for its greenery and fertility and, where not covered with olive trees, its glens and ravines are choked and lush with wild plants. Here, too, grows wild moly, or rather a plant that botanists conjecture might be the magical plant 'black at the root, but with a milky flower' which protected Ulysses from Circe's sorcery. It is a species of *allium*, a plant related to garlic, and three varieties of *allium* are to be found on Paxos.

Just one Paxiot legend has survived since classical times and this could perhaps have some bearing on

Ulysses' adventure with the goddess Circe. The tale is that the pilot of a ship in the reign of Tiberius heard a great and mysterious voice calling out his name as his vessel sailed past Paxos. The voice told him to proclaim that the great god Pan was dead. When the pilot did so, a great wailing arose from Paxos. This story may be pure fabrication, but the association of Pan with Paxos is odd. Pan, the shepherd's god, half-goat, half-man, was always linked with rampant nature. He was a primaeval figure, exercising power over wild creatures of the forest and field and involved in love affairs with the nymphs of nature, the spirits of the woodland and rivers and streams. The same nymphs were found with Circe, attending her household and preparing food and baths for Ulysses, and it is striking how Circe's role as a goddess of nature exactly complements Pan's qualities. Circe could also charm animals like the wolves and lions who fawned on her; her home was deep in the wild forest; and her lovemaking with Ulysses presents the same picture of elemental fertility as Pan's amorous behaviour. Finally, Pan was the son of Hermes, and of course it was Hermes who met Ulysses on Circe's island and gave him the moly. We are left with the two green islands of Aeaea and Paxos being associated with related gods of wild nature, animals and magic plants.

In one respect, however, Paxos fails to agree with Homer's description of Aeaea. Ulysses said that when he climbed up a rocky promontory to look around the island there was nothing but sea to the horizon. But from the highest point on Paxos you can easily see the mainland and also the island of Corfu to the north. On the other hand, Ulysses' information is contradictory because his ship took only a day to sail to the mouth of the Acheron, and a day's sail would normally be well within the line of sight. Paxos' position fourteen miles off the Acheron puts it easily within this range. From

Paxos Ulysses and his men could comfortably have used the north wind to sail into the harbour at the mouth of the river five or six hours later. This may seem rather short as 'a day's sail', but it is in keeping with the *Odyssey*'s standard measurement of distance by sea. The story never mentions 'an hour's sail', or 'a morning's sail': a day is the shortest measure used in calculation, and even King Menelaus on his voyage back from Egypt goes 'a day's sail' to an offshore island which was so close to the shore that it has now been joined to the expanding delta.

If Paxos was indeed Circe's island of Aeaea, then there is one logical spot to seek her home. The key is the presence of fresh water. On the whole of Paxos the most reliable source of drinking water lies at the head of the narrow valley at Ipapandi. Here a natural cliff topped by cypress trees encloses a small glen. In the distance is a glimpse of the blue water of the tranquil bay of Lakka, an ideal harbour to drag ashore a galley and store her for the winter. A trickle of water emerges into the head of the glen and is caught in a small arched well, shaped like a bread oven, built into the rock wall. The place is full of the smell of wild mint, the buzzing of bees, and birdsong. Wild cyclamens grow there, and a cool breeze blows up from the sea and rustles the leaves of the dense undergrowth. It seems isolated from the rest of the world. Here, if anywhere, legend would have located a sylvan fairy-figure like Circe, goddess of the golden hair.

After his visit to the Oracle of the Dead, Ulysses went back to Circe's island to bury a comrade, Elpenor. Youngest of all his crew and 'not much of a fighting man nor very strong in the head', Elpenor had drunk too much during the final night's celebrations at Circe's home. He wandered away on his own to sleep off his excess and climbed a ladder to the flat roof of Circe's

Circe's Glen, Ipapandi, Paxos

home. There he fell asleep and in the morning woke to the clatter and noise of the crew getting ready to depart. Leaping up to join them, he forgot where he was and fell headlong off the roof, breaking his neck. His ghost had appeared to Ulysses at the Oracle of the Dead and beseeched his former captain to go back to Aeaea, burn his corpse and raise a grave mound for him 'on the shore of the grey sea . . . to mark the spot for future voyagers'.

As we would anticipate, the site Ulysses picked for the grave mound was a cape, 'the summit of the boldest headland of the coast', just as a cape had been the last resting place for Phrontis, the master pilot of Menelaus. Ulysses' men marked the place with a stone and planted Elpenor's oar on top of the barrow. When their work was done, Circe came to meet them, her servants bringing supplies of food and wine, and suggested they should stay the night. Next morning they could sail on for Ithaca, following a route that she would carefully explain. This track and its landmarks offered the climax of our search because here were the majority of the most famous episodes of the 'Great Wanderings': man-luring Sirens, the vortex Charybdis and the many-headed monster Scylla. The whereabouts of these legendary creatures was the most startling sequence of discoveries of the Ulysses Voyage.

10
The Roving Rocks

☐ 'Spend the rest of the day where you are, enjoying this food and wine, and at the first peep of dawn you shall sail. I myself will make every landmark clear, to save you from the disasters you would suffer if you ran into the snares that may be laid for you on sea or land.' ☐

This was Circe's friendly offer to Ulysses, and she was as good as her word. She warned him that after he left her island of Aeaea, he would come first to the Sirens, those 'enchanters of all mankind' who sat in a meadow by the seashore. The sweetness of their singing so beguiled men that they lingered there, never leaving, and the beach was piled with the bones of men now rotted away. Once past the Sirens, he would have two choices of route to take him to Ithaca. Either he could sail by way of the Roving or Wandering Rocks against which the sea crashed in great swells, wrecking many ships and carrying away the shattered timbers and the bodies of the dead sailors on great waves or licking them up with 'tempestuous and destroying flames'; or he could choose to sail down a narrow channel and run the gauntlet between the awful vortex Charybdis which sucked down ships, and the man-snatching monster Scylla who preyed on passing vessels. Scylla lived in a cave halfway up a steep cliff on the flank of a tall rock. The peak of this rock was capped by perpetual cloud. Scylla's monstrous body was tucked inside the cave and her six heads on their long necks dangled out over the cliff perpetually searching for victims. She snatched sailors off the deck of any ship that passed down the channel and, Circe warned, nothing that Ulysses could do would save several of his crew from her jaws.

I had read that Greek mythology sometimes made a connection between the witch Circe and the she-monster Scylla. There was a story that Scylla had once been a beautiful young woman, a rival to Circe for the love of the sea-god Glaucus. To dispose of the competition, Circe used her powers as a sorceress to turn the unfortunate girl into a hideous nightmare with six ravening heads on six long necks and a six-legged misshapen body, now tucked like a hermit crab into its cave. It occurred to me that if Circe and Scylla had been close rivals for the love of the same god, then perhaps their two legendary homes might not lie far apart and I should look for Scylla in the general region of Aeaea/Paxos and the mouth of the Acheron. This seemed such a straightforward line of inquiry that I felt rather foolish as I consulted the relevant volume of the Admiralty Sailing Directions describing the west coast of Greece, and looked up the word 'Scylla' in the index. Surely I was being very naïve in hoping that perhaps there was a local name which commemorated the legend. I had ploughed through all the classical directories and reference works without any luck. My feeling of naïvety changed to astonishment when I found that there was a Cape Skilla halfway between the mouth of the Acheron river and Ulysses' home island of Ithaca!

It was a stunning discovery. This 'Cape Skilla' lay exactly on the coasting route a galley would take. Hadn't someone spotted the existence of this cape before, and thought about its possible significance to the *Odyssey*? But no, I could find no reference to it in the mass of learned books discussing the background to the *Odyssey*. In ancient times there had been Cape

Scylla or Scillaeum off the east coast of the Peloponnese, but that was in the Aegean Sea and much too far away. Perhaps, I thought to myself, the Cape Skilla of the Admiralty Sailing Directions was a very recent name and had nothing whatever to do with Homer's six-headed monster. The chart on which it appeared was the first comprehensive chart of the area and drawn by those same painstaking nineteenth-century surveyors of the Victorian Navy whose work had been so important for Schliemann's discovery of Troy and for the archaeological work on Crete. Indeed it was prepared under the supervision of Captain Mansell who, as a lieutenant on the Mediterranean Survey, had assisted Captain Spratt in his superb survey of Crete. Perhaps Cape Skilla on the west coast of Greece had been named after a Royal Navy ship, HMS *Skilla* maybe. There had been a famous Antarctic Survey ship, the *Erebus*, a place-name in the *Odyssey* for the faraway realm in the west where went the souls of the dead. I contacted the offices of the Navy Hydrographer. I was told that as far as they knew Cape Skilla in western Greece was not named after any particular vessel. The normal procedure at that time was for the naval surveyors to ask local inhabitants for their names for prominent coastal features and keep the same names on the maps. As far as the Hydrographer's office was aware, Cape Skilla was what the cape had been called by local Greeks in the mid-nineteenth century.

I was to discover that the name Cape Skilla, still neatly printed on the charts, preserves a tradition now totally forgotten by the local residents. When I eventually sailed to Cape Skilla with *Argo* to investigate, I failed to find anyone in the area, fisherman or schoolmaster, who was aware of its nineteenth century name. This was reassuring. It meant that no one was likely to have invented a local tradition to justify or create an artificial link with the *Odyssey*. Instead the material we found near Cape Skilla was vital information that had lain there, blatant but unremarked, for a very long time.

Why had no one sought Scylla near the Acheron before? The answer was that for more than 2,000 years scarcely any classical scholar had seriously questioned the long-held belief that both Scylla and Charybdis were in the Straits of Messina between the toe of Italy and Sicily. It was said that the Straits themselves were obviously the narrow channel which Circe had described. On the Italian side was the rock of Scylla; on the other side, off the coast of Sicily, a series of whirlpools known as *tagli* had given rise to the legend of Charybdis the spouting vortex. Over the centuries this location had become a principle of faith in Homeric geography. If Homer knew of the conditions of the Messina Straits, then his geographical details were genuine. To question whether Scylla and Charybdis were really in the Straits was to cast doubt on whether Homer was writing about real places at all. No one seemed to offer the possibility that the Messina Straits had been misidentified and this mistake had distorted the entire framework of the geography of the *Odyssey*. Far from destroying the reality in the *Odyssey*, a more convincing strait with more plausible homes for Scylla and Charybdis would make better sense of Homer's geography.

Indeed there was much to criticize about putting Scylla and Charybdis in the Straits of Messina. Scylla was a ravening monster, to be avoided by all sailors, yet the cliff pointed out as 'Scylla's cliff' in Italy overlooked two small harbours used by local boats as places of safety. The Reverend William Smith, editor in 1854 of the *Dictionary of Greek and Roman Geography*, commented dryly: 'it is difficult to understand how, even in the infancy of navigation, it could have offered any obstacles more formidable than a hundred other headlands whose names are unknown to fame'. If Cape Scylla was unimpressive, the Messina Straits were even less suitable. They are far too wide to be the channel of which Circe warned Ulysses. In her description the passage is so narrow that a fig tree hung over the whirlpool of Charybdis. But the Straits of Messina are *more than two miles wide at their narrowest point*. The notion of the overhanging fig tree is absurd and, to make matters worse, at the point known as the rock of Scylla the width of the strait has increased to three and a half miles. This flatly breaks the first law of myth-making which is that myths and legends do not make men or places smaller or less spectacular. Instead they make them larger than life. It was the same lesson we had learned at the start of our voyage when Homer's 'beetling Ilium' proved to be a village-sized settlement on a low ridge scarcely 100 feet high above the plain.

From a sailor's point of view not merely are the Straits of Messina far too wide, but it is difficult to understand how they could ever have been a threat to the passage of a galley. Again it is partly a question of scale. Passing through the Messina Straits in a small vessel is easy. Like many other modern yachtsmen, I had done so aboard a small sailing boat without the slightest hazard. There are no natural difficulties or dangers. One is scarcely aware of passing through any 'narrows' because the shore seems too far away on either side. The Messina Straits are twice as wide as the narrows of the Dardanelles and Homer makes no great matter of sailing through the Dardanelles. Nor is there the slightest need, as Circe advised Ulysses, for a small boat to hug one shore in order to avoid the whirlpool of Charybdis. The *tagli*, the tidal whirlpools, are not even in the narrows of the Straits, and there is ample room to avoid them. To be caught in a *tagli* is no great calamity. *Tagli* are slowly gyrating patches of water and, at worst, merely make the vessel spin round ponderously.

The classical commentators were often puzzled how these *tagli* could have once represented a threat to a vessel. They supposed that the whirlpools were much less fierce than in ancient times because earthquakes had changed the profile of the sea floor whose irregularities caused the *tagli* as the tides flowed over them. But recently this reasoning too has lost its force. Satellite photographs of the tides in the Messina Straits have explained the mechanism of the *tagli*. They are not the result of irregularities in the sea floor, but occur because the water in the Tyrrhenian Sea is lighter and less salty than the water of the Ionian Sea to the south. There is a surface current of lighter, fresher water flowing southward on the surface while deeper down there is a counter-current of the heavier, salty water going north. *Tagli* are set up when this regular exchange of water is disturbed by the tidal rhythm which is out of phase at the north and south ends of the Straits. The effect is enhanced near the Sicilian town of Ganzirra where the moving water is further disturbed as it flows past the tip of a small peninsula. The conditions which create the famous *tagli* – the tides and the salinity of the seawater – have not changed over the millennia. The 'whirlpools' are the same today as in Homer's time or when the Greeks attacked Troy, and pale candidates to be ship-swallowing Charybdis.

The moment was long overdue to question the ancient tradition when, on 31 July, I set *Argo*'s course towards the intriguing 'Cape Skilla' of western Greece. I had no idea what we would find there, but after two months' searching the 'logical route' from the deck of a galley we had detected a pattern of coastal sites which consistently echoed the legendary material of the *Odyssey*. For the Cyclopes there were the three-eyed *triamates* in Crete, for Aeolus, Ruler of the Winds, there was the Island of the Leather Bag; one mouth of Hell lay at Taenarum, another had long been known at the *nekymanteion*. Blegen had discovered the Palace of Nestor in a vicinity where local tradition told of a 'Nestor's Cave', but not where orthodox classical opinion put it. One other fact was irrefutably in favour of *Argo*'s present quest for Scylla and Charybdis: the Straits of Messina were more than 250 miles from the *nekymanteion* which modern archaeology now supported as the 'Halls of Hades'. Cape Skilla is barely fifteen miles from Ulysses' previous landfall. It would be interesting to see whether the practical experiment of sailing a replica galley into those waters would reveal any answers to the ancient riddle.

Nazem left us at the port of Methoni. He had to return to his job in Bahrain and it was a sad moment for all the crew as we waved goodbye to the small, rather dejected-looking figure standing on the end of the jetty. Nazem was wearing a large baggy pair of shorts that made his tiny figure look all the more fragile, and he seemed crushed by the bulk of an enormous shoulder bag containing his cameras. We had all grown very fond of him, and as he turned away and tramped wanly down the quay Cormac roared 'Goodbye, Nazem! I'll come and visit you in Bahrain!' He must have heard, for the little figure turned and gave one last wave. From that day the cuisine aboard *Argo* never again achieved the same distinction. We had to make do with much more modest fare, taking it in turns to help Jonathan, a new recruit from England who was in his second year at London University. At least my responsibilities as captain were eased because another arrival for this final stage of our voyage was Peter Wheeler, second-in-command from the Jason Voyage. He could take over the running of *Argo* after Doc John returned to his hospital post and when my research into the *Odyssey* took me ashore. The other veteran from the Jason Voyage, rowing-master Mark Richards, burnished his muscular reputation by arriving with a bicycle. When the Ulysses Voyage was over, he proposed pedalling back to Oxford to keep himself fit. The rest of us quietly noted that to add to his effort he had brought with him several heavy reference books which were stuffed in his cycle panniers and would surely add to his burden.

Argo headed towards the tantalizing Cape Skilla marked on the Admiralty chart. Our track took us along the west coast of the island of Levkas, and as we travelled up the coast we passed inside the small island of Sesola. The name is Venetian and means 'the baling scoop', and it is the only island off the west coast of Levkas. My attention was caught by a bright column of light apparently shining right through the rock at the southern end of the island. 'Change of course!' I called out to the crew. 'Let's have a closer look at that cave! It looks peculiar.' As we approached, we saw that the column of daylight was coming through a remarkable cleft in the rock. It was not so much a cave as a massive crack that pierced clear through Sesola from one side to the other. It gave the impression that Sesola was in two segments, a larger portion to the north, and a smaller, separate part to the south. The two parts of the island only touched at the top of the three-metre-wide cleft where the rock formed a natural bridge some forty feet above the surface of the sea which lapped through the gap. It was as if two quite separate pieces of rock had smacked together and stuck in position. As I gazed at the remarkable formation, a single thought leapt into my mind: Sesola looked exactly like the image of the Roving or Wandering Rocks that feature in Jason's story.

In Greek mythology the Roving Rocks were two

masses of rock which had floated loose on the surface of the sea. They clashed together whenever a ship tried to pass between them and smashed the vessel to splinters. For this reason they were also known as the Clashing Rocks, and it was said that Jason and the Argonauts had been the first seamen ever to sail between them successfully. Thereafter the Wandering Rocks had been rooted to the sea floor. Circe had described the danger of the Roving Rocks to Ulysses, because they lay on one route from Aeaea towards Ithaca. Now, suddenly here at Sesola, we were seeing the perfect image of the legend – an image as obvious as the Ram's Forehead at Cape Krio.

Rick went to investigate the cleft. In the rubber dinghy he drove into the great cleft, stopped for a few minutes to peer down into the sea, and then continued right through the island before circling round to rejoin *Argo*. 'It's a huge crack which seems to go on and on downwards underwater,' he reported as he came back aboard. 'The two sides stay the same distance apart, and they are so flat that they look like someone's taken an axe and split the rock. As far as I was able to see, the cleft goes right down to the sea floor.'

I checked the chart. The depth in this area was marked at 29 fathoms, more than 170 feet deep. What bizarre geology had created this huge underwater cleft I could only guess. Possibly the island had split apart long ago under the shattering stress of one of the numerous earthquakes which rock this area. But the reason for this extraordinary formation was unimportant. What mattered was that here, off Levkas and only seventeen miles from the tantalizing Cape Skilla, was a perfect candidate for the Roving Rocks which had been mentioned by Circe when she gave Ulysses his directions to get home. The coincidence, I felt, was not accidental.

The Roving Rocks

To understand the significance of the Roving Rocks, we need to look at Circe's own words to Ulysses as he was about to depart homeward for Ithaca. Once he had passed the Sirens, she had warned him,

□ two ways will lie before you, and you must choose between them as you see fit, though I will tell you both. One leads to those sheer cliffs which the blessed gods know as the Wandering Rocks. Here blue-eyed Amphitrite sends her great breakers thundering in, and the very birds cannot fly by in safety. Even from the shy doves that bring ambrosia to Father Zeus the beetling rocks take toll each time they pass, and the Father has to send one more to make up their number; while for such sailors as bring their ship to this spot, there is no escape whatever. They end as flotsam on the sea, timbers and corpses tossed in confusion by the waves or licked up by tempestuous and destroying flames. Of all ships that go down to the sea one only has made the passage, and that was the celebrated Argo, homeward bound . . . □

This is the only occasion in the *Oydssey* that Jason's *Argo* is specifically mentioned, though as we saw with the spring of Artacie and the Laestrygonian massacre it seems that the *Odyssey* borrowed extracts from the saga of Jason and the Argonauts. But the Clashing Rocks of Jason's story are placed in the Bosphorus, nowhere near the island of Levkas or, for that matter, the Straits of Messina. In 1984 Mark Richards and I had clambered up on top of those original Clashing Rocks at a place called Rumeli Fener, sixteen miles north of Istanbul on the European shore of the Bosphorus. We had found a Roman pillar erected where the Greeks had made offerings for safe passage through the dangers of the Black or inhospitable Sea. How could Jason's Rovers or Clashing

Rocks suddenly turn up in the *Odyssey* and, according to Circe, when Jason was *homeward bound*, that is after he had seized the Golden Fleece and was returning to Greece? Everything seemed topsy turvy and it was a question that had baffled commentators. Now, thanks to our modern *Argo* and Sesola, I believed I saw the answer.

The most complete surviving version of the Argonaut legend was written down by the Greek savant Apollonius Rhodius in the third century BC. He claimed that after Jason and the Argonauts stole the Golden Fleece from the Kingdom of Colchis (modern Soviet Georgia at the eastern end of the Black Sea) they were chased by the fleet of its ruler, King Aeetes. The king wanted to recover not only the fleece but also his daughter Princess Medea who had run away with Jason. To escape the pursuit, according to this tradition, the Argonauts sailed back across the Black Sea, rowed up the Danube and emerged with their ship into the Adriatic Sea. In reality this feat is physically impossible because the portage across the mountains of what is now Yugoslavia does not exist. Nevertheless Apollonius and now, it seemed, Homer or his predecessors had believed in this return route. An archipelago in the north end of the Adriatic was named the Apsyrtides Islands in memory of Prince Apsyrtus, commander of the Colchian fleet. Here, according to this belief, he had been lured into an ambush by his sister, Medea, and foully murdered by Jason even though he was protected by a truce. Traditionally Jason's *Argo* then passed on down the length of the Adriatic, and Jason and Medea visited the island of a powerful sorceress to try to obtain expiation for their foul crime. That island, of course, was Aeaea and the sorceress was Circe. Thus the Argonaut story too placed Aeaea/Paxos very neatly off the mouth of the river Acheron.

As the *Odyssey* said, the Argonaut story was very well-known and Jason's *Argo* was 'in all men's minds'. Circe had mentioned the 'tremulous doves' which carried nectar to Zeus and were snapped between the Roving Rocks. They harked back to the dove which Jason had released. Flying between the two rocks, the dove had caused them to clash together and, as the rocks moved apart, Jason and his oarsmen had rowed through the gap. Thereafter, said the legend, the Roving Rocks had been 'rooted to the ground'. So when sailors saw the remarkable half-split profile of Sesola they naturally thought of the story of Jason's Clashing Rocks, just as I had done, and imported to western Greece a legend whose original home was in the Bosphorus. Sesola with its two parts rooted to the sea floor at the base of that remarkable cleft really did look just as if Jason's *Argo* had recently slipped through. Sesola was the legend petrified and, by transfer of the tale, became the Wandering Rocks.

Subsequently I was able to confirm that other parts of Circe's description of the Roving Rocks fit Sesola Island. She warned Ulysses that Amphitrite the sea goddess sent 'her great breakers thundering in' against the rocks where 'for such sailors as bring their ships to the spot, there is no escape whatever'. In classical writings the waters off the west coast of Levkas were notorious for their bad weather. The great white headland of Cape Ducato eight miles away was particularly feared for its sudden gales. In the *Aeneid* the poet Virgil calls it 'a stormy peak where dread Apollo appears', and Smith's *Dictionary* roundly declared 'it still retains among Greek mariners of the present day the evil fame which it bore of old in consequence of the dark water, the strong currents, and the fierce gales which they there encounter'. As for the 'storms of ravening fire' which Circe said carried away the broken timbers and bodies of the sailors, they were to puzzle me until I saw a geological map of the area. Levkas lies close to a fault-line in the earth's crust, one of the 'plate lines' whose grinding dislocation causes the earthquakes that shake the Ionian Islands. It is possible that submarine volcanic activity has taken place along this fault-line. There is a local, but unverified, belief in Levkas that an underwater volcano exists to the north of the island, and this could perhaps have produced 'flames in the sea'. More scientifically the same Admiralty Sailing Directions that had noted Cape Skilla also record two volcanic eruptions thirty miles away at the eastern end of the Gulf of Ambracia. Great numbers of fish were killed, and the sea was covered with sulphur. 'Small amounts of sulphur are still discharged occasionally,' concluded the Pilot, 'often making the water phosphorescent at the head of the bay.'

The revelations of that sunny afternoon of 31 July were not yet over. When Rick came back aboard *Argo* and described the great submarine crack through Sesola, I took another look at the Admiralty chart of the area. The realization that Sesola Island matched the image of the Roving Rocks gave me another piece to add to the jigsaw of Circe's instructions to Ulysses about his route home. To the north-east we now had a headland called Cape Skilla on the mainland, while to the north Paxos was probably Circe's island of Aeaea lying off the mouth of the river Acheron. Sesola, as the Clashing Rocks, lay off the west coast of Levkas, while to the south was Ithaca, Ulysses' home. In the centre of that roughly diamond-shaped area lay the island of Levkas. Perhaps because I was in the right place and in the right situation – aboard a galley – and perhaps also because I had wondered for so long about the different parts of the puzzle, the answer leaped off the chart. The entire pattern of Circe's directions to Ulysses fell into place. I had been asking myself what and where were the Sirens, Scylla, Charybdis and the others, and suddenly I saw the solution:

Circe had been telling Ulysses that as he sailed south from her island, he could choose between two routes for passing Levkas. Either he could go down its west coast, by the open sea route, in which case he had to pass Sesola, which looked exactly like the Roving Rocks from the legend of Jason and the Argonauts. Or he could go *inside* Levkas down the narrow twisting channel, now silted up but very evident from the old Admiralty chart, which separated Levkas from the mainland. It was along this channel, barely fifty yards wide in places, that we should go to look for Scylla and Charybdis. The shape of the pattern was so clear that I knew we would find the missing pieces there.

As if to confirm this intuition, I noticed the name of the steep hill which overlooks the ancient channel from the east. It was marked on the chart as Mount Lamia.

'Costas,' I asked our Greek crew member, 'does "Lamia" mean anything?'

'Lamia? Why yes,' he answered, pausing as he considered his explanation. 'A Lamia's a sort of female monster of old mythology. With a long neck. It swallows babies and has a bad reputation. Even today if two women are having a row and one wants to insult the other that she's got a nasty voice and is unpleasant she might shout at her "Lamia!" ' At this point Theodor the Bulgarian broke in. 'We also have a monster called Lamia in Thracian mythology which I think must be inherited from the Greek legends. Our Lamia also has a long neck, maybe like a dragon, and it attacks the hero.'

I was elated. 'There it is then! We're looking for a narrow strait on one side of which lives Scylla, a monster with six long necks who snatches up men, and what do we find right here beside the old, very narrow ship channel separating Levkas and the mainland but a steep hill named after a long-necked man-eating monster of antiquity. Doesn't that sound like Scylla? Let's go there and investigate!'

Kevin Fleming, the photographer who had joined our team on behalf of the *National Geographic Magazine*, was looking over my shoulder at the chart as I explained how Circe's instructions added up to the two different ways of sailing past Levkas, out to sea or via the inshore channel. After I had pointed out how the names of mythology were still there for all to see, he looked up and said, 'But it's so obvious. Are you sure that no one has noticed this before?'

'I don't think so,' I answered. 'Sometimes the most obvious things are overlooked because they're so plain.'

And that, I thought to myself, was why we had brought *Argo* to that spot. Previous commentators had been too immersed in their learning to look for something really very uncomplicated and close at hand. The deck of a replica Bronze Age galley gave a very much more matter-of-fact perspective.

11

The Sirens, Scylla and Charybdis

Sailing south by the route that Ulysses would have taken from Aeaea and the Acheron, Levkas soon appears tall on the horizon, a lofty island with a bold north face where cliffs rise sheer from the sea. But when the navigator is within a mile or so, he sees that he has been mistaken. The cliffs are set back, the real shoreline is a low foreland barely visible above sea level which extends out towards him as a thin smudge. It is not a dangerous error because the water shallows only gradually, and there is plenty of time to alter course and enough depth for a galley to sail only a stone's throw from the beach. This is a strange, rather lonely, strand made of low dunes and a few clumps of wind-racked trees. On the far side of the dunes, scarcely interrupted by the land, the sea seems to continue in a muddy grey sheet, where a shallow lagoon is trapped between the dunes and the main island. Scattered lines of stakes mark the shapes of fish-traps, and a flat-bottomed skiff like a bean pod can sometimes be seen moving across the lagoon as a fisherman checks his catch. It is a scene of marshes and fens rather than of the sea, and in the dawn calm there are birds wading, frogs croaking, and abrupt, rather unnerving splashes as fish suddenly leap and fall back into the turgid water. But every summer afternoon the wind comes in briskly from the west, across the Ionian Sea. It strikes white caps from the blue water of the open sea, heaps waves against the sands of the low foreland, and then cuts the surface of the lagoon into a queasy chop that obliges the lake fishermen in their little boats to seek shelter. So regular and strong is this wind that the only structures on the promontory are windmills, still facing into the breeze though their arms are long since broken and the mechanism rusty, adding to the atmosphere of decay.

Windmill Rock is the name the Victorians of the Mediterranean Survey gave to the only minor off-shore danger, a shallow patch ten yards off the tip of the promontory. The point itself they called by a Greek word, Cape Yrapetra, the 'Cape of the Rock of Turning'. Presumably this was the name they heard locally, and today the inhabitants of Levkas claim that the cape was the place where a man, walking on his way to the mainland, changed direction. But this is a very roundabout way to go to the mainland; there was a more direct causeway and stepping stones even in Turkish times. It seems much more likely that the Rock of Turning is a much older name and was a sailor's description. This was a promontory where a coast navigator had to choose to turn left or right, either to select the outside passage of Levkas or take the narrow inner channel between Levkas and the mainland. It is literally the Cape of 'veering aside'. Circe had said the meadow of the Sirens would be found near the place where the two routes to Ithaca diverged and so it seemed to me that the most likely site for the place of the Sirens would be here, on the low sandy beach.

Circe explained to Ulysses how he could enjoy, yet escape, the deadly sweet singing of the Sirens. He could ravish his senses by listening to the Sirens' song, but still evade destruction, if he plugged the ears of all his crew with wax and they tied him firmly to the ship's mast. Then, heedless of their song, the deaf crew could row him past the Sirens in their meadow, and however much Ulysses longed to join them his bonds would hold him fast, and he and his men would not end their lives on that beach 'piled high with the mouldering skeletons of men.'

'Three tumuli' were plainly marked on the Admiralty Chart, at the very tip of Yrapetra Point. Three ancient burial mounds! What more could one have wanted to identify the meadow 'piled high with the mouldering skeletons of men'? What place could be more suitable for the legend of the Sirens to take hold? It seemed too good to be true.

So, in a way, it was. Edging *Argo* past Yrapetra Point in no more than five feet of water, I could not see any ancient barrow graves among the nondescript undulations of the beach. Had the tumuli been eroded, covered with wind-blown sand, or were they figments of the surveyors' imaginations? That didn't seem very likely for men trained under Captain Spratt. I went ashore to investigate and found what I thought must be the tumuli, or rather their remains. In exactly the correct place according to the map were two low, quite distinct humps of sand, about eight yards across, but flat-topped where the surface had been scraped away. Had they been excavated by archaeologists or perhaps robbed for sand? The third mound was even more battered, and had a squarer outline. This worried me. Were these really 'tumuli', as the nineteenth-century map claimed, or were they the foundations of former windmills which the naval surveyors had mistaken for ancient burial tombs? There was no trace of mill workings, and two of the 'tumuli' were too close together to have allowed space between them for the whirling arms of windmills. Yet though I was to search, I never did find any mention of these three 'tumuli' in the archaeological records of Levkas, and local informants insisted that they knew of no ancient burial grounds here. The only relics on the point, they assured me, were the remains of former gun emplacements. That explanation, however, I could

'Sirens' Beach' (Cape Yrapetra, 1250 BC)

reject. A Victorian marine surveyor of the Royal Navy knew the difference between a gun battery and a grave barrow.

The comparatively modest size of the 'tumuli' presented no difficulty. The scale of the Mycenaean world, as we had repeatedly seen, was very modest by our standards, and the site at the tip of Yrapetra was exactly where the ancients would have buried their dead. Elpenor, Ulysses' youngest crewman, had been buried in a mound 'overlooking the grey sea' on Aeaea, and Phrontis, Menelaus' stricken helmsman, had been interred at Cape Sounion, both headlands on the sea route. The low foreland at Yrapetra matched the pattern. One day, perhaps, professional archaeologists will find time to dig here and check the nineteenth century map reference.

Other factors would locate the Sirens in this part of Greece. The Sirens were the daughters of the ancient river god Achelous, depicted as having a tail like a stout conger eel with a human torso and head sprouting the horns of a bull. The Sirens were either born from his union with a nymph or one of the muses, or they arose from the drops of blood which leaked out when one of his horns was snapped off in a fight with Hercules.

Achelous' home was in north-western Greece, and the river Achelous, named after him, is forty miles away, its mouth level with Ithaca. So the Sirens ought, by descent anyway, to be found in the Ionian Islands. Myth claims that the Sirens were given wings so that they could better search for Persephone, queen of the Underworld, snatched away by Hades. Again, as we have seen, the abode of Hades and Persephone was located in the north-west, on the Acheron not far from Levkas. Finally there may be another echo of their association with Levkas in the way the Sirens themselves perished. The Sirens committed suicide either from bitter chagrin at losing a music contest against the Muses or because they had allowed Ulysses (some say Jason) to escape unscathed. Like the Clashing Rocks which become immobile when the first ship succeeded in sailing past, the menace of the Sirens ended when the first sailor escaped their clutches. The Sirens committed suicide by casting themselves into the sea from a tall, white cliff. Although an island off Crete has been claimed as the spot, by far the most renowned suicide cliff to fit this description is the tall white cliff of 'storm clouded' Cape Ducato at the south-west corner of Levkas. Here Sappho the poet is said to have thrown herself off the precipice still known as Sappho's Leap. There is a clear parallel between the cliff suicide of a woman-poet and the legendary death of the singing Sirens.

Only two Sirens were waiting to lure Ulysses and his men, according to the *Odyssey*. Later authorities usually list three of these mythical creatures and tell us they had the faces and bodies of beautiful virgins but from the waist down the legs and feathers of birds. All sources agree that it was the quality of their voices, sometimes accompanied by sweet music on the lyre and flute, which brought men to their deaths, entrancing them so that they forgot their homes and families and remained there captivated until they died.

Circe's clever scheme, however, protected Ulysses well. She gave him a fair following wind to blow his galley swiftly from Aeaea homeward towards Ithaca. As the vessel approached the Sirens' meadow the breeze suddenly died away. The sailors lowered and stowed the sails, Ulysses stopped their ears with softened wax, and they lashed him to the mast. Then they got out oars and rowed until they 'had just come within call of the shore' when the Sirens caught sight of them and directed their beguiling song towards the passing galley. At the sound of their voices said Ulysses,

□ my heart was filled with such a longing to listen that with nod and frown I signed to my men to set me free. But they swung forward to their oars and rowed ahead, while Perimedes and Eurylochus jumped, tightened my bonds and added more. However, when they had rowed past the Sirens and we could no longer hear their voices and the burden of their song, my good companions were quick to clear their ears of the wax I had used to stop them, and to free me from my shackles. □

Turning to port, therefore, Ulysses and his crew had chosen to take the second route Circe had offered – the inside passage through the narrow twisting channel separating Levkas from the mainland district of Greece known as Arcania. Thus they avoided the dangers of the open-water passage, past Sesola/The Rovers and stormy Cape Ducato, and now we must imagine them following the beach eastward from Cape Yrapetra, where today windsurfers skim past using the same stiff breeze that once spun the arms of the windmills. Only two and a quarter miles ahead is a spectacular hazard:

☐ We had no sooner put this island behind us than
I saw a cloud of smoke ahead and a raging surf, the
roar of which I could already hear. My men were so
terrified that the oars all dropped from their grasp
and fell with a splash in the wash of the ship; while
the ship herself, now that the hands that pulled the
long blades were idle, was brought to a standstill. I
made a tour of the vessel, and with a soothing word
for each man I tried to put heart into my company.

'My friends,' I said, 'we are men who have met
trouble before. And I cannot see that we are faced
here by anything worse than when the Cyclops used
his brutal strength to imprison us in his cave. Yet my
courage and presence of mind found a way out for
us even from there; and I am sure that this too will
be a memory for us one day. So now I appeal to you
all to do exactly as I say. Oarsmen, stick to your
benches, striking hard with your blades through the
broken water, and we may have the luck to slip by
and for once avoid disaster. Helmsman, your orders
are these. Get them by heart, for the good ship's
steering oar is under your control. Give a wide berth
to that smoke and surf you see, and hug these cliffs,
or before you can stop her the ship will take it into
her head to make a dash over there and you'll wreck
us.' ☐

The 'smoke and raging surf' that so scared Ulysses' men
is still there today. It is the band of surf and spray
breaking in a line over the reef called Plaka Spit. The
same wind of the surfers and the mills builds up a swell
which rolls in from the west. This swell hits the two-
mile-long reef which projects, ruler-straight, from the
shore and directly into the path of the wind. The reef
is just a foot above sea level and is so straight that it
looks artificial, a submerged jetty or training wall. Even

after the wind has dropped, the swell continues to heave in so that on a calm sea there is the strange sight of the line of Plaka Spit marked by a bar of surf and breaking waves when all else is calm. Beyond this obstacle lies the goal that Ulysses sought – the entrance to the ancient channel.

Three months earlier, at Troy, I had promised Kevin a photograph of *Argo* negotiating a reef, and here was the ideal spot for him. After all, this would have been the same hazard that Ulysses struggled to avoid, ordering his men to ignore the Plaka's surf and row straight for the entrance to the channel. So Kevin went ahead in the dinghy to find a footing on the reef, waist deep among the breaking waves, and set up his camera while we idled with *Argo* at a safe distance. Kevin waved that he was ready, and I called to the crew to unloose the sail from its cross-yard. The late afternoon breeze was blowing steadily from the west, and the sail's portrait of the young nobleman of Pylos swelled out vigorously. *Argo* gathered speed and began to race towards the end of the rocky spit. My intention was to shave the reef as close as I dared, just avoiding the breaking waves and then round up into the protected calm on the far side. It was an exhilarating run as the slim hull accelerated forward. Ahead and not far from Kevin I could see a small open fishing boat bobbing up and down in the swell, sometimes lost from view between the waves, sometimes plainly visible on the crests. There were two men aboard and they were standing up, shading their eyes against the sun, watching with amazement the sight of a Bronze Age galley blazing in out of the west. The gap was closing very rapidly. Kevin's head was bowed down over his viewfinder. Peter Wheeler was in the bows peering ahead through the water, trying to spot any outlying boulders, Jonathan and Derry were standing alert to handle the sheets. Just then, as *Argo* hit her stride, I saw directly in her path the line of half-submerged floats of the fishing net that the boatmen were tending. The net lay directly in our path, extending nearly to the edge of the reef. If *Argo* hit the net at that speed, her twin rudders projecting downward below the hull would be snagged as if she had hurtled into a tripwire. She could be pulled aside and smashed into the reef. There was no way to stop her scalding rush, so I prayed that there was enough room to squeak through the gap between the end of the net and the rocks if *Argo* could be made to respond fast enough. I wrenched the twin rudders over to maximum deflection, and *Argo* swerved crazily. I hung on to the helm, my heart in my mouth. The crew were frozen in place, not moving a muscle as we waited for the rending crash. A round-shouldered swell lifted the galley up, and she went careering headlong past Kevin, who was standing amid the swirling water on the reef, so astonished that he even omitted to press the shutter for a final frame. I glimpsed the black path of *Argo*'s shadow flicker across the darker line of rocks, and we were across the Plaka Spit.

'Let go sheets!!' Never had the crew reacted so fast. The billowing sail flapped out to spill the wind. 'Brail up!' The crew ran to haul on the buntlines that gathered the canvas to the cross-yard. Peter came aft from his lookout's perch. 'I calculate that you had about six inches between the tip of the rudders and the top of the rocks,' he announced calmly. Kevin came back aboard with his cameras. 'My God,' he said in shock, 'I never thought you would come that close. For the first time in my life as a photographer, I won't say "Just one more time".'

Once a vessel was safely behind Plaka Spit it would have to turn right-handed to enter the mouth of the old channel, which the Venetians later called Canali Stretti.

Today that channel is severed by an artificial causeway built to carry the main road from Arcania into Levkas. But the line of the ancient channel, now barely a foot deep in places, is clear both on the map and to the eye. Canali Stretti meanders through back-waters and cut-offs before petering out near the causeway.

The extent, depth and changing position of this channel excited a famous controversy among Homeric archaeologists, which reached its climax in the 1920s. Oddly enough the fierce arguments were nothing to do with Scylla and Charybdis but a completely different problem of the *Odyssey:* whether Levkas qualified as an island at all, or was really only a peninsula in Ulysses' time. Wilhelm Dorpfeld was the man who unleashed the heated debate. Dorpfeld had achieved a towering reputation as a result of taking over Heinrich Schliemann's excavations of Troy, applying the scientific assessment that corrected Schliemann's errors and ending up with his proclamation that the ruins of Troy VI were the city that Ulysses helped to sack. After concluding his work at Troy, Dorpfeld – in the manner of the Homeric archaeologists – could not resist looking for other Homeric sites. Like Blegen and Schliemann he searched for King Nestor's palace, but without success. Then he took up the quest for Ulysses' home itself. Dorpfeld went to Ithaca (where we shall shortly follow him) and dug in the north of the island. But again he found nothing conclusive, and proceeded to announce a theory which left his contemporaries thunderstruck. Modern Ithaca, Dorpfeld declared, was not Homer's Ithaca. The island where Ulysses had actually lived was Levkas. The names of the two islands had been switched around by the migrations of the early inhabitants who moved from one island to another and took the names with them. Homer's Ithaca was really the modern island

'The Place of Turning'

of Levkas and he, Dorpfeld, would prove it by finding Ulysses' home there.

The intense row created by this maverick theory was to rumble on for fifty years, with claim, counter-claim, argument and deep personal quarrels. To many, Dorpfeld's idea was heresy. For 2,000 years no one had doubted that Ithaca was Ithaca. But Dorpfeld had to be taken seriously. He was the senior Homeric archaeologist of his day. He had worked with the great Schliemann. He had an impeccable record as an excavator, and he had ample funds and expertise available. Backed by the German Kaiser, who sent him a special portable villa which Dorpfeld erected on Levkas on a lovely headland (overlooking what would later become the private island of the millionaire Onassis), he doggedly settled in to *prove* that he was right. Dorpfeld summoned teams of experts – surveyors, geologists, geomorphologists, linguists, pottery experts and engineers – to help him in his single-minded search. The quest became an obsession, and Dorpfeld pursued it to the end of his days, even when the tide of evidence began to run against him. It was a strange destiny for a man whose training and inclination up until then had been towards cool, rational analysis of the facts; and it affected Dorpfeld. The American consul in Athens, Irving Manatt, called on him in Levkas in 1905 and found him quite obsessed with his Levkas theory. 'Here in Levkas was Ulysses' home, and I *shall* prove it,' Dorpfeld repeated several times to his visitor, who refrained from pointing out that five years earlier on his previous excursion to the Ionian Islands he had found Dorpfeld digging on Ithaca, equally convinced that he had found Ulysses' home there.

The benefit to me of this famous wrangle was that Levkas' topography had been minutely studied for clues to the *Odyssey*, and the inland channel between Levkas and the mainland had received particularly close scrutiny. One major attack by Dorpfeld's critics was that the channel had not existed either in Homer's day or at the time of the Trojan War. Thus Levkas could not have been an island, and therefore could not be Ulysses' homeland which was quite clearly an island. The critics cited Thucydides who said that during the Peloponnesian War in the fifth century BC the inhabitants of Levkas had been obliged to dig out a channel, the *dioryktus*, to get their vessels over the neck of the land. Dorpfeld counter-attacked by asking his geologists and

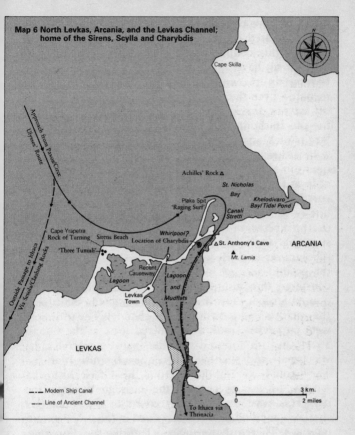

Map 6 North Levkas, Arcania, and the Levkas Channel; home of the Sirens, Scylla and Charybdis

hydrographic experts to make a detailed map of the isthmus. It showed quite clearly that the isthmus was made up of silt and sedimentary material which could well have been deposited after the Bronze Age. At the time of the Trojan War, Dorpfeld stoutly maintained, Levkas had been an island.

It is curious that in all this flurry of argument no one

seems to have considered the possibility that if Levkas was separated from Arcania by a narrow channel, perhaps this channel itself might have been unusual enough to have appeared in the geography of the *Odyssey* in its own right. But the scholars were locked in battle over the Ithaca versus Levkas dispute, firing off salvoes of scholarship at one another and, besides, the old tradition that Scylla and Charybdis lay in the Straits of Messina was too strong to be challenged.

It is strange, too, that there was ever any serious question about the existence of the channel, navigable at least for the very shallow draft vessels of the time. A cursory overview of the Canali Stretti today shows the line of the ancient waterway. It is even more obvious on the nineteenth century charts of the area. Generally speaking, the clash was the old division of armchair scholars versus those who had taken the trouble to walk the ground and see for themselves. The stay-at-homes consulted the libraries and the written histories and quoted Strabo, Pliny and Thucydides to the effect that the ancients had cut an artificial channel. The travellers went to Levkas, took a considered look at the Canali Stretti and pronounced that the main line of channel was small and shallow, but quite obviously natural. They could counter-quote from the Greek historian Arrian, to the effect that the passage through the *dioryktus* was intricate on account of the numerous shallows, marked out by stakes fixed in the sea at certain intervals. Therefore the ancients had dug the *dioryktus*, because the natural channel always tended to silt up (as its successor – the modern ship channel cut in 1902 – does to this day) and had to be cleared from time to time.

Colonel William Leake, a reliable classical scholar known for his 'wonderful topographical eye and instinct', visited Levkas in 1809-10 and was ahead of

Dorpfeld's scientific conclusion by nearly a century when he summed up his observations on the spot:

> I am disposed to believe . . . that Leucas (Levkas) was never more of a peninsula nor less of an island than it is at present; that is to say, that it has always been separated by a narrow fordable channel and that the changes which appear from history to have occurred were all covered by the natural obstruction and artificial clearing of the entrance of the deep channel.

I was so confident that we were on the brink of solving the riddle of the narrow straits of Scylla and Charybdis on Ulysses' journey that I went ashore to search for Scylla's Cave feeling certain that it would be there. I had compared the description of the cave in the *Odyssey* with the large-scale chart and knew just where to start looking. The rock in whose side Scylla dwelt, Circe said, 'rears its sharp peak up to the very sky and is capped by black clouds that never stream away nor leave clear weather round the top, even in summer or in harvest time.'

Of course Homer was exaggerating the lofty peak with its perpetual cloud, just as he had exaggerated and embroidered the 'walls of bronze' at Gramvousa to make the island of Aeolus, and the size and height of 'beetling Ilium'. Nevertheless there was the peak of Mount Lamia standing above the bay, and the usual west wind blowing in from the sea struck the summit and left a trail of orographic cloud streaming from its crest in an otherwise clear sky. Scylla's cave had to be in the flank of Mount Lamia, the Mountain of the Long-Necked Devouring Monster. The directions within the legend were there in front of me; I had only to apply them to the physical reality, reading the poet's word pictures as a description of the countryside.

The flank of Mount Lamia was steep but not as unclimbable as Homer would have us believe: 'no man on earth could climb it, up or down, not even with twenty hands and feet to help him; for the rock is as smooth as it if had been polished'.

The steepest section of Mount Lamia's flank was close above the modern road, a promising-looking crag of near vertical cliff. The gentler lower slope was covered with bushes growing in the detritus that had slumped down the hillside. The crag itself was in exactly the right position, for it faced west out over the bay where *Argo* had anchored behind Plaka Spit, and Circe had told Ulysses that 'halfway up the crag is a misty cavern, facing the West and running down to Erebus, past which, my lord Odysseus, you must steer your ship'.

Erebus was the land of the departed spirits, to the west, and Scylla's cave had to be fairly high up, for Circe continued that 'the strongest bowman could not reach the gaping mouth of the cave with an arrow shot from a ship below'.

Two men were in a punt below me as I walked along the road between Canali Stretti and the section of cliff. They were poised with immensely long-handled fish tridents and stared intently at the water, fishing for eels in the shallows of the waterway. 'The cave!' I shouted down to them. 'Where's the cave?' They looked up, startled. I realized that I was so sure that I would find the cave that I hadn't even asked, 'Is there any cave near here?' or some such general question. 'The cave? Where?' I yelled again. The fishermen were clearly annoyed to be disturbed. They turned their backs. I persisted. 'The cave? Please, the cave?' hoping that my very clumsy Greek pronunciation would be understood. The cave *had* to be nearby. I saw the two men confer, witnessed an irritated shrug. Obviously they thought I was a crazy tourist, and I caught the word 'Antonis'

[Anthony]. Then in final exasperation before he turned back to his eel-spearing, one of the men gestured at the cliff behind me. Turning, I could just make out the corner of some sort of balcony with an iron railing projecting beyond the branches of an ancient olive tree, high up the crag. With growing excitement I hurried down the tarmac road until I found a footpath leading up the hillside. The path zigzagged back and forth, and hadn't been used recently for I pushed through cobwebs spun between the bushes. The fat spiders reminded me of Scylla, sitting in her lair waiting to seize the passing victims, for I *knew* that I was on the right track.

The path brought me to a short flight of steps, and these led me up on to the concrete balcony which I had noticed earlier. The balcony was something to do with a church, for there was a crude cross made of two extra pieces of the metal rail welded together, and a large bell was hung on a frame of metal pipes. A tiled roof had been built out from the cliff face as a sort of porch, and at the back of the balcony were two small windows and a brown painted door led into the cliff face. On closer inspection I saw that the door was set in a section of man-made wall which had been constructed to fill in the overhang of rock. Above the door was a large iron key on a nail. I unlocked the door and, feeling like Alice walking through the looking glass, stepped inside.

I was standing in a cave. It had been turned into a chapel, but the shape and atmosphere of the original grotto were not masked in any way. Its walls were grotesque. They were blobbed and runnelled like melted wax and streaked with smoke from the offertory candles. The highest point of the cave was about fifteen feet and it was some twelve feet deep and about thirty feet wide, a gloomy hole scooped in the cliff face. It was the perfect den for Scylla. Nor was I surprised that the cave was now a chapel. Just as the Church of St

John the Forerunner had been sited over the ancient House of Hades at the *nekymanteion*, here too the new religion had taken over an ancient pagan holy place. Scylla's Cave was now a chapel to the hermit St Anthony, and I had to smile to myself when I caught sight of a crude little icon depicting St George killing the dragon. It was the perfect metaphor for the new religion versus the old, and some folklorists believe that the long-necked dragon fighting St George evolved from the pagan notion of the mounted knight battling with Lamia the long-necked monster who attacks the hero.

I turned and walked back on to the balcony, with my back to the cave mouth. Circe's directions fitted perfectly. Below me I could distinguish the line of the ancient channel where it wound close against the foot of the cliff. From my vantage point I could look down like an osprey and see the wriggling patterns of small eels disturbing the fine pale yellow mud of the shallows of Canali Stretti. Directly ahead was the Plaka Spit with its straight line of waves still breaking in foam, though it was evening and the wind had calmed. Beyond the spit in the distance was the nose of Yrapetra Point, the place of the mysterious tumuli and the likely beach of the Sirens. I was standing just as Circe had said, in a cave, halfway up the cliff face, over the channel, and looking towards the west. Below me the eel fishermen had packed up for the day and were poling their way out of the shallows, using the ancient waterway. Scylla's Cave was found.

If Scylla's Cave lies in the flank of present-day Mount Lamia on the Arcanian shore, where would Charybdis, the swallowing whirlpool of the channel, have been? Circe said it lay so close on the other side of the channel that 'you could even cast an arrow across'. Today, with the Canali Stretti completely blocked and no more than a calm backwater, there is no current, no tide, no mechanism to create a whirlpool. So to get even close to an answer it is necessary to reconstruct the line and tidal pattern of the navigation channel in the time of the Trojan War. Much has to be conjecture, for massive silting has taken place in the Levkas lagoons on a scale to match the infill of the bay before Troy.

But there are some clues. Today there is a tide run, from south to north, in the modern ship channel where it cuts through the base of Plaka Spit. The current is modest, only one and a half knots, but it shows that a tidal current would have been part of the mechanism which set up the 'swallowing vortex' of Charybdis. More important, though, are the two bays of St Nicholas and Khelodivaro a mile to the north of Scylla's Cave. These two bays serve as holding ponds. Filling up with wind-driven water in the afternoon, they release their pent-up water through the rocks and shoals of 'Port St Nicholas'. 'The sea breeze forces a considerable quantity of water into Ormos Ayiou Nikolaou (St Nicholas' Bay)', say the Admiralty Sailing Directions, 'which, when the breeze dies away at sunset, runs out with some strength.' This peculiarity, a *wind-driven current*, may explain the strange characteristic of Charybdis which has baffled all commentators. The *Odyssey* says that 'dread Charybdis sucks the water down. *Three times* a day she spews them up, and *three times* she swallows them down once more in her horrible way.'

A triple-phase whirlpool had seemed impossible. Commentators like Strabo dismissed it as mere fabrication for the sake of exaggeration because tides usually flow only twice a day. But here, just south of Cape Skilla at the head of the narrow Levkas channel, is the possibility of that third tide. On some days, depending on the times of low and high tide, the wind would push water into St Nicholas' Bay, the normal tide would ebb and flow, and when the wind dropped in the evening the pent-up water would rush out of its reservoir in the bay to create a third tidal flow. Unquestionably the storage capacity of Khelodivaro Bay in the Late Bronze Age would have been far greater, before silt filled in the bay, and additional water may have gushed from Voulkaria lagoon, which is still linked to Khelodivaro by a narrow cut along the line of an ancient channel. The unexpected flow of water out of this reservoir, following on the usual tidal rhythm, would have been quiet literally the stuff of legend to a small-boat navigator of the Bronze Age.

Where, then, to place the actual phenomenon of the thrice-active whirlpool? Again, we can only make a reasoned guess, and draw a comparison with a somewhat similar situation, six miles to the north, where the waters of the Gulf of Ambracia empty out through a narrow channel at Preveza. Here on spring tides the outflow produces a large gyration, a spinning of the water, just inside Aktion Point. Fishermen claim that the current can run so strongly that occasionally it is impossible to get their nets back aboard, so powerful is the grip of the current. In the Canali Stretti between Levkas and the mainland the most likely spot for such a whirlpool effect would be at a choke point where the rush of water was accelerated and deflected. This would happen either alongside a low islet in mid-channel or at one of the gaps between the huge boulders of the Plaka Reef where the tidal water would gush through, setting up a whirling current on the edge of the narrow channel. This phenomenon would have been terrifying for a galley, already threading its way through the gullet. The vortex would have been nothing like as dangerous as the *Odyssey* claimed — capable of swallowing down a vessel — but enough to create the legend of Charybdis.

Skirting the whirlpool and gazing at the terrifying

'Scylla's Cave', facing west over the Channel, 1250 BC

rush of water, says the *Odyssey*, Ulysses forgot all about
Scylla as his galley passed close under the steep foot of
Mount Lamia. The long-necked she-monster struck, and

☐ snatched out of my boat the six ablest hands I had

on board. I swung round, to glance at the ship and run my eye over the crew, just in time to see the arms and legs of her victims dangled high in the air above my head. 'Odysseus!' they called out to me in their agony. But it was the last time they used my name. For like an angler on a jutting point, who with a long rod casts his ox-horn lure into the sea as bait for the little fish below, gets a bite, and whips his struggling prey to land, Scylla had whisked my comrades up and swept them struggling to the rocks, where she devoured them at her own door, shrieking and stretching out their hands to me in their last desperate throes. In all that I have gone through as I made my way across the seas, I have never had to witness a more pitiable sight than that. □

So another six sailors were lost. But the worst was yet to come. Next Ulysses was to witness the destruction of his ship, the last vessel of his squadron, and his entire crew.

12

Cattle of the Sun King

□ From the perils of the Rocks, from Scylla, and from the terrors of Charybdis we had now escaped; and it was not long before we reached the Sun God's favoured island, where Hyperion kept his splendid broad-browed cattle and his flocks of sturdy sheep. From where I was on board, right out to sea, I could hear the lowing of cows as they were stalled for the night, and the bleating of sheep. □

Circe had strictly warned Ulysses to steer well clear of the island of the Sun God's cattle. A terrible fate would befall anyone who dared touch the sacred animals that grazed there. Seven herds of cattle, each with fifty animals, and seven flocks of sheep were tended by two daughters of the Sun God, the nymphs Lampetie and Phaethousa. If Ulysses could only succeed in passing by Thrinacia, as the island was called, all would be well and his company would get home safely. But if, as Circe implied, his crew got into their usual mischief, it was to be their last adventure. They would all perish, and Ulysses alone would reach home.

Inevitably, Ulysses' accident-prone crew refused to bypass Thrinacia and sail past. Their spokesman was Eurylochus, the same mutinous crew member who had jibbed at visiting Circe's home in the interior of Aeaea. Now he told Ulysses that the crew insisted on landing. They complained that Ulysses was driving them too hard. He was sailing dangerously by expecting them to voyage at night when it was impossible to see a storm coming. A sudden onrush of wind could easily over-whelm the boat. Eurylochus argued that the crew was exhausted by hard work and lack of sleep. They wanted to have a proper meal cooked ashore and to sleep on dry land. They need only halt for one night and the next morning they could proceed to Ithaca. Bowing to their demands, Ulysses reluctantly agreed to put in to Thrinacia, but first he made the sailors swear on no account to touch the sacred cattle of Helios Hyperion, the Sun God, for fear of bringing disaster on the whole enterprise.

Having made this pledge, the crew turned the galley towards the island and disembarked. That night, however, such a fierce south wind sprang up that they were obliged to haul the galley out of the water for safety. For a whole month the same south wind continued unabated so, unable to relaunch their boat, they were pinned on land waiting for a break in the weather. Gradually the supplies of food given to them by Circe ran out, and they were obliged to scavenge. They tried fishing and catching wild birds, but eventu-ally came to the verge of starvation. At this crucial moment Ulysses very unwisely went inland to pray to the gods for help, and left his men unsupervised. During his absence the mischief-making Eurylochus incited his colleagues to break their oath. Why should they starve to death on the island, he asked them, when they could feast on the sacred cattle? He would rather die by drowning at sea than waste away uselessly by famine. Surely Helios Hyperion would be sufficiently placated if the proper sacrifices were made undertaking to build a fine temple in his honour when they got home to Ithaca. Fecklessly the crew fell in with his suggestion and cut out the best animals from the herds. The ravenous sailors drove the beasts down to the beach, and since there was no barley grain left to offer to the god in accordance with the correct ritual sacrifice they made do with a makeshift dedication of tender leaves plucked from an oak tree. Then they slaughtered the cattle, flayed them and, after making a burnt offering of the meat from the thighs wrapped in fat, began to roast the meat on spits over the fire. At this juncture Ulysses returned. He had fallen asleep after his prayers and now, as he approached the beach, he smelled the roasting meat and realized that the worst had happened. It was too late. Even the wayward sailors realized their mistake when the ghastly portents began. The flayed skins of the dead oxen started to crawl, and the meat, whether raw or on the spits, bellowed with the noise of live cattle. The nymph Lampetie, says the *Odyssey*, had run off to report the sacrilege to her father Helios Hyperion, and Zeus swore to the Sun God that he would exact fatal retribution on the blasphemous sailors.

For six days, so the *Odyssey* recounts, the sailors compounded their unholy insolence. They killed more cattle and feasted on the flesh until, on the seventh morning, the wind finally dropped and they were able to manhandle the galley back into the water and put to sea. The mast was set upright in its mast box and the sail hoisted. Then, as the ship moved across the wide sea, Zeus struck. A blue-black cloud hovered over the galley darkening the surface of the sea with menace. A sudden squall rushed in from the west and snapped both forestays of the mast which collapsed backwards. All the rigging went overboard, and the toppling mast crashed down on the steersman's head crushing his skull so that 'he like a diver dropped from the high deck, and the proud life left his bones there'. Thunder and lightning erupted from the cloud and the ship was sent spinning in a circle. She was breaking up and foundering. The sailors were flung into the water and 'bobbing like sea crows, they were washed away on the running waves all around the black ship, and the god took away their homecoming'.

Only Ulysses survived. As the galley began to disintegrate he seized the leather backstay and lashed together the two largest pieces of flotsam, the keel and the broken mast, and clung to this emergency life-raft. When the westerly gale abated, the south wind returned so that all through the night Ulysses drifted, aware that he was being blown back towards the terror of Charybdis the whirlpool. At daybreak he was on the edge of the vortex, just as Charybdis was beginning to suck down the water in its regular triple rhythm. At the very last instant Ulysses reached up and grabbed the strong branch of the massive fig tree which leaned out over the whirlpool and, abandoning the life-raft, hauled himself to safety. There he hung like a bat.

This is the archetypal story of the sailor's shipwreck and miraculous survival, the ultimate mariner's yarn from Ulysses to Sindbad the Sailor and Moby Dick. Yet, if one allows for the fanciful exaggerations of the convenient fig tree and the swallowing power of the whirlpool of Charybdis, the sea-sense of this adventure is very credible. Once again the compiler of the *Odyssey* reveals that he knew all about the cramped reality of life on a galley. The pleas of the weary galley-men ring very true: their exhaustion, their reluctance to sail at night when it is impossible to see the tell-tale whitecaps that warn of a sudden squall approaching an open boat, the enticing thought of a hot meal on shore followed by the chance to stretch out on the beach and get some proper sleep instead of having to curl up on the cramped oarbenches of a galley – *Argo*'s own crew remembered all these from the long taxing slog to Soviet Georgia during the Jason Voyage. Just as deft is the description of the sudden squall that destroyed the ship. Where tall mountains run very close to the sea on the Greek coast there is a risk of a sudden violent blasting wind associated with a local weather disturbance. These local squalls are rare, but once experienced they are never forgotten. On the south coast of Crete they can be so shockingly sudden that the wind leaps from a gentle force two up to force eight or nine in less than a minute, and a modern yacht under bare masts has been knocked down by the blast out of an apparently tranquil sky.

The *Odyssey* is describing something similar in Ulysses' tempest, and the effect on a Bronze Age galley would have been catastrophic. Her rigging worn and weak, Ulysses' galley is taken flat aback by the sudden switch in wind direction. The square sail slams the wrong way against the mast so that the forestays which support the mast snap under the sudden pressure. The entire mast then pivots on its foot and comes slicing backwards like a giant mace on the skull of the unfortunate helmsman. The technical details of the calamity are remarkably well-drawn, and so is the behaviour of the stricken vessel. Dismasted, with wind from dead ahead and the helmsman killed, the galley spins round crazily until she comes broadside to the squall and abruptly tips over so that the crew are thrown into the water. Unless they can grab for the ship or hang on to flotsam, they stand little chance in the raging waves. The vessel continues to heel and the gunwale dips under water. The sea rushes in and the craft begins to swamp. Lightly built and made entirely of wood, a galley was almost unsinkable unless she had a very heavy lading. But if she began to break up then the only chance was to seize on to broken flotsam and cling on until washed ashore in whichever direction the wind was blowing.

The direction of the wind tells us where to start looking for Thrinacia, the island of Helios Hyperion, the Sun God. First, the south wind blowing for a month prevented the boat from reaching Ithaca and kept the crew on the island. Thrinacia therefore had to lie north of Ithaca. After the tempest destroyed the vessel a gentle wind, again from the south, blew the shipwrecked Ulysses on his lifesaving raft back into the vortex of Charybdis. Knowing the position of the island of Ithaca on the one hand, and the location of the Levkas channel on the other, we can identify the general whereabouts of Thrinacia. It had to lie on the normal route a Bronze Age galley captain would have followed as he brought his ship out from the southern end of the Levkas channel and steered on the last lap of the journey to Ithaca. It is only a short distance from the channel to Ithaca, just twenty miles by sea, but here again we are dealing with Homeric geography in its local, small-scale perspective and, as the *Odyssey* states, 'it was not long' after passing Scylla that Ulysses heard the lowing of the cattle on Thrinacia. The challenge is to pinpoint the right island from the dozen or so on the route. Some of them are very small, barely half a mile across, others are five or six times the size. One of them was apparently the place where herds of cattle and sheep dedicated to the Sun God were tended by priestesses to Helios Hyperion.

A second, faint, clue to the identity of the island may be its Homeric name – Thrinacia. Scholars have been divided about the meaning of the word. Some see in it a connection with the numeral three, either three-cornered or perhaps three-pronged or maybe even like a *thrinax*, a fish spear. Supporters of a three-cornered island have put forward the suggestion that Thrinacia was the great triangular island of Sicily. But Sicily is so vast by Bronze Age standards – as large as the entire Peloponnese – that its triangular shape is virtually meaningless in Bronze Age geographical terms. Moreover the impression is that when Ulysses walks inland to pray he is on an island of modest size, not a huge land mass. As some of those advocating the claims of Sicily place other adventures like the meeting with the Cyclops on Sicily, it would make it very unlikely that this was also the Island of the Sun God's cattle. Finally the Siculi, apparently the inhabitants of Sicily, are mentioned quite separately by Homer. So we must look elsewhere for Thrinacia.

As an experiment I decided to try out the name Thrinacia on an expert who knew the waters around Levkas, to see if the name made any sense from a seafaring point of view. The reply was revealing.

Gerassimos Robotis was patiently attaching shrimp-bait to the hooks of a long-line which he was coiling in a basket by his side when I first met him. He was sitting beside the deckhouse of his small motor fishing boat which was moored in the muddy backwaters of Levkas lagoon. Through an interpreter, I asked him if he had time to answer some questions about the sea around Levkas. No, he replied matter-of-factly, he was too busy and wanted to get some rest before he went out to the night fishing grounds. As soon as his lines were freshly baited and the boats tidied up, he intended to go home for a meal and a siesta. Could he perhaps find time to meet me in the evening? By all means. At six o'clock in the main square.

When we met there at six o'clock, I had an excellent interpreter to help me, a native of Levkas who was a graduate student in London University studying for a research degree. Over a glass of ouzo Robotis the fisherman was shy and hesitant to begin with, but when told that I was the captain of *Argo* he relaxed and was pleased to have an audience. He had first gone to sea at the age of ten, and for fifty-five years had fished in the Ionian Sea, particularly in the waters around Levkas where he based his boat.

'Have you ever heard of an island called Thrinacie or Thrinacia or some such name?' I asked him.

'No, never.'

'Does the name remind you of any island or place in this area?' He shook his head.

'What about a place connected with the number three, like a three-cornered island or a three-pronged island?' Robotis thought for a moment, obviously trying to work out the point of this strange question.

'Well,' I added, 'can you think of an island which has three of anything which you would use to describe the island? Three hill tops? Three cliffs? Natural features which would be obvious as you sailed by in your boat and which you would use to identify the island when talking to another fisherman and he would know at once the island you meant?'

'Oh, I know the place you mean! You are talking about the three headlands of Meganisi.'

'I've never been to Meganisi,' I said. 'What do you mean, the three headlands?'

'They are on the way south from Levkas, steering outside Sparti towards Ithaca. You see the three head-lands on Meganisi. You can't mistake them, one after another. There are bays between them which make good anchorages. The best is at Point Elia which is a good place to spend the night when you have set your nets and are waiting for the dawn.'

Gerassimos Robotis was not to know that Meganisi is something of an archaeological enigma. Sylvia Benton, an archaeologist working from the British School at Athens on a survey of the Ionian Islands, observed in Meganisi 'several fields covered with the fragments of Late Bronze Age *pithoi* [large jars]', as well as broken pieces of Mycenaean cups. Meganisi, a comparatively insignificant island, had apparently been important in the Late Bronze Age. But why this was so the archaeologists could not explain. I wondered if perhaps Meganisi had been a special place, a sacred island connected with sun worship. In very early Greek myth the cattle of the Sun God are stolen from the island of Erytheia (Red Island) by the giant Alcyoneus. According to early Greek mythology Erytheia lay in the general region of Ambracia, the lake just to the north of Levkas. Mythology was later to transfer the Sun King's Cattle much further west, all the way to Spain. But here we are dealing with Mycenaean myths, created before Greek navigators had reached the Iberian peninsula. Could Thrinacia and the original Erytheia both be the Island of Meganisi?

I went to Meganisi to check Robotis' description of the island and in particular of the last headland, the one which Robotis said was the best anchorage. It is now called Cape Elia, nominally in honour of St Elias or Elijah. But some scholars, among them Patrick Leigh Fermor, have pointed out that numerous places in Greece now named after Elias would previously have been sites dedicated to Helios the Sun God. Elias was the natural Christian successor to Helios the Sun God because the names were virtually interchangeable. Also it is striking how St Elias is associated with the same kind of site – mountain peaks and places like capes and headlands which in pagan times were the sacred places of sun worship. To support this theory Leigh Fermor pointed out how in Greece, where the sun god was known as Helios, there are a great many St Elias sites. By contrast in Italy where the sun god was known as Apollo there are comparatively few places named Elias. Was it possible, then, that Elia Point had once been a cape sacred to Helios Hyperion the Sun God?

I climbed the hill beside the island's main settlement of Vathy and looked towards the channel down which the Bronze Age ships would have approached from

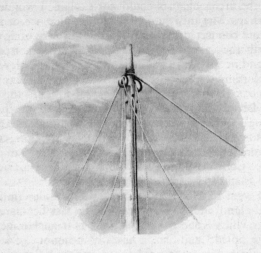

Levkas. From the summit I could see the peculiar shape
of Meganisi. A long, rocky and uninhabitable ridge like
a long thin rat tail makes up more than half the length
of the island. This tail widens to a blunt centrebody
which then terminates on its north-east shore in a series
of finger-like peninsulas, separated by the three deep
bays. The last three headlands were the ones Robotis
had said stood out and were readily identified as
seamarks. From where I was, looking out from the spot
where the Bronze Age inhabitants would have judged
it, it was difficult to tell that the long tail of Meganisi
is set askew to the main body. Instead it looks like the
'handle' of the island, and the points of the headlands
with the bays between them appear like the prongs of
a fish-spear thrusting at the gullet that leads to the
Levkas channel. In short, Meganisi could be imagined
as *thrinax*, the fish spear.

The loss of Ulysses' last galley brought *Argo*'s unique
method of investigation to a natural conclusion. Because

Cattle of the Sun King

Ulysses never again sailed aboard a galley of a normal type after the catastrophe near Thrinacia, we could no longer use our galley in our experiment to follow the likely track of our Bronze Age navigator, comparing his experiences against our own. So at the end of August we laid up *Argo* in her winter quarters, hauled out on the bank of the new Levkas ship canal. She had served as well and carried us without mishap along the 'logical route' and all its discoveries. From now forwards Ulysses' track was not to be based on logic because he would have little control over his movements as he drifts helplessly on a raft, sails a homemade one-man boat, and finally comes home fast asleep aboard a magic fifty-oared galley that did not need a human intelligence at the helm. As we try to follow him on the last lap of the Great Wanderings, he becomes increasingly elusive until he reappears in his island home of Ithaca where we can place him with certainty.

13
Calypso, Alcinous and Ithaca

At last encounter our heroic traveller was left hanging
like a bat in the branches of the fig tree which overhung
the whirlpool of Charybdis.

☐ I could find no foothold to support me, nor any
means of climbing into the tree, for its roots were
far away below, and the great long branches that
overshadowed Charybdis stretched high above my
head. However, I stuck grimly on until such time as
she should spew me up my mast and keel once more.
My hope was justified . . . at last the timbers reappeared on the surface of the pool. I flung my arms
and legs down for a plunge, and with a splash fell in
the water clear of the great logs, which I then bestrode
and rowed along with my hands. And thanks to the
Father of men and gods I was spared another sight
of Scylla. Otherwise nothing could have saved me
from certain death. Nine days of drifting followed;
but in the night of the tenth the gods washed me up
on the Isle of Ogygia, the home of fair Calypso. ☐

Ogygia means 'the ancient place' and there is a very
strong flavour of fantasy about it. It was extremely
remote, 'a lonely island far away in the middle of the
seas', and there Calypso lived in a fairytale cave,

☐ sheltered by a verdant copse of alders, aspens and
fragrant cypresses, which was the roosting place of
feathered creatures, horned owls and falcons and

garrulous choughs, birds of the coast whose daily business takes them down to the sea. Trailing round the very mouth of the cavern, a garden vine ran riot, with great bunches of ripe grapes; while from four separate but neighbouring springs four crystal rivulets were trained to run this way and that; and in soft meadows on either side the iris and the parsley flourished. It was indeed a spot where even an immortal visitor must pause and gaze in wonder and delight. □

In this dreamlike setting Calypso sheltered Ulysses and indeed her name is also a metaphor, for it means 'the sheltering one' or 'the hider'. Here the *Odyssey* consigns Ulysses to a seven-year-long limbo. We are not told what he did or how he passed his time except that he shared the bed of Calypso and gradually became more and more homesick. He sat on the rocks beside the seashore 'with sighs and tears and heartache, and looking out across the barren sea with streaming eyes'.

Finally, with the encouragement of the gods on Olympus, Calypso took pity on Ulysses and provided him with tools and instructions how to make a small boat. At once the *Odyssey* comes alive and explicit as it spells out the boatbuilding details, just as it did when describing life aboard ship during the earlier voyaging. Ulysses may be in a never-never land, but the compiler of the *Odyssey* cannot resist showing off his knowledge of ancient boatcraft. Given a good double-edged bronze axe on an olive wood handle, Ulysses felled twenty tall trees which were dead at their roots and had seasoned into dry light timber suitable for boatbuilding. He marked out and trimmed the wood true and straight with chalk line and adze to make the timbers for his vessel. With an auger he bored holes so that he could peg the timbers together and then added extra lashings to strengthen the joints. To the flat bottom he fixed vertical side planks and topped them off with wattles of osier to increase the freeboard above the sea just as some small cargo boats still increase their freeboard with canvas strips to fend off the wave tops. He made a mast, fitted a steering oar, and with sailcloth provided by Calypso stitched a sail. Then he 'lashed the braces, halyards and sheets in their places on board' and finally, using rollers, he worked his makeshift vessel down the beach and launched her. The entire description is realistic, functional and matter-of-fact, a complete contrast to the vague and insubstantial treatment of Ogygia. The only magic in the boatbuilding is that the vessel is built in just four days.

Calypso, so the story runs, gave him two skin bottles, one of wine and the other of water, as well as a sack of corn and 'appetising meats' to supply him on his single-handed voyage. Also, being a goddess, she arranged for a fair following wind to waft him on his way. For seventeen days and nights he sat at the steering oar,

☐ and never closed his eyes in sleep, but kept them on the Pleiades, or watched Bootes slowly set, or the Great Bear nicknamed the Wain, which always wheels round in the same place, and looks across at Orion the Hunter with a wary eye. It was this constellation, the only one which never bathes in Ocean's Stream that the wise goddess Calypso had told him to keep on his left hand as he made across the sea. ☐

Here, for the first and only time in the *Odyssey*, we have a reasonably precise sailing direction based on the stars, and this is something curious enough to arouse our suspicions. Suddenly we are presented with astro-navigational technique when until now the directions of the voyage have been left vague, implied by wind directions or marked by physical features like headlands, just as one would expect with Mycenaean navigation. This star-derived course jars with all the rest of the *Odyssey*'s navigation passages. The list of constellations – Orion, Bootes, the Great Bear, and the Pleiades – have a much later ring, perhaps from Homer's time in the eighth or seventh century BC. Indeed the entire journey from Calypso's island sits uneasily with the rest of the Great Wanderings. Here is a trip in a small, hastily constructed boat designed merely to free Ulysses from mysterious Ogygia, and yet its seventeen-day voyage is by far the longest sector Ulysses ever travels. It exceeds all the other sectors, either when he is with the complete Ithacan squadron or when he is aboard the single galley. Their journey times were left vague or were divided into short practicable stages. Yet here, going from Calypso's mystical island towards his home, Ulysses on his own spends twice as long at sea. It is an open-sea passage, and this again contrasts with the coasting habits of the Mycenaean galleys. After reaching Calypso's mystical island by the near-impossible feat of hanging on to the broken keel and mast for nine days, he then leaves it by a voyage that is either impracticable or imaginary or both. The entire passage has the ring of a later addition to the story.

The suspicion deepens when we try to work out the star directions and how far Ulysses would have travelled in seventeen days. A sailor in the Mediterranean who keeps the Great Bear – the only constellation 'which never bathed in Ocean's Stream', i.e. never went below the horizon – on his left hand and heads towards the constellations of the Pleiades or setting Bootes, is sailing east-north-east. Given a seventeen-day passage in a small boat at forty miles a day he would have come

680 miles, a very modest distance bearing in mind that there were no overnight halts on beaches. But there is immediately something very wrong. In the Mediterranean it is virtually impossible to sail east-north-east for more than 400 miles without running into land. There is just not enough open sea. Decrease Ulysses' average speed to a near-drift, say twenty miles a day, and the 350-mile voyage can *just* be fitted into a sensible range, though this means ignoring the claim that Calypso gave her departing guest a fair wind for the entire seventeen days. On the basis of this spectacularly slow pace the island of Gozo, 350 miles south-west of Ithaca, has traditionally been identified as Calypso's home.

Gozo offers nothing to support such identification. 'Calypso's Cave' is still pointed out on the north-west coast of Gozo and overlooks a pleasant beach of reddish sand. But the 'cave' is now so tumbled down by erosion that only a shallow overhang remains, and there is no archaeological discovery or local folktale to sustain the theory. Apollonius Rhodius, who wrote down the story of Jason and the Argonauts, believed that Calypso's home (which he called Nymphaea) lay somewhere in the southern approaches of the Adriatic Sea, and there is a chance that he might be correct. He said that as Jason and his men sailed south along what is now the coast of Albania they passed 'out on the horizon, Nymphaea the home of the powerful Calypso'. Although Apollonius was writing much later than Homer, he may have had access to an earlier, less corrupt version of the legend. An Ogygia in the entrance to the Adriatic (the Albanian island of Saseno has been proposed) would fit in with the other identifications of the *Odyssey* which cluster around north-western Greece. But in the final analysis the magical island of Ogygia 'the ancient place' remains insubstantial. We are given only stylized topography and scenery, and the details of Ulysses' arrival and departure, the time and direction of his journey, do not stand up to any practical test. Calypso's idyllic island does not find its place in a real world.

The same sense of the fabulous tinges Ulysses' next and penultimate landfall, with the added frustration that we are presented with enough physical details to make us think that we should be able to identify the place. On the eighteenth day of his singlehanded voyage from Ogygia Ulysses saw a distant land that 'looked like a shield laid on the misty sea'. He steered towards it but was observed by his implacable enemy the sea god Poseidon, who made one last attempt to destroy the wanderer. Stirring up the waves with his trident, Poseidon unleashed a tremendous storm. Cloud covered the sky, the wind blew from every direction, and a great squall from the north raced down on the makeshift craft. A massive wave twisted the boat round, tearing the steering oar from Ulysses' hands and flinging him into the water. A gust of wind snapped the mast and blew the cross-yard and sail overboard. After a long time underwater, Ulysses spluttered to the surface and managed to scramble back on to the boat. There he clung on while the waves tossed the little skiff this way and that. Next, says the *Odyssey*, a sea nymph appeared rising from the waves 'like a sea mew on the wing', and settled on the boat. She offered Ulysses her veil which she said would protect him if he wrapped it around himself and swam for shore. Then she plunged back into the water.

Ulysses was debating whether to follow her advice and risk swimming for land when the matter was decided for him. Poseidon sent a huge wave which overwhelmed the boat, scattering its timbers 'as a boisterous wind will tumble a parched heap of chaff' and Ulysses once again found himself riding on a piece of driftwood. Wrapping the sea nymph's veil around his waist, he dived into the sea and struck out. For a superhuman two days and nights he swam. Luckily Poseidon had lost interest in his fate and the goddess Athena, who favoured Ulysses' cause, smoothed the seas with a north wind and this enabled Ulysses to get to land. But a tremendous swell was still running, and it beat upon a rocky shore. When Ulysses tried to land, he was sluiced off by the backwash, leaving pieces of skin from his hands sticking to the rough rock surface. He decided it was wiser to swim along the shore to find a safer spot, and eventually came to a place where a stream entered the sea. Feeling its current he realized it was his best hope and at his request the stream checked its course so that he managed to swim to the beach. There he dropped the sea nymph's veil into the stream which washed it back out to sea to its owner, and Ulysses himself staggered naked to the shelter of some bushes where he collapsed and fell asleep.

He awoke to a female shriek, and peering out from the bushes saw a group of young women playing with a ball on the beach at the mouth of the stream. Laundry they had washed in the stream's pools was laid out in the sun and they were amusing themselves while waiting for it to dry. Breaking off a leafy branch to cover his nakedness, Ulysses emerged from the bushes and asked for their help. After their initial alarm the group of girls, led by Nausicaa, daughter of the local king, took Ulysses to their town, travelling with their cart full of clean laundry. Nausicaa wanted Ulysses to meet her father, King Alcinous, but did not wish to be seen entering the town with a strange man. So when the group reached the outskirts of the town, the maidens went forward, leaving Ulysses to wait in a grove of poplar trees until he could enter by himself and find his way to the palace. 'Our city,' Nausicaa told him,

> □ is surrounded by high battlements; it has an excellent harbour on each side and is approached by a narrow causeway where the curved ships are drawn up to the road and each owner has his separate slip. Here is the people's meeting place, built up on either side of the fine temple of Poseidon with blocks of quarried stone bedded deeply in the ground. It is here too that the sailors attend to the rigging of the black ships, to their cables and their sails, and the smoothing of their oars. For the Phaeacians have no use for the bow and quiver, but spend their energy on masts and oars and on the graceful craft they love to sail across the foam-flecked sea. □

Here, at first sight, we have all the clues needed to identify the city of King Alcinous, more details than for any other spot since Ulysses and his luckless squadron were driven off-course at Cape Malea. The kingdom of Alcinous was well wooded, on a land whose profile was 'like a shield laid upon the misty sea', with a rocky coast where a stream entered the sea at a sheltered spot with washing pools for laundry. A long ride away by mule cart was the main town with its double port, a central causeway with the ships drawn up, a meeting square, and a fine palace for the king. In theory, Phaeacia should be easy to locate.

Indeed since classical times the inhabitants of Corfu Island have firmly claimed that they were descended from the Phaeacians. Drawn by this long-established claim Heinrich Schliemann paid a lightning visit to Corfu in 1868 to find Alcinous' palace for himself. This was before he went to Troy, and Schliemann was in the first flush of his Homeric enthusiasm, so although he visited the place for barely forty-eight hours he had no difficulty in locating Ulysses' adventures on Corfu in detail. The peninsula south of the modern town of Corfu he declared was the site of Alcinous' palace. As they were master-seamen the Phaeacians were clearly descended from the Phoenicians. His main coup was to identify the actual beach where Ulysses met Nausicaa. Dashing off his steamer and hastening around the capital and the immediate area, Schliemann hired a guide to take him to the nearest stream. This was simply the only stream close enough for Schliemann to visit on his brief stay. Halfway through the promenade, when the guide baulked at wading across some muddy irrigation channels, Schliemann stripped off and plunged on his way alone. Splashing across the fields only in his shirt, he spotted two large stones fifty yards from the stream mouth. They were, he claimed, the very rocks on which Nausicaa and her companions had done their laundry. 'There can be no doubt that this stream is the same as the Homeric stream,' he wrote, 'as this is the only stream near the ancient town.'

Fifty years later a Frenchman, Victor Berard, after spending years sifting through all the evidence of the *Odyssey*, came to the conclusion that the traditional identifications of the *Odyssey* – the Straits of Messina as Scylla and Charybdis and so forth – were correct and that Corfu was indeed Phaeacia as the ancients had claimed. Berard announced that he too had certainly found the site of Alcinous' palace, but on the opposite side of Corfu. Berard had done his homework very thoroughly, and at Paleocastritsa on the west shore of Corfu he pointed to a remarkable formation of two peninsulas, which sheltered not two but three harbours, ideally suited for galleys. Here was a sandy central spit for galleys to be drawn up, and a pair of soaring headlands, each of which looked perfect for the royal palace.

The washing pools for Nausicaa's laundry which the *Odyssey* said were 'far from the palace' Berard located five miles down the coast at the entrance of a small stream that entered the bay at a place called Ermones.

Paleocastritsa seemed so suitable as the site of Alcinous' palace that Wilhelm Dorpfeld, again on the track of yet another Homeric site, searched the headlands for traces of a royal building. But neither he, nor a later investigation by a German archaeological team, found any traces of the legendary ruler's magnificent home there. So either Alcinous' palace existed elsewhere on Corfu or it was as much fairyland as Calypso's island of Ogygia. It is suspicious that, just as Calypso's name was symbolic, so too are the names of the Phaeacians. Ulysses met men by the names of Coxswain, Swiftsea, Seabord, Launcher, Shiprich, Pilot, Sailor, Boatchampion and so forth, almost the maritime equivalents of the knights of King Arthur's round table. Alcinous' realm itself has a Camelot quality. This ideal king is almost too good to be true. Unlike the real King Nestor, who is garrulous and talks of real events, King Alcinous is faultless. He lives in peace and tranquillity far away from the intrusions of men. His ships range far and wide and could find their way across the sea without the help of steersmen. His palace is more magnificent and luxurious than any that have been described elsewhere. Its doors are of gold turning on silver pillars, a band of blue enamel tops the outer wall, and gold and silver dogs guard the entrance. Alcinous and his wife embody all the kingly virtues: they are just and reasonable, peaceable and courteous, generous and caring. They entertain Ulysses lavishly, never asking the castaway who or what he might be until Ulysses himself chooses to recount to them the full story of his wanderings since the day he left Troy. It is in his tale to Alcinous that we learn of the Lotus-eaters, the Cyclops, the fierce

Laestrygonians, and the rest of Ulysses' adventures on his travels.

When his guest was rested and refreshed, the kindly Alcinous arranged for one of the special fifty-oared Phaeacian ships to carry the hero home. He gave the castaway splendid treasures: gifts of gold and silver and thirteen bronze tripods which represented great prestige. Ulysses fell asleep almost as soon as he was aboard, and so he did not witness how the swift black ship brought him at a magical pace to his own island of Ithaca, skimming along so fast that she drove half a keel's length up the beach with her speed. There, at the cove named after Phorcys, the Old Man of the Sea, the Phaeacian sailors carried the still-sleeping Ulysses on to the beach, unloaded his presents and stacked them against the trunk of an olive tree. Then the magical ship silently withdrew, leaving Ulysses to face his home-coming.

Argo was no magic ship, so we could not emulate the Phaeacians. Nor when we came to Ithaca did I feel that we were equipped to improve on the attempts which historians, archaeologists and Homeric scholars had made for more than 2,000 years to pin down Ulysses' adventures in his homeland. I did feel, however, that the degree to which these experts succeeded might provide a last backward look on our own, seaborne research, because the story of Ulysses on Ithaca shows how geography can both confirm and blur the *Odyssey*'s picture of Ulysses' own realm, a last conundrum within a small island no more than twelve miles long and just over three miles wide.

'I confess that despite my fatigue and hunger I felt an immense joy at finding myself in the land of heroes whose adventures I had read and re-read a hundred times with the most lively enthusiasm.' So enthused Heinrich Schliemann describing the moment he first stepped ashore on Ithaca on the evening of 9 July 1868. He was, as always, in a headlong rush. He had left Corfu and his researches into Nausicaa's washplace and Alcinous' palace barely forty-eight hours earlier. Met on the landing place by the local miller, he hired an ass for four francs to carry his bags across to the capital at Vathy. While he walked he bombarded his companion with a rapid fire of questions about the *Odyssey* and Ithaca. Was this really the mountain peak where Ulysses' palace had stood? Where was the farm to which Laertes, Ulysses' father, had retired? Could this be the harbour of Phorcys where the Phaeacians had left the sleeping traveller on the beach? In which direction lay the Cave of the Nymphs where Ulysses had hidden the treasure given to him by King Alcinous? To Schliemann's chagrin he could get no useful information out of his guide, only a tedious repetition of the plot of the *Odyssey*. 'The road was long,' Schliemann noted wryly, 'but the miller's story was long too.'

Schliemann did not come to Ithaca expecting to make any major discoveries. There was, in his opinion, little to find. Ithaca had been thoroughly ransacked for Ulysses' relics. Troy might have vanished to the point that its very existence was doubted, but Ithaca had always been on the map and the favourite hunting ground for touring savants and classicists. They had discussed and dissected every possible location of Ulysses' adventures which were now dotted all over the landscape. The experts did not always come away from Ithaca with exactly the same opinions, but a broad consensus about the major sites had emerged. The best that Schliemann hoped for was to confirm the Homeric geography of Ithaca with a bit of casual digging.

According to most visitors, a locality in the south of the island near a place called Raven's Cliff was where Ulysses – after hiding his treasure – went to find his loyal swineherd Eumaeus. Here, also, he was said to have plotted the destruction of the 108 suitors who were laying siege to his patient wife, Penelope. There was some disagreement about precisely which was the Bay of Phorcys where he had been landed, whether it was the main harbour of Ithaca at Vathy or the smaller bay of Dexia just beside it. But by and large the salient features of Ithaca appeared to fit the places that Homer had described. A stalactite-hung cave seemed very suitable as the 'Cave of the Nymphs' where Ulysses hid his treasure, and most authorities believed that Ulysses' home had occupied the saddle of Ithaca's isthmus, a strategic ridge of land where the two halves of the island join in a wasp waist. Any chieftain who fortified this ridge controlled land communications between the two halves of the island and would be the effective overlord of Ithaca. There were ancient ruins on the ridge, which the locals called 'Ulysses' Castle', and the morning after his arrival Schliemann was already up there, prospecting for Homeric remains. He noted a Cyclopean wall and in his fertile imagination saw Ulysses' palace extending up the hillside in a splendid multi-storeyed edifice. He had brought no tools with him so he could only daydream, muse over the relevant passage of the *Odyssey*, admire the breathtaking view across the Ionian Islands, and hurry back to Vathy in time to make his arrangements for a dawn attack.

Daybreak on his second full day on the island saw him once again hastening up the steep climb to the ridge. This time he was mounted on horseback and leading a small caravan of four Greek workmen, a donkey laden with tools, and a boy and a girl whom he had hired to fetch water and wine for the digging gang. By 7 a.m. they were on the site and hard at work. Schliemann set the men to pulling up the brushwood at the north-east corner of the ancient ruins. With endearing and literal-minded optimism he calculated that this was the spot where Ulysses had his bedroom. The *Odyssey* claimed that Ulysses used the trunk of a living olive tree as a bedpost so Schliemann confidently hoped to uncover the olive tree itself. His extraordinary naïvety was soon disappointed. The workmen found nothing but a debris of old tiles and pottery and then hit bedrock. Scratching around with a knife, Schliemann exposed some building foundations but it was obvious that they were much more recent than the Bronze Age. Then his knife blade uncovered a small jar, and he took a pickaxe to try to free it. The jar was broken in the attempt, but Schliemann claimed he recognized its contents as human ashes. More jars turned up, twenty in all. Schliemann broke all but five in trying to get them out of the ground, but was unrepentant. This was what he had come to find. Reverently he identified his discovery as probably the last remains of Ulysses and Penelope or the ashes of their descendants.

Not surprisingly, subsequent archaeological research on Ithaca made mincemeat of Schliemann's headlong and ingenuous research at 'Ulysses' Castle'. His site was dismissed as being later in date than Ulysses' era, and over the next eighty years a long campaign of excavations at various points around Ithaca led most professional archaeologists to identify Ulysses' home at a spot called Pelikata in the north of the island where the battered remains of a small Mycenaean manor house were located. Greeks, Germans, Britons, Americans, team after team tramped over Ithaca, dug, analysed and produced their theories about Homer's geography. Even when *Argo* was setting out from Troy to conduct her own investigations into the Great Wanderings, the most recent archaeological investigation of Ithaca was in the field. An American–Greek team from St Louis, Missouri, and Athens came to re-examine the evidence.

Map 7 Ithaca

After J.V. Luce
Homer and The Heroic Age

Ironically, they were returning to dig again at Schliemann's old site on the ridge in the belief that this might
after all turn out to be the 'real' home of Ulysses. A
new controversy was beginning.

The truth is that Ithaca presents all the problems and
illusions of the *Odyssey*'s geography in miniature –
contradictions, anachronisms, double clues, deceptions.
Some of the places that Homer described do seem to
find an exact fit. A few ravens still flap and caw around
the ledges of Korax, the 'Raven's Crag', at the south
end of the island where the swineherd Eumaeus had his
hut. There too is Arethusa's Spring where Eumaeus is
said to have watered his swine, though in summer time
the spring is virtually dry. The stalactite-hung grotto at

Marmarospilia, which Schliemann examined by the light of a brushwood fire, is still an excellent candidate for the 'Cave of the Nymphs' where Ulysses hid his Phaeacian treasure for safekeeping. The cave was said to have two entrances, one for humans and one farther south for the gods. The human entrance is a cleft in the rocks, just wide enough to squeeze through, and the gods' entrance is a round hole in the roof. The strange shapes of the stalactites hanging from the cave ceiling and dripping down its walls would account for the idea that in the cave the nymphs wove draperies and hangings of purple. Sherds of pottery show that the cave was used for the worship of the nymphs in later, classical times.

But doubts soon rear up. A century ago a quite different cave was reported right next to the cove at Dexia where Ulysses is said to have been landed by the Phaeacians. This cave would have been a much more convenient place to hide the treasure which included the thirteen unwieldy tripods. This cave was said also to have had a double entrance and niches in a rock that looked like the nymphs' basins. Unfortunately no one can now check on this cave because it was destroyed when the townsfolk of Vathy used it as a quarry for building stone. Even more confusing was a report that a local landowner and an amateur archaeologist had found a bronze tripod just like the ones that Ulysses was supposed to have brought back from Phaeacia. But the find was made at the opposite end of the island, at least four hours' walk away from the cave of the stalactites or the quarried-out cave, but close to the Mycenaean manor house at Pelikata. A British team went to the spot and conducted a fully-fledged excavation. They identified a collapsed cave on the edge of the shore, brought in pumps to suck out the seepage, and were rewarded with the squashed remains of twelve more tripods of almost pure copper, making with the original tripod discovered earlier the correct total for Ulysses' property. Here too was ample pottery evidence of the worship of the nymphs. Dramatically a tiny sherd of clay showed up, scratched with Ulysses' name. If the cave had been located in the right spot, say near Dexia Cove, there would have been universal agreement that this was the true Cave of the Nymphs. But on examination the tripods turned out to be from the ninth and eighth centuries BC, later in date than the Trojan War, and the sherd was more recent still, from the second or first century BC. Nevertheless whoever left the tripods in a cave, or his successor who scratched a dedication to Ulysses, clearly believed that this northern cave was the Cave of the Nymphs.

The riddle of the three possible 'nymph caves' at least can be solved with an easily credible answer: Ulysses' original Cave of the Nymphs was the stalactite cave at Marmarospilia, but when Homer compiled his version of the *Odyssey* he added details of the collapsed Cave of the Tripods which he had heard about. The vanished cave of Dexia was probably a red herring. Here was a fact, embellished with mistaken poetic detail, and finally hidden behind rumour. Other puzzles of the *Odyssey*'s description of Ithaca are far more stubborn. To resolve them, scholars for two millennia have conjured up arcane explanations, fought sharp quarrels, and many still confess to being baffled.

The most notorious case is the small island Homer called Asteris. He said it lay midway in the channel between Ithaca and the neighbouring island of Same. Here a murderous detachment of Penelope's suitors laid an unsuccessful ambush to kill Ulysses' son Telemachus on his return from visiting King Nestor. The island is described as being rocky and having two harbours, and the suitors kept a lookout from its 'windy heights'. Only one island is found in the long narrow channel between Ithaca and the neighbouring island of Cephallonia which most scholars take to be ancient Same. Unfortunately this little island, called Daskalio, has not got a single harbour, is barely six feet above water level, and would make a singularly useless observation post. By no stretch of the imagination could it be described as having the 'windy heights' on which the suitors posted their lookouts. The suitors would have found it difficult to moor their boats on this barren reef, let alone mount a watchful guard there.

Ample ingenuity has gone into trying to explain away the problem. The first suggestion was that the real Asteris had disappeared as the result of an earthquake, vanishing like a miniature Atlantis beneath the waves. Later this idea was adapted to the belief that the island of Asteris had been planed down by erosion and submerged by land movement or a combination of both. When this solution too was rejected by geomorphologists, Homer's original text was retranslated to make the circumstances fit better. Homer, it was said, did not write that the suitors set up guard *on* the island but *opposite* the island. Reading the lines a different way it could be said that their watchpost was on Cephallonia close to Daskalio where indeed there is a double harbour and plenty of convenient peaks to serve as observation posts.

Wilhelm Dorpfeld's notorious solution – that Ulysses' Ithaca was really Levkas – disposed of the problem in the grand manner by locating the ambush site on the totally different island of Arkudi. Dorpfeld's key argument was that the *Odyssey*'s Ithaca was said to be in a group of four islands among which it lay 'uppermost of all towards the Darkness, while the others face the Dawn and the sun'. Most authorities translated this as meaning that Homer thought of Ithaca as being the

Raven's Crag

most northerly or north-westerly island of the group –
which it is not – and that he had merely got his
geography mixed up and was not aware of the true
relationship of the four islands. Dorpfeld, on the other
hand, believed that Homer had got his compass points
right, and that Levkas which fits the description more
nearly had to be Homer's Ithaca. It all came down to a
question of the weight of the evidence. Was the detailed
evidence on Ithaca – the Raven's Crag, the Nymph
Cave, Dexia Bay and so forth – more convincingly
found on modern Ithaca than at Dorpfeld's locations
on modern Levkas? If so, did that mean one could

disregard the fact that Ithaca was not the northernmost island of the group? Over the years – and Dorpfeld did not die until 1930 – the archaeological record seemed more and more to confirm that today's Ithaca was Homer's Ithaca. Recently a distinguished Homeric expert, Professor J. V. Luce, who carefully walked the entire terrain of Ithaca, observed that Homer's words can make sense if they are interpreted from the point of view of the 'palace' site on the northern end of Ithaca. Here Ithaca does seem 'furthest out' towards the north-west, with only open sea lying in the direction of the setting sun. Professor Luce contends that Homer only introduced topographical details into the *Odyssey* when they were necessary to the unfolding of his plot, and that, in the main, Homer's geography was sound.

14

The Greek Odyssey

If Homer's local topography of Ithaca is understandable to an observer who carefully walks the ground with the *Odyssey* in hand, had we found the same degree of accuracy in his sea-going geography now that we had sailed *Argo* home from Troy by the 'logical route'? And if we had, why had the *Odyssey* been a geographical conundrum for so long? The answers lie partly in the origins of Homer's tale and partly in the treatment that it received at the hands of one man who, it might be said, was the chief culprit. He started a hare that has been chased in circles ever since, without being caught.

The purpose of the *Odyssey* was to entertain audiences with intriguing tales about the famed hero's homeward voyage from the distant foreign war. The bards who composed the original strands of the tale, and Homer who wove them together, did not think in cartographical terms, and may not even have had maps. Even if they had, they would have found them inappropriate to the composition of an epic voyage. Their aim was to give a notion of travelling, of going from one strange place to the next, without necessarily plotting the landfalls on a chart. But did they follow a logical sequence? Victor Berard, the French savant who found Nausicaa's laundry and Alcinous' palace on the west coast of Corfu, postulated that Homer had somehow got hold of a Phoenician pilot book and strung together his landfalls based on the trade routes of the Phoenicians. Such a convenient reference work (for which there is not the slightest evidence) is unnecessary. Modern archaeological research has shown that Mycenaean traded goods reached as far afield as Sardinia and that a major trade artery ran from Crete up the west side of the Peloponnese and to the heel of Italy. There was no need for Phoenician knowledge to be involved at all if the Mycenaeans were trading on their own account and bringing back their own stories.

The *Odyssey* is a seafaring story composed by men who certainly knew something of galley sailing. Time and again it betrays knowledge of the sea, of voyages, of boats. The bards would have obtained their material from the oral tradition of one or more voyages, from report of real events, from sailors' yarns, and from the resources of their own imaginations working on the subtle mixture of history and folklore related to the sea. This must be the starting point when we address ourselves to the mystery of where Ulysses is supposed to be going as he wanders from one strange location to the next. Anything else is a quicksand as we have seen with the difficulties of sorting out the locations of Ithaca or Levkas where it is possible to invoke mistakes in translation, transfer of place names from one spot to another, earthquakes, vanished caves, and a whole host of variables. Aboard *Argo* we applied the single fundamental test that the *Odyssey* was a sailor's story and if it contained any truth it should be capable of being investigated by practical experiment. After three months at sea with the replica of a Bronze Age galley following the 'logical route' we had come up with a unique series of identifications, sometimes where we had least expected them.

The first fact we could confirm was that the *Odyssey* is demonstrably true to the realities of sailing and rowing a galley in the Mediterranean. The seagoing authenticity of the tale corroborates the hard-learned lessons and limitations of Late Bronze Age navigation as we had shared it. The *Odyssey* is about a coasting voyage from headland to headland, landfall to landfall with relatively short stages in between. How else could large crews in open boats proceed except by coming ashore frequently to replenish water and to try to find food and rest? This cannot be the story of some far-off journey, as some have suggested, to the Outer Hebrides, Scandinavia or even Canada's Bay of Fundy.

It must be remembered that for half the journey Ulysses was not travelling alone, but in company with a squadron of eleven other vessels, all heavily laden with booty, all well-worn by a long voyage and an alleged ten-year campaign. Such a squadron had to proceed at the pace of the slowest vessel, halt at rendezvous after rendezvous to regroup, allow the slowest to catch up with the leaders. They travelled slowly, grudgingly and cautiously.

Nor should we overlook the constraints of a galley's seagoing performance. On *Argo* we found it impossible to row against a headwind, and very hard work to make any significant progress in a calm. Ulysses' sailors repeatedly show themselves to be reluctant travellers and they would certainly have preferred to sail than to row, waiting for a favourable wind rather than slogging through a calm unless obliged to do so, and they would never have risked any lee shore when there was a chance of a foul wind. All this adds up to a cautious, stage-by-stage voyage waiting at each stop-over for the weather to favour the next sector. This was how a wise commander proceeded, and all the evidence points to the fact that Ulysses was cautious except when curiosity or brief outbursts of bravado got the better of him.

So we need not look far afield for the sites of the *Odyssey*'s landfalls even when they seem as exotic as the homes of Lotus-eaters, one-eyed giants or death-dealing Laestrygonians. If the *Odyssey* is a sailor's story, then such places ought to be within the normal sailor's horizon of a return voyage from Troy to Ithaca by the logical coasting route. Mycenaean vessels were capable of venturing into the western Mediterranean on long-distance voyages, but these were *trading* vessels proceeding almost certainly under sail. Long-distance voyages were not made in heavily crewed war galleys any more than the famed Viking voyages across the North Atlantic were made by longships rather than seaworthy merchantmen. The Mycenaean war galleys, like the Viking longships, could cross stretches of open water when they had to, but prudent captains preferred to wait for favourable weather, just as Menelaus and Nestor delayed at the island of Chios for the right conditions to cut across the Aegean Sea towards the coast of Greece. Given this pattern of coasting, waiting at key points for the right wind and sea state and then making a dash for the next good shelter, we have the rhythm and framework for Ulysses' homeward voyage.

Within this framework we directed *Argo*'s course for the space of the single Mediterranean season's sailing. This is all the sailing time the *Odyssey* allows. Ulysses' notorious nineteen-year absence evaporates under scrutiny to a few weeks at sea, and many years at war or with agreeable hostesses. We proved that a few weeks, a sailing season from June to August or September, was ample time for the homeward voyage even if Ulysses' squadron strayed down to the coast of North Africa.

So it was that, out of our own experience, a remarkable consistency emerged. We could fix the stories in the *Odyssey* in two ways: by reference to turning points and memorable physical features on the coasting route – such headlands and islands as would have been of navigational significance to a Bronze Age sailor – or by association with a particular local folktale. More often than not, both seamark and folktale coincided.

Setting out, therefore, from the great bay at Troy, Ulysses' squadron of twelve ships struck off on their own. They abandoned the main fleet to their direct homeward voyage, and chose the logical and safe alternative coasting route around the northern Aegean looking for plunder among Troy's weak and defeated allies. Their victims were to be the Cicones of Ismarus.

After the Ciconian raid the squadron swung south and took the much-travelled sea highway via the northern Sporades that led to the Doro channel. There it joined the same track that took Nestor and Menelaus past Cape Sounion and on to Cape Malea. Nestor with his large fleet rounded Cape Malea without accident, but both Ulysses and Menelaus in turn were blown away southward, probably by the *meltemi*, the seasonal north wind, that was too strong for the unwieldy squadrons. Several of Menelaus' vessels were wrecked on Crete by the gale. Ulysses' squadron was luckier. The north wind carried it clear of the dangers of Crete, and it followed the standard tactics of galleys in heavy weather. The ships reduced sail to a minimum and kept together like a flock of gulls resting on the water as they drifted southward. They were forced down to the coast of North Africa, most probably in Cyrenaica which has the high range of the Jebel Akhdar standing as a beacon to guide the castaway ships to land. Here they replenished their badly depleted water supplies and rested. Their scouts, exploring inland, came across primitive African tribes whose use of seedra fruit from the jujube gave rise to stories of the Lotus-eaters.

Anxious to return to their homeward track and with neither motive nor time to go exploring unknown lands, the galleys reversed their drift course and headed back along the same track that the northerly winds had brought them. By design or accident they made the shortest sea crossing from Africa to the Greek world, from Cyrenaica to Crete, where their first landfall was on an offshore islet populated by gri-gri, the wild goats of Crete, which firmly locate their position for us. The famished sailors hunted for fresh food and feasted while Ulysses and a single ship went off to visit the mainland. This area of south Crete was already known to the Mycenaeans and possibly a report of the abandoned towns and fields of the Late Minoan settlements, now shown by archaeologists to have been recently deserted at that time, gave rise to the notion that the Cyclopes people did not have to till the land but lived off naturally growing crops. More important, this was the legendary home of the *triamates*, the three-eyed, cave-dwelling, man-eating ogres. Their reputation for being giants was very likely to have been founded on discoveries of the fossil bones of large extinct mammals, such as elephants and hippopotami, which have been exhumed in Cretan caves. The folklore story of the *triamates* coloured the *Odyssey*'s version of Ulysses' encounter with the primitive shepherd folk living in caves along the limestone south coast.

Proceeding on their way home the squadron rounded the south-west corner of Crete beyond 'the Ram's Forehead', Cape Krio, a key headland whose name is noted in the Mycenaean clay tablets found at Pylos. The Ithacans were again on a known sea road, the trade route that linked southern Crete with the western seaboard of Greece, and they followed the rocky west coast of Crete until they reached the jumping-off point for ships crossing towards the Greek mainland. Here was the natural harbour sheltered by Gramvousa Island, whose soaring cliffs of bronze-coloured rock, impregnable acropolis, and convenient area of pasturage made it an ideal lair for an independent Bronze Age chieftain. Gramvousa harbour was where ships habitually waited for a fair wind, often for weeks on end, before they got a break in the prevailing summer northerlies. Thus Gramvousa's ruler had acquired the reputation in sailors' folklore of being the man who controlled the winds. This was Aeolus, and at his island the Ithacans had to wait a month. Like the *triamates*, a local folktale could now be worked into the *Odyssey* at this pivotal halting place. The visitors got their fair wind because hospitable Aeolus imprisoned the other breezes in his famous leather bag. The local folktale was perpetuated in the island's ancient name of Korykos – 'the leather bag'.

With the fair breeze the squadron left Korykos and set out for home. The wind lasted them so well that they steered a course along the Peloponnesian coast and may even have had the Ionian islands in view when the weather abruptly turned against them and they were driven back to Gramvousa. The ruler's hospitality had worn thin after already entertaining a dozen shiploads of armed men for a month, and they were no longer welcome. Dreading making the same mistake with the *meltemi* a second time, they determined to keep within touch of the Greek coast. They toiled north, this time under oars. At Cape Matapan, the ancient Taenarum and the next main headland, they passed the ultimate point on the Greek mainland, sacred to the Sun God and a fabled entrance to the Underworld. Here, mythology claimed, the Sun disappeared into the Underworld and black night emerged, so this was where the *Odyssey* said 'the paths of Day and Night crossed at the portals'.

A day's hard rowing further on, past the dangerous cliffs of Cape Grosso, the bone-weary squadron came to the remarkable enclosed harbour of Mesapo. Packing into the claustrophobic barrel-like cove, eleven ships were ambushed by the natives who, like their successors on this cruel peninsula, had a well-deserved reputation as bloodthirsty brigands. These were the Laestrygonians, who blocked the tiny exit to Mesapo harbour, and dropped rocks from the cliff edge so that the missiles tore through the hulls and sank the galleys. This was the end of the Ithacan squadron and the conclusion of the return from Troy for all but one man in twelve.

Up to this point the route of Ulysses' squadron has followed a totally logical path, coasting from headland to headland as always it tries to reach Ithaca after the misfortune of the gale at Cape Malea. Each stop-over is embellished with a flourish of local folklore to enliven the sailor's account of the journey. Here is the classic technique of the yarn-spinning mariner recounting the myths and folktales of all the places he has visited.

As we have shown earlier, the continuity of the narrative abruptly breaks here. The *Odyssey* suddenly jumps from the Laestrygonian massacre on the logical route to Ithaca, and arrives on the island of Circe, which is on the opposite side of Ithaca. If Ulysses had been sailing home to Ithaca along the natural route from the south, why should he now appear to the north of his home island as though he had sailed straight by his homeland?

The solution can be found in a new strand in the *Odyssey*. From Troy to Mesapo we have the story of the squadron's return. This is the report of the events that happened to the Ithacan contingent of twelve ships on the homeward trip from the foreign war. That story ended when the squadron was wiped out.

By contrast, the events on Circe's island and the subsequent events leading to the final wreck off the island of the Sun King's cattle form a separate cycle of tales relating to a *single* ship and specifically to the Ionian Islands. The switch from one story-line to the other is very obvious. The narrative does not even attempt to say how far or in what direction Ulysses and his sole surviving ship went from the Laestrygonian harbour to reach Circe's island so abruptly. He suddenly arrives at a place he knows not. 'East and West mean nothing to us here. Where the Sun is rising from when he comes to light the world, and where he is sinking, we do not know.' This is a new beginning. We are now to be treated to the Ionian epic cycle.

Ulysses is the greatest hero of western Greece. Nothing would be more natural than to include in his epic story the folktales and myths from the area in which he lived. Starting from Circe's island the *Odyssey* traces a route based on the maritime folklore of Ithaca and the surrounding archipelago. Here is a rich collection of sea tales associated with the homeland of the hero. The yarns tell of the dangers and bogeys of the archipelago for sailors coasting in its waters, but every tale is still associated with a particular locality. Archaeology supports Pausanias' 1,800-year-old suggestion that the river Acheron we visited on *Argo* is the same river Acheron of the *Odyssey*. There the Oracle of the Dead stands on its famous rock at whose foot the Streams of Lamentation and Flaming Fire unite. A Mycenaean grave inside the Oracle walls and a Mycenaean fort nearby confirm that the place was settled by Ulysses' contemporaries. From there the green and charming island of Paxos seems best placed to be Circe's island.

Argo, peering with her inquisitive 'lucky eye' into every bay and inlet between the Acheron and Ithaca, now stumbled on the most surprising revelations of all: the raw material of the folklore of the *Odyssey* still exists. The first surprise was Sesola Islet, perfect image of the Rovers, the feared Clashing Rocks of antiquity frozen in place off the coast of Levkas. In rapid succession and in their correct sequence came Cape Yrapetra, the Cape of the Rock of Turning, as the meadow of the Sirens but with the new mystery of the destroyed tumuli that could explain the 'mouldering

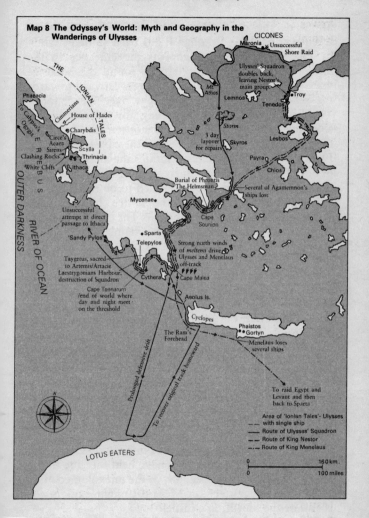

Map 8 The Odyssey's World: Myth and Geography in the Wanderings of Ulysses

CICONES
Maronia — Unsuccessful
Shore Raid

Ulysses' Squadron
doubles back,
leaving Nestor's
main group.

THE IONIAN TALES

Phaeacia

To Calypso's Ogygia

Mt
Athos

Lemnos

Troy

Tenedos

Storm

3 day
layover
for repairs

Skyros

Lesbos

House of Hades

Charybdis

Circe's
Aeaea

Sirens

Clashing Rocks

White Cliffs

Scylla

Thrinacia

Ithaca

Psyra

Chios

Burial of Phrontis
The Helmsman

Several of Agamemnon's
ships lost

E R E B U S

Mycenae

Cape
Sounion

OUTER DARKNESS

RIVER OF OCEAN

Unsuccessful
attempt at direct
passage to Ithaca

'Sandy Pylos'
Telepylos

Sparta

Strong north winds
of *meltemi* drive
Ulysses and Menelaus
off-track

Taygetus, sacred
to Artemis/Artacie
Laestrygonians Harbour,
destruction of Squadron

Cythera

Cape Malea

Cape Taenarum
/end of world where
day and night meet
on the threshold

Aeolus Is.

Cyclopes

Phaistos
Gortyn

The Ram's
Forehead

Menelaus loses
several ships

N

Prolonged defensive drift

To recover original track homeward

To raid Egypt and
Levant and then
back to Sparta

Area of 'Ionian Tales'- Ulysses
— — with single ship
———— Route of Ulysses' Squadron
———— Route of King Nestor
-·-·- Route of King Menelaus

LOTUS EATERS

| 0 | | 160 km |
| 0 | | 100 miles |

bones of the dead'. Nearby Cape Skilla retains its legendary name and though it has been shifted slightly by coastal changes, it signposts the entrance to the ancient Levkas Channel. Here we found the home of many-headed Scylla, the cave facing westward towards the setting sun and perched right over the channel. There is no difficulty in imagining how passing sailors spun tales about the horrendous monster that lurked in that sinister cavern mouth. Behind the cave rises Mount Lamia, whose name commemorates the alleged mother of Scylla. Astonishingly, much of that folklore was even marked on the map. It only needed to be read.

Geography corroborated the match between surviving folknames and Homer's tale. The curious twisting channel between Levkas and the mainland, the ruler-straight reef of Plaka Spit with its breaking waves, and the low nub of Yrapetra make a unique combination. They occur nowhere else, either in Greece or on the Italian coast, and they accord perfectly with the sailing directions given in the *Odyssey*. What is more, there is no evidence that the place-names are falsified to gratify the inquirer. The inhabitants of Levkas have no inkling that their region is depicted in the Great Wanderings of the *Odyssey*. The evidence was genuine and unadulterated.

Of course, some problems remain. What happened to the three mound graves recorded by the Royal Navy in 1864 on Yrapetra Point? Were they dug by an amateur archaeologist or by grave robbers? Dorpfeld's team did not record them, working on Levkas forty years later. These tumuli may have held the clue to the Sirens' meadow by the sea, just as the unexplained mass of Mycenaean pottery on Meganisi might explain the island of the Sun King's cattle.

The strange and empty tale of Calypso interrupts the cycle of Ionian tales within the *Odyssey*. Ogygia, the nymphs' dwelling place, reads like pure insubstantial fairyland. Getting there by clinging for nine days to flotsam is unlikely. Returning by an eighteen-day passage is impossible within the confines of the Mediterranean. Ogygia is beyond the real horizon and in the opinion of Professor Alan Wace, joint author of the standard *Companion to Homer*, Calypso was Homer's 'own invention to explain the hero's long absence'.

Did the landing on Phaeacia and Ulysses' romantic rescue by gentle Nausicaa happen on Corfu? Maybe, maybe not. No Mycenaean remains have yet been found there, and in Corfu we could have passed beyond the limit of the Mycenaean world although, as Professor Wace also noted, 'it appears to be a general characteristic of epic poetry that major events of sagas have firm local attachments'. From the moment that the Ithacan squadron was destroyed, these attachments are clustered in the north-west of Greece.

How, then, did the sites of Ulysses' adventures, which are first on the logical coasting route homeward-bound from Troy and then in his native archipelago, come to be transferred hundreds of miles to the western Mediterranean, usually to the Tyrrhenian Sea between Sicily and the coast of Italy. The answer lies in the great migration of the Greeks at the time that Homer was assembling the amalgamated version of the story. The Greeks were migrating westward to establish their colonies in Magna Graecia and they took their folktales with them. Greater Greece is precisely where they applied the tales to local features in their new homes, regardless of the inconsistencies, because in their tradition Ulysses was the unsurpassed traveller and so must have been there before them. Eight hundred years earlier in the Bronze Age the truth would have been very different. As a small squadron of Mycenaean war galleys plodded home, their route would have been prudent, close to land, and as short as possible. Transferring the *Odyssey* to Sicily and Italy only made the voyage a conundrum.

The chief culprit can be identified. Ironically for me, he is the same brilliant geographer whose interpretation of Jason's voyage in search of the Golden Fleece led *Argo* to Georgia in the year before her Ulysses Voyage. Strabo was the most perceptive geographer of his age. He guessed correctly that the notion of the Golden Fleece was linked with the practice of collecting grains of gold by placing sheepskins in the mountain streams of the Caucasus. In that instance Strabo wrote from experience. He came from Asia Minor and knew the Black Sea area at first hand. Later he moved to Rome, lived in Alexandria, and travelled so widely that he could claim to have travelled 'from east to west, from Armenia to the Tuscan region facing Sardinia, and north to south from the Black Sea to the borders of Ethiopia'. But clearly he never visited Ithaca, Mycenae or northwest Greece. Here his writings are riddled with mistakes: he says there is no Cave of the Nymphs on Ithaca; he does not know whether Daskalio Island exists or not; he reduces the Gulf of Ambracia to a mere lagoon; and he gets into a terrible muddle over the crucial channel between Levkas and the mainland, misplacing towns and bridges. It is evident that he was never there himself. Most damning of all, he pointed to the wrong site for Nestor's palace.

Yet Strabo has to be forgiven. Stoutly he maintained against the critics that the *Odyssey* was based on real lands and history, erroneously citing Monte Circeo, the Straits of Messina and all the sites of Magna Graecia. Strabo's *Geography* was the only major work of early geography to survive, mistakes included, and had tremendous influence. From ignorance of the terrain and with the best intentions he poisoned the well of information on the *Odyssey*. Had Strabo visited north-west Greece and seen the topography for himself I believe he would have revised his opinion.

Yet we must acknowledge that the geographical concepts which underpin the *Odyssey* are of a far different order to Strabo's critical and descriptive approach. The *Odyssey*'s myths and folktales go back to a much earlier and more primitive time, to a world that believed in monsters and witches and the notion of a small habitable landmass surrounded by the all-encircling world river. To the east the Greeks looked across the Aegean Sea and knew of Asia Minor, south-ward they were in contact with Crete and with Egypt. But the west was terra incognita. The unknown began at the very fringe of Greece itself. This was the margin of the Ocean River. Ulysses came from that outermost fringe, from the western frontier of the Mycenaean world, close to the 'outer darkness' as the *Odyssey* says, and on his way back he ran the gauntlet of these dangers. Here were found mysterious places like the Halls of Hades and misty Erebus where went the departing spirits. The souls of the dead suitors, whom Ulysses killed in a frightful slaughter when he got home, had not far to go. The *Odyssey* says they fled out past 'the white cliff', Cape Ducato at Levkas, and came to the Halls of Hades where they were led into the Underworld. Very close indeed to Ithaca lay the lands of magic, superstition and myth.

The Greek poet Cafavy wrote of Ithaca as a goal that could never be attained:

Setting out on the voyage to Ithaca
You must pray that the way be long,
Full of adventures and experiences.
The Laestrygonians and the Cyclops,
Angry Poseidon – don't be afraid of them;

You will never find such things on your way
If only your thoughts be high, and a select
Emotion touch your spirit and your body.
The Laestrygonians, the Cyclops,
Poseidon raging – you will never meet them,
Unless you carry them with you in your soul,
If your spirit does not raise them up before you.*

Perversely we *had* carried the image of Homer's
monsters with us during our voyage on *Argo* and we
had been rewarded. Our galley had carried us to
locations for the Cyclops, the Laestrygonians, Circe's
island and the Sirens, Scylla and Charybdis and the rest
because it turned out that the geographies of folklore
and navigation overlapped. This was the lesson we had
learned from our own odyssey as *Argo* retrieved the
story of Ulysses from the disarray of hyperbole, doubts
and contradictions. In the end it proved very straightforward – *Argo* had brought the *Odyssey* home to Greece.

* *Ithaka*, taken from *Poems* by C.P. Cavafy, translated by John
Mavrogordato, reproduced here by kind permission of Chatto and
Windus and The Hogarth Press.

Index

283

Index

Index

Index

Index